CHARACTER 'THAT' COUNTS

ROD HANDLEY

CHARACTER THAT COUNTS—WHO'S COUNTING YOURS?

Copyright © 2012 by Cross Training Publishing

Library of Congress Cataloging-in-Publication Data

978-1-938254-03-1
Rod Handley

CHARACTER THAT COUNTS—WHO'S COUNTING YOURS? / Rod Handley
Published by Cross Training Publishing, Omaha, Nebraska 68137
Distributed in the United States and Canada by Cross Training
Publishing

Unless otherwise indicated, all Scripture quotations are from the
Holy Bible, New International Version, © 1973, 1978, 1984,
International Bible Society. Used by permission of Zondervan Bible
Publishers. Other quotations are taken from *New American
Standard Bible,* (NASB) © The Lockman Foundation 1960, 1962,
1963, 1968, 1971, 1972, 1973, 1975, 1977, the *Revised Standard
Version of the Bible* (RSV) © 1946, 1952, 1971, 1973, the
Authorized/King James Version (KJV).

Printed in the United States of America

Contents

CROSSTRAINING
PUBLISHING

For additional books and resources available
through Cross Training Publishing contact us at:

Cross Training Publishing
15418 Weir Street #177
Omaha, NE 68137
(308) 293-3891
www.crosstrainingpublishing.com

For more information on Rod Handley
and Character That Counts contact us at:

Character That Counts
512 N.E. Victoria Drive
Lee's Summit, MO 64086
www.characterthatcounts.org

FOREWORD

In the United States, athletes are thought of as role models, icons, super heroes and even spiritual mentors. This kind of adulation puts much pressure on those athletes who desire to live up to the expectations, hopes and dreams of their families, friends and fans. However, there is only one set of eyes that everyone should gaze into to find guidance, direction and approval—the eyes of Jesus Christ. The big question is: "How can we accomplish this?"

After reading Rod's book, I embraced and applied the ideas and principles to my life. What came of it was a changed man. Application of this brilliant piece to my life has not only influenced my relationship with God but deepened my friendships with my accountability partners. To me, this is a "win-win" situation.

Two books have had a significant impact on my life, stretching me as a man to be more like Jesus on and off the field. Rod's book stands second only to a book that I'm sure you've read: the precious Holy Bible. If you want to excel as a believer and have an even stronger desire to look into the eyes of our "Audience of One," to be shaped and molded into what He wants you to be, you're holding a book that is a wonderful beginning. Enjoy the journey!!

Mike Sweeney
Retired, 5-Time All-Star MLB First Baseman

Rod Handley has addressed the area of personal accountability in a very candid and practical manner. He writes as though he is talking with you one-on-one. He gives the basic principles of developing an accountability relationship and the disciplines of living a genuine Christian life.

Over the past several years, accountability partners have helped and encouraged me in many ways. Each of them has played a part in my own journey to serve and love the Lord Jesus Christ.

The tough questions that John Wesley used almost 300 years ago and the accountability model suggested by Rod work. People who lead lives of integrity will embrace accountability because they hide nothing from the Lord and people. Unfortunately, there are people lacking character in the world today—people leading lives of "secret" sin and worldly pleasures, with no one asking hard questions directed at the very soul. It is a true blessing to look your partners in the eye after making a covenant of accountability.

This is a practical tool to make a real impact in the lives of men and women who desire to be people of integrity. With accountability you will confront areas of your life which need to be addressed. You will not regret making a commitment to accountability. Character Counts—especially if it is Christ's character living in and through you.

Dal Shealy
Past President, Fellowship of Christian Athletes

INTRODUCTION

When I was in Seoul, Korea, as a chaplain at the 1988 Summer Olympic Games, people would come up to me and ask, "Where are you from?" I would say, "America." They would then respond by saying, "Oh, USA! Number one country."

One cannot dismiss the fact that although America is the richest, most powerful country on earth, we are in a serious crisis. Problems of family dissolution, crime, teen pregnancy, substance abuse and unemployment are a few symptoms of a far deeper crisis. If there is a problem that is thread throughout our society, it is the lack of character, among Christians and non-Christians alike. Dr. Martin Luther King Jr., who championed the civil rights movement in the late 1950s and 1960s, said, "America is obeying the Eleventh Commandment, 'Thou shalt not get caught.' "

Edwin Louis Cole states in his book *Communication, Sex and Money*, "Compromise is the rule of the day. Our society deals with images, not issues. We suffer from the recompense of having leaders who have great personal charisma but who seem totally devoid of upright character."

As the former pastor of Lawndale Community Church in North Lawndale (Chicago), my family and I lived in the 15th poorest community in America (the church was one of former President George Bush's "Points of Light"). The most effective book, other than the Bible, was *Character That Counts: Who's Counting Yours?*, in teaching our "Kingdom Men" Monday night Bible study. This book transcended race, economics and educational backgrounds. It was so exciting to see how the men desired to have their own personal copy. These men, who function in a society that emphasizes "do whatever you can to get by," began to realize that character really does count and is the major way out of some very despairing situations.

If you desire a personal, practical and powerful resource in your journey with Christ and your fellow man, get into this book. Rod's approach will reinforce scriptural values that are so sadly missed in a changing world.

Carey Casey
President, National Center for Fathering

TESTIMONIALS

"This is a tremendous tool for people wanting to start an accountability group or for those wanting to take their current accountability group to a deeper level."
—Ray Hilbert, President, Truth @ Work

"Rod wonderfully inspires the horizontal accountability needed to be a champion on God's team—man to man. This helps motivate me to the all-important vertical fellowship with my 'Coach'—Jesus Christ."
—Ron Brown, University of Nebraska Assistant Football Coach

"*Character That Counts* is a tremendous tool for anyone seeking to truly walk in the light. This book breaks down the principles of accountability and makes them practical."
—Sue Semrau, Florida State University Head Basketball Coach

"Small group accountability is vital for successful Christian living. This book is perfect for helping build that accountability system."
—Trent Dilfer, Former NFL Quarterback

"*Character That Counts* takes character out of the world of aspirations and moves it into the world of reality. It's a game plan that will provide victory for those who choose to participate."
—Mike Gaffney, Vice President College Ministries, Young Life

"This book is the textual cornerstone of our men's ministry. Rod reaches deep inside us and demonstrates a clear understanding of what drives us as men. A 'must read' for every man."
—Greg Lindsey, Pastor, Colorado Springs, CO

"Reading *Character That Counts* encouraged me to find an accountability partner and to apply the principles of real accountability. Rod Handley's book has made a tremendous difference in my walk with Christ."
—Betsy King, LPGA Hall of Fame

"Rod has an incredible gift for understanding and communicating the issues of character and integrity. The greatest part of his ministry is that he is everything that he speaks about. Rod lives a life that shows *Character That Counts* for everything. It count it a privilege to have him as a brother."
—Chuck Stecker, President, A Chosen Generation

"Thoreau observed, 'How vain it is to sit down and write when you have not stood up to live.' Rod Handley has stood up, lives a life of character and contribution, and writes effectively on the subject. I strongly recommend Rod, his ministry, and this book!"
—Joe Calhoon, CSP, Founder and President of Priority Advantage

"Rod Handley has written this book to help men face up to the challenges of our day in a way that sets men free to follow the Lord in the power of His Spirit. Only God in Christ can produce character that counts in the lives of our dear ones and friends. His life and ministry back up the "character that counts."
—Dr. Jerry Kirk, Founder of the National Coalition for the Protection of Children and Families

"Character That Counts is an incredible resource for people who have a passion for living a life of integrity. Its rich content caused me to reflect on many facets of my character that I don't normally spend time thinking about. This book, and the ministry of Character that Counts, has impacted countless lives and is a critical resource for today's weak moral climate."
—Rick Boxx, Founder and President of Integrity Resource Center

"Rod Handley's Character That Counts ministry has been a true blessing to my life and many others (as I've seen firsthand). In order to progress in life, I have realized (and it is confirmed in his books) that we have to, first, set our road to the Lord's direction and plan based on scripture. To many people that is a given, but the crucial focal point covered is the need for Accountability. I am more apt to stay on track when I know I have to answer to others. "Who's Counting Yours?," just the Title alone, displays that fact. I love Rod, his family and his ministry. God has called him into a much needed area that we all need. His "Character" continues to be a light throughout each of his books.""
—Danan Hughes, former NFL player (Kansas City Chiefs/New Orleans Saints)

"I have known Rod Handley for over 30 years. He is a man who honors his commitments and lives his faith with integrity. His character counts and I'm proud to support him."
—Denny Rydberg, President of Young Life

"Rod Handley's Character that Counts is on target as it gives biblically based practical handles for an accountability process that is easily applied in real life. This book, coupled with the Bible Study Guide is sure to be a help to anyone of any age who seeks a godly life. Rod's message is clear, his writing concise and his style is engaging. No matter your age or stage in life, you will find Character that Counts to be an important life-guide that will help you live a life that honors God and lifts others to Him."
—John Garner, Lifeway Recreation Sports and Family Ministry

ACKNOWLEDGMENTS

Every day we are faced with decisions. Each decision made either enhances or damages our character. Character also deals with the issues pertaining to making and keeping your commitments. Former FCA staff member Larry Medcalfe formed an accountability group several years ago which he described as an "ABC Group." ABC stood for "Accountability Builds Character." If you want to take a huge step in building your character, then this book is for you.

Character That Counts: Who's Counting Yours? has been a 25-year journey. During that time, I have learned so many lessons. This is a concise look at the issue of accountability. *Accountability* is a buzz word, yet when it really gets down to the specifics, very few know how to implement it into daily life. Here is my attempt to bring it into one book.

You will not find the word *accountability* very often in the Bible, yet the principles are found throughout. Accountability is asking someone to help enhance your relationship with Jesus Christ. As you place your trust in Christ, He is the only one who can meet your needs. He has to be the first one you turn to for instruction and guidance. Your accountability partners play an important secondary role in your spiritual growth and maturity. One person described being in an accountability group as a "buried treasure" and that many treasures are available to each one of us if we would allow people to ask difficult questions.

Character That Counts: Who's Counting Yours? is broken into two sections. The first section defines accountability by breaking down the who, what, where, when and why issues. The second section breaks down the 10 questions that our group answers each week. Each chapter ends with a special story, lesson or poem which ties back to the chapter topic. Ideally, you will get through this book in a few days and have a solid basis for beginning your own group with ideas to put it together. The next section is a Bible Study Guide to be used with each of the chapters in this book. The final section is appendices filled with practical tools, as well as a section on the Character That Counts ministry.

Because the chapters could be one or several volumes in and of themselves, I have only given you basic information to help you get started. If you want to get into more detail on the areas mentioned in Chapters 8-17, I encourage you to seek out your local church or Christian bookstore for resources to aid you.

Though written primarily for men, this book should help meet the needs of both males and females, young and old, as well as crossing cultural and denominational lines. Though it is not intended to be all things to all people, you can refer to the Scripture references and various suggestions to help guide you in your daily life.

A special thanks to my accountability group for their input to the project. Also, my wife, Janna, was so supportive of this effort during the entire time and also provided her insight and prayers. I am also thankful for my editor, Don Hilkemeier and Laura Maxwell, who not only provided the final touches but they are wonderful friends and co-laborers in the Gospel. George Toles was responsible for providing the title of this book, along with some key editorial comments and much encouragement. I also want to thank my publisher, Gordon Thiessen, for agreeing to do this book—sight unseen. What a wonderful blessing to have someone catch a vision with you even when the dream is still in the infancy stages!

Many other people along the way gave me encouragement and valuable information. Chuck Snyder, Chip Lambert, Scott Kessler, Deb Shepley, Becky Bowman, Dan Dolquist, Jake Combs, Craig Hamilton, Kathy Van Horn, David Holdsworth, George Gilliam, Joe Calhoon, Dan Erickson, Chuck Stecker, the entire Character That Counts board, and numerous FCA staff members and volunteers across the country were helpful in many ways. A special thanks to Tom Nelson, senior pastor of Christ Community Church in Overland Park, Kansas, and Doug Brown, pastor of Lee's Summit Community Church in Lee's Summit, Missouri, for their wisdom on this subject. All in all, it was a true team effort and to God be the glory! My prayer from the beginning has been from John 3:30, "He must become greater; I must become less."

Rod Handley
Founder and President, Character That Counts

Chapter One

CHARACTER COUNTS

Sal had always been "the man." Growing up, he excelled far above his peers. Sal dominated in athletics, being named all-state in three sports. He had a 4.0 GPA and was class valedictorian. He was popular, smooth and savvy. He got everything he wanted, including his pick of all the girls. It's no surprise that he graduated from college with honors and made his mark on the business world. In just a few years, he'd flown through the ranks and was named president of a large international multimillion-dollar organization. He and his wife traveled around the world, living a life of luxury. They had all the money and power anyone would envy. Because he was recognized worldwide, people applauded when he was named Secretary of State. Yes, Sal had it all, but deep in his heart he felt an empty discontentment he could not explain.

Joe, on the other hand, grew up with a series of bad breaks. Joe fell victim to abuse at an early age and ended up spending his adolescent years in a foster home. Through great determination he achieved in spite of insurmountable odds. His exceptional work ethic caught the attention of his boss, landing him a substantial promotion just before his life unraveled. One night while working late on a special project, the boss' very attractive wife made unwanted advances which he resisted. Imagine the shock in the office the following day when federal agents entered Joe's workplace and arrested him for sexual harassment. He sat in jail trying to sort out his life.

Preston had built a mega-church ministry from scratch. People were always eager to hear the Word of God preached by this spiritual giant. As one of the most in-demand speakers in America, he traveled frequently spending many nights away from home. One lonely night Preston couldn't resist the temptation and slipped out of his hotel during the wee hours and entered a topless bar in a city where he wasn't recognized. Although the first encounter was supposed to be his last, he began sliding deeper into the addictive patterns of sexual misconduct. At his lowest point Preston found himself sitting in a peep booth only hours before addressing a large evangelical gathering. As he stepped onto the platform, all he could see in his mind was a nameless woman who'd just entertained him.

It appears each of these men are deep in crisis. Although Sal had all the external signs of success, it was only a matter of time until he was dismissed from his position after an independent counsel sleuthed out a number of his criminal offenses including heavy drug dealing and fraud.

Joe didn't have anyone to validate his story about the boss' wife during his trial, but eventually the facts came out, and the case was thrown out by the jury. Amazingly, while in prison he befriended a man who, after his release, put in a good word to some key people. One thing led to another, and years later Joe was elected governor. Eventually he was joyously reunited with his once-estranged birth family.

Preston, after a 10-year battle with heavy pornography, decided to come clean and reveal his secret struggle to a fellow minister of impeccable character whom he could trust. As he confessed his sin, the listener broke down and began to sob. Through his tears, he confessed that he, too, was involved in even deeper sexual sins.

Perhaps you've figured out that Sal and Joe are updated versions of the biblical accounts of Saul and Joseph. 1 Samuel 16:7 reminds us, "...man looks at the outward appearance, but the Lord looks at the heart." On the surface Saul was the obvious choice of Israel's desire for a king, but, like a ticking bomb, his true character was soon uncovered. Joseph established himself as one of the heroes of the faith and died as one of the Bible's all-time greats.

Unfortunately, Preston's story isn't fictional. The most read article in the history of *Leadership* magazine, "The War Within: The Anatomy of Lust," written in 1982, reveals an unnamed individual's struggle with lust.[1] His terrible patterns were hidden for years, but it struck a chord with a significant number of people inside and outside the church. The awful reality is that many people are sinking in quicksand situations which grieve the spirit of God. Their character is questionable at best.

CHARACTER COUNTS: COUNT ON IT!!

As I've traveled the country the last 25 years, I've attentively listened to people speak on the importance of character. By reading only the polls, it's hard to determine if character truly matters anymore. Does character count? I propose that it does and that society will place a higher premium on character in the upcoming years. We see indicators of this as moral issues gain greater emphasis during political elections, in the media, from the pulpits and on the talk shows. There is even a resurgence of teaching character within the public school system.

It has been said that ability may get you to the top, but character keeps you there. A person of character is marked by notable and conspicuous traits. Character cannot be purchased. It's a quality of life lived. Horace Greeley said it this way, "Fame is a vapor. Popularity is an accident. Money takes wings. Those who cheer you today will curse you tomorrow. The only thing that endures is character."2

I'm greatly concerned about situations where character is lacking, especially when it involves believers. Our local paper reported about a man in the Northeast who claimed to have kidney, lung and prostate cancer. Apparently he was good at faking seizures, had shaved his head to show the effects of chemotherapy and would drop red food coloring in the toilet to indicate blood in his urine. What got my attention was that this individual was a deacon in his church, and his congregation had given a significant amount of money to help with his "supposed" mounting health bills. What a shock it was for people to discover the lie.

There are numerous studies which indicate that Christians are as likely as non-Christians to falsify tax returns, to plagiarize, bribe, shift blame, ignore construction specifications, illegally copy software, steal from the workplace and to selectively obey the laws of the land. Many believers have convinced themselves that their questionable and inappropriate actions are justified. A Kansas City company called Integrity Resource Center is committed to teaching people how to live a life of character. Many of its clients are Christians.

Character development prior to the 1960s was learned early in life with a strong sense of right and wrong. Appropriate behaviors were taught in the homes, schools and churches. Somewhere we lost it as we moved from developing internal character to teaching external appearances of charisma and personality techniques. Success models were designed to help people achieve results without impacting one's deep fiber. We exchanged truth for a lie, and today in America we're reaping what we've sown with the highest levels of immorality, drug/alcohol abuse, suicide, abortion, teenage pregnancy, murder, divorce and pornography in our nation's history.

Until we return to old-fashioned character—and the church of Jesus Christ would be an excellent place to start—we'll continue to see deterioration of our society. In fact, true character is based entirely on Jesus Christ. Man-made character will crumble, while character developed and molded through Christ can withstand any situation.

What is character? The dictionary lists more than 20 different definitions which focus primarily on ethical behaviors. Pittsburgh businessman Bruce Bickel developed a wonderful list of character qualities. Some of which are noted Appendix A. A number of excellent books and other resources detail what character looks like and how we can attain it. The word "character" comes from the idea of an engraving in a printing business. The printed letter (the engraving) is called a character. The idea is that each letter leaves a distinctive mark. So a person's character is defined by the mark he or she leaves behind. Our character is the sum of a person's value, actions and attitudes. Thus, character is not a style, but is a reflection of one's spirit and heart. From our heart, flows a variety of character traits including our courage, compassion, conviction, etc. Therefore, I often refer to people of character as those who choose to do the right thing (right attitudes, right responses, right actions and re-actions). It's my strong conviction that when our character and our conduct are Christlike, there will be converts. Your character plays a crucial role in furthering the good news of Jesus Christ. Daniel Taylor reminds us, "Character is not something you have; it is something you are that inevitably shows itself in what you do. It is determined by the stories of which you are a part. As the concept of character makes a highly visible comeback in our public conversation, we must rescue it from glib politicians, do-gooders and busy-body moralizers."[3]

INTEGRITY: "BEING," NOT JUST "DOING"[4]

Many times "integrity" is substituted for the word "character." Integrity comes from the Latin word *integritas,* which means wholeness, entireness or completeness. The root word "integer" is used often in math to represent a whole number, meaning untouched, intact and entire. Literally, integrity means you have a complete soul. It's not synonymous with ethical behavior, though ethics will often follow, but is more related to the whole concept of "being" rather than "doing." You don't attain true integrity through a series of behaviors (doing) but by being internally transformed through a personal relationship with Jesus.

God is into making integers; Satan is into making fractions. God desires to bring people to wholeness, putting all the pieces together which will ultimately take place in heaven when we're united with Him. Satan, working through the vehicle of sin, tears things apart, dividing people and bringing confusion and conflict. Remember, God's plan will ultimately succeed, and His universe will one day become one glorious integer (whole and complete). But until that happens, you and I must live in a fractional world and experience the problems that come from fragmentation.

There are 16 references in the Bible about integrity. Four of these occur in the book of Job describing his character. Several are contained in the Psalms and Proverbs, and King David is equated with integrity in a few passages. But the first time it's mentioned is in Genesis 20 and is attributed to a pagan king (Abimelech, King of Gerar), against God's servants (Abraham and Sarah).

The story unfolds with Abraham and Sarah lying to the king about Sarah's identity as a married woman. Because they said that Sarah was Abraham's sister, verse two tells us, "Abimelech...sent for Sarah and took her." When God threatened to kill Abimelech if he committed adultery, he replied, "Lord, will you destroy an innocent nation? Did he not say to me, 'she is my sister,' and didn't she say, 'he is my brother'? I have done this with a clear conscience and clean hands." (In the NASB the word *integrity* is used.) God spared Abimelech's life, and it illustrates several points:

1) *Integrity is a serious issue.* A lack of integrity can kill those involved. From time to time even innocent bystanders get caught in the shrapnel.
2) *Unbelievers can often exhibit greater integrity than believers.* Even God's servants have feet of clay and often fall painfully short of leading lives of integrity.
3) *God delights in those who demonstrate integrity.* I love the Lord's reply in Psalm 15 where the psalmist inquires as to what delights a holy God. The answer is, "He whose walk is blameless and who does what is righteous, who speaks truth from his heart and has no slander on his tongue, who does his neighbor no wrong...who keeps his oath even when it hurts...He who does these things will never be shaken."

Integrity is at the heart and core of survival for nations and individuals. Yet why do so many dismiss it as merely an option? The Bible is filled with examples of people who thought living a life of integrity didn't really matter—people like Adam and Eve, Cain, Esau, Rueben, Moses, Aaron's two sons, Samson, King Saul, Judas Iscariot, Ananias and Sapphira and others. Even David, who in Psalm 78:70-72 is described as a man of integrity, lacked it when he sinned with Bathsheba and had her husband Uriah murdered, resulting in the death of David's son and a blood-filled curse.

David's life reminds us that integrity must continually be built in our lives through the disciplines of our faith in Jesus Christ. We cannot place confidence in our own integrity and relax and become lazy, or we will soon regress into a pitiful state. Ted Engstrom said, "No matter how much we try to hide our actions, our integrity (or lack of it) always shows through."[5]

CHARACTER MANIFESTATION: LOVE ONE ANOTHER AS OURSELVES

In the Bible we see strong examples of character lived out in the lives of Daniel, Joseph and Ruth. After his conversion Paul's transformed life shows his character even while chained, stoned and whipped. Their character emerges because of who they were (again back to the "being"). They made right decisions and exhibited character because they had a right relationship with God.

Today, character is manifested in many ways. Karl Day describes it as "returning extra change at the grocery store. Keeping appointments. Being on time. Honoring your commitments. Choosing the harder right instead of the easier wrong. Setting priorities that honor God, family, country and then career. Telling a business associate that you can't stop for a drink after work because you have to be at your kid's Little League game or dance recital. Working through the tough times of marriage rather than throwing in the proverbial towel. Being committed to the well-being of others even if it is personally costly. Setting a good example—even if it requires playing a difficult and unfamiliar role. Sacrificing personal pleasures, if necessary, in order to provide for the well-being of the family. It is being truthful in all things, while being sensitive to the fact that sometimes the truth hurts and needs not be spoken. Character is being selfless rather than selfish. Being accountable for one's actions and accepting the consequences. Ultimately, true character is a willingness to do as God commanded us to do—to love one another as we love ourselves."[6]

The bottom line is, "Do the right thing." Dr. Jack Graham said it like this, "Character is doing right no matter what the consequences or cost."[7] For example, what would you do if you had been given money which is not rightfully yours and nobody knows about it except for you and God? Several years ago I found myself facing this situation.

My odyssey began when I purchased a few file drawers and some hanging folders at Office Depot. Later I realized I didn't need one of the file drawers, so I returned it for a cash refund. The clerk was very willing to take back the item, handing me $10.63 along with my original receipt. When I got home, I looked at the receipt and realized that I'd been refunded for the wrong item. I'd been given more than $6 too much.

My mind raced with conflicting thoughts of good ("I need to go return the money") and evil ("Too bad, Office Depot"). It's amazing how we can so quickly try to justify something which isn't right. I tried to put the incident out of my mind, but all I could think about was a saying above my desk at work which says, "Character is who you are when no one but God is watching." Frankly, my character was worth more than $6, or any amount of money. I vowed that evening that I would return to the store to take care of the situation. I called one of my accountability partners to help me follow through with this commitment.

Why was it important for me to right this wrong? The following Scriptures give me plenty of reasons:

"Do what is right and good in the Lord's sight…"(Deuteronomy 6:18).
"Blessed are they who maintain justice, who constantly do what is right" (Psalm 106:3).
"…the ways of the Lord are right; the righteous walk in them, but the rebellious stumble in them" (Hosea 14:9).
"Be careful to do what is right in the eyes of everybody" (Romans 12:17b).
"For we are taking pains to do what is right, not only in the eyes of the Lord but also in the eyes of men" (2 Corinthians 8:21).
"…never tire of doing what is right" (2 Thessalonians 3:13).

A few days later I walked into Office Depot, told the manager my story and that I wanted to return the money. As I walked out of the store that day, I knew God was pleased, and I was relieved. Author Mark Twain said, "Always do what is right. This will surprise some people and astonish the rest."[8]

Character and integrity are not short-term disciplines. They're established, tried and true for a duration of time in multiple situations and many different environments. Dwight L. Moody said, "Character is what you are in the dark."⁹ The private life should match the public lifestyle. During our lives, our character will be established as we encounter conflict, adversity, pain and humility. In fact, some of the greatest growth in our character development takes place through situations similar to the following.

ADVERSITY: TURNING TRAGEDY INTO TRIUMPH

Years ago I found myself in the middle of a very difficult situation, and my character was challenged greatly. My prayer during the ordeal was that the truth would emerge, and God would be glorified. Through it all I asked the Lord to reveal His ways and purposes so that I could learn and grow in my faith. Early on in this ordeal I realized that my battle was "not against flesh and blood, but against the rulers, against the authorities, against the powers of this dark world and against the spiritual forces of evil in the heavenly realms" (Ephesians 6:12). My battle was against the Devil who was attempting to discredit and nullify my testimony and witness. This attack was straight from the pit of hell. When I figured out who my real opponent was, I mobilized the full armor of God as noted in Ephesians 6:13-18 (See Appendix K). The Word of God became my refuge and hope. I identified with David when he said in Psalm 62:5-8, "Find rest, O my soul, in God alone; my hope comes from him. He alone is my rock and my salvation; he is my fortress, I will not be shaken. My salvation and my honor depend on God; he is my mighty rock, my refuge. Trust in him at all times, O people; pour out your hearts to him, for God is our refuge."

Many times in the Scriptures David found himself in precarious situations. Saul pursued him, seeking his death. He helplessly watched an infant son die, and he had a major conflict with a rebellious son. Though David had many successes, he encountered adversity. Perhaps you can relate. Can you find common ground with any of the following? You're in the midst of a terrible job predicament; you're dealing with a family frustration; you have mounting bills and debt; you're limited by physical ailments; you have a major conflict with a friend; you've watched death overtake someone you love dearly. It's been said that adversity can make us or break us. What can we do during adverse times?

1) *Do not become prideful and vindictive by taking things into your own hands.* Romans 12:19 says we should not avenge because the Lord will repay. God is still in charge of your situation. Seek Him through prayer and humility, asking God to give you wisdom and strength.

2) *Don't react, reflect!* Psalm 46:10 reminds us to be still (or "cease striving") and know that He is God. Calmly place your anxiety in the hands of an all-knowing God who's still on the throne. Patiently wait for God to lead and direct.

3) *Let God deepen you; don't allow Satan to destroy you.* Realize that God uses even the worst jams to orchestrate His perfect and holy will for our lives. Through the pain we're strengthened, becoming the person God created us to be. Romans 8:28 tells us that when it comes to those who love Him, God causes all things to work together for good. Don't give Satan a shot at tearing away at your faith.

4) *Let God make you better; not Satan making you bitter.* Unfortunately, so many times we allow a root of bitterness to rob us of what God is trying to accomplish in our lives. Satan would love to cause us to lose focus. Absolutely nothing can separate us from the love of Christ (Romans 8:35-39).

5) *Don't be self-absorbed; be self-abandoned.* Follow the example of Jesus who came not to be served, but to serve (Mark 10:45). When we relinquish our plans and desires to the Lord, He can do an internal work in our lives that truly will bring glory to our Father.

Adversity is a necessary part of life as trust and faith develop. Remember 1 Peter 4:12-13, "Do not be surprised at the painful trial you are suffering, as though something strange were happening to you. But rejoice that you participate in the sufferings of Christ, so that you may be overjoyed when his glory is revealed." When you find yourself in the middle of a character-building opportunity and you begin to wonder where God is in the middle of your crisis, be assured that God is in control. Through it all God will truly enhance our character as we identify more with His Son and His sufferings.

Charles Spurgeon described it this way, "As sure as God puts His children into the furnace of affliction, He will be with them in it."[10] Here are some of the ways God will use adversity in our lives:

1) *God uses adversity to teach us obedience (Hebrews 5:8).* Jesus learned obedience through suffering. Don't take matters into your own hands. Learn to say no to sin and even to the good things, so you can say yes to righteousness and the best things. God simply desires us to be obedient.

2) *God uses adversity to train us for reigning days (1 Peter 4:7-11).* One day the believers will reign with Jesus Christ. Therefore, while on earth, we're to learn from situations we're placed in and have an attitude of sound judgment, prayer, fervent love, hospitality, serving one another and using our talents to glorify God. The afflictions we face are temporary and will soon pass, compared to the eternity and glory that await us.

3) *God uses adversity to test our faith (1 Peter 4:19).* The genuineness of our faith is revealed through adversity. We can see our faith deepen and be radically transformed if we put our hope and trust in God alone. The illustration of the oyster which is irritated by the sand and the ultimate development of a beautiful pearl is one example of how this testing can accomplish its complete purpose.

4) *God uses adversity to turn tragedy into ultimate triumph (1 Peter 5:8-11).* Though Satan prowls around seeking to destroy believers (v.8), we experience victory when we resist him. We're promised in the depths of these dilemmas that we'll be "perfected, confirmed, strengthened and established." Precious metals are purified through a tedious process of heat and sweeping the dross. Heat and sweep, heat and sweep,

heat and sweep. The metalworker knows the purification is complete only when he can look in the metal pool and see his face without distortion. Until then the process of being refined is incomplete.

FAILURES: TAKING RESPONSIBILITY FOR SIN

King David is a wonderful example of someone who failed, yet God says David was a man of integrity. How can this be? David was a murderer, he committed adultery, he had trials as a father, he had trouble controlling his anger, and the list goes on and on. Though his battles with his human flesh are well documented, it's also apparent that God had a special place for David because of his strong love relationship with the Father. Intimacy, trust and forgiveness were involved. Fortunately for David (and all of us), we serve a God who is rich in mercy and grace.

David's character grew despite the failures. Part of the reason his godly character emerged was that he took responsibility for his sin. He was transparent before God with his failures. True character begins with acknowledging who you really are and what you don't have. So often we have a false impression of who we are, and we view ourselves under a different set of standards than we judge others. Then when we fail, we blame others or justify our actions, rather than taking personal responsibility and willingly accepting the consequences.

Some of my greatest character-building moments have occurred through my darkest experiences, simply because I've learned and grown from them. I've been benched, demoted, rejected and mocked more times than I want to admit. These humbling moments have proven to be some of the most teachable times. One of my life goals is to learn from bad situations the first time around rather than encountering it over and over because of my refusal to learn. When handled appropriately, failure can be a catalyst for a healthy soul as you embrace the freedom which can only come through confession, complete forgiveness and restoration from the Lord Jesus Christ.

Let's be honest with ourselves and realize that we're going to blow it often. When I'm gut-level honest with myself, others and God, I know I don't always make the right decisions. I allow temptations and sin into my private world. I compromise my values and belief system. I live out Romans 3:23, "For all have sinned and fall short of the glory of God." I'm in the same battle you are.

Howard Hendricks says it well, "It is not about where you are but in what direction you're moving. God is into character, not credentials."[11] Therefore, the next time you find yourself in the midst of a failure, confess it to the Lord and move boldly ahead, intending not to repeat your mistake. Paul W. Powell reminds us, "God is more concerned about our character than our comfort. His goal is not to pamper us physically but to perfect us spiritually."[2]

OBSCURITY: AN OPPORTUNITY, NOT AN OBSTACLE

In 1 Samuel 16:1-13 we see Jesse bringing seven sons before Samuel to determine which would be king. One by one, they were passed over. Eventually, Samuel asked Jesse if all of his sons were present. As it turned out, the youngest, David, was still in the fields tending the sheep. David was so obscure that he was not invited to be part of the anointing service. Out of public view is often where fertile soil can be nurtured by God, allowing His plans to become established in our lives. David's character had been forged in depth while alone in the wilderness.

How do you deal with the temptation to exalt yourself? There's something in each of us that makes us want to be noticed, acknowledged and praised. We fight anonymity! This has reared its ugly head with me many times. For whatever reason I often find myself inserting foot into mouth as I seek the applause from others rather than the applause of heaven. Afterwards, I ashamedly confess to God that I've blown it again.

We need to view obscurity as an opportunity, not an obstacle. Allow situations to develop where the possibility of self-exaltation blows by like the wind. Don't jump ahead, placing yourself in a visible position until God does it. Unfortunately, we often get ahead of Him through self-promotion. John 12:24-25 challenges us to lose our life, and when we do so, God gives it back to us at just the right time. We change from being self-absorbed to being self-abandoned for Christ. Unless we die, we cannot live. This is true Christianity. To remind myself of this truth, I often sign my name with Galatians 2:20, which says, "I have been crucified with Christ and I no longer live, but Christ lives in me..." That's what I'm striving for.

It's been said that before you can have true public victory, you need to have private success. Look for opportunities to sit in the shadows and learn lessons which can only be understood out of the spotlight. If you're used to being noticed, this can be difficult. I urge you to commit to the biblical challenge to "die to self" and truly learn from the Lord the life-changing lessons that come with taking a back seat.

Thomas B. Macaulay said, "The measure of a man's real character is what he would do if he knew he would never be found out."[12] One of the practical ways to do this is by honoring and blessing people without fanfare. My good friend Don Hilkemeier used to say, "I'm going to do something nice for someone, and if they find out, it doesn't count." That's an excellent way to practice obscurity.

SUCCESS: EGO "EDGING GOD OUT"

Handling success and accolades can be equally as difficult as going unnoticed, and our true character often emerges. During my single years, I had a roommate who played in the NFL, and I was always amazed that he wouldn't read the newspapers. Through both successes and failures he'd learned to not rely on press clippings to determine his value. He said, "I'm not nearly as good or bad as the press believes." He graciously handled praise, realizing he was only a few bad plays away from the "boo" birds.

Being a winner often brings great pride and self-centeredness. It's easy to begin thinking of yourself as able to handle any situation. As our ego grows, our reliance on the Lord and His strength diminishes. Do you know what "EGO" stands for? *Edging God*

Out! Success is something we all should strive for, yet we need to remain humble and grateful.

Humility is one of those words that's easy to say but hard to live out. We cannot make ourselves humble. It's impossible! Only God can humble us. Nor can we talk about being humble for that merely proves our pride. But we can discuss the attitudes and disciplines of life that allow us to work in harmony with God as He teaches us humility. We can choose to remember where our success really lies, in the Lord's provision and mercy.

Thankfulness is a key to remaining humble. If you've gained a favored position and find yourself relying on worldly accomplishments, remember Who our example is—Jesus Christ. Though He had equal status with God, He did not cling to His awesome perks. He set aside the privileges of deity and took on the role of a slave by becoming human. Then, just as amazing, He stayed human. It was an incredibly humbling process. He lived a selfless, obedient life, then died a selfless, obedient death. Because of His obedience, God honored Him far above anyone or anything ever, so that all created beings in heaven and on earth—even those long ago dead and buried—will bow in worship before Jesus, calling out in praise that He is the Master of all, to the glorious honor of God the Father (Philippians 2:1-11).

There are several principles that enable believers to honor God enroute to becoming humble:

1) Listening allows us to hear what God, His Word, the Holy Spirit and others are trying to tell us.
2) Self-examination allows us to prayerfully process decisions and events, helping us choose the right response.
3) Confession allows us to cast off sin and guilt as we admit we're nothing without His strength, forgiveness, mercy and love.

Putting these three attitudes into practice as we follow Jesus Christ will definitely change the way we view success. I love the old Native American saying, "When you were born you cried and the world rejoiced. Live your life in such a manner that when you die the world cries and you rejoice."[13]

COMPROMISED CHARACTER: A CRACK IN THE DAM THREATENS ALL

Here are some of the consequences which emerge when character is compromised:

1) *Our courage is crushed.* I've seen people from all segments of society, inside and outside of the church, lose confidence in themselves and their decision-making ability through compromise. A knockout punch results from a crushed character.

2) *God's blessing is withheld.* You may have temporary success, but eternally you're on a destructive path, and God will not bless your life.

3) *Our secrets will be revealed and exposed to all.* Devastating consequences await those who have small cracks in the dam of integrity. Everything in time, in this world or on Judgment Day, will be made fully known.

The *Daily Walk Bible* devotional gets right to the point: "Nothing is quite as comforting—and at the same time quite disconcerting—as the truth that God knows everything. He knows your thoughts; he knows your actions; he knows your words. He knows when you get up and when you go to bed. He understands your motives and intentions even when no one else on earth does. But at the same time he knows your secret sins that no one else ever sees: pride, lust, jealousy, coveting. And he holds you just as accountable for your secret sins as for those that others know about. Similarly, God's presence can be both a comfort and a concern. There is no mountain you can climb, or depth you can descend, where he is not there. His presence shines through the darkness and transcends distance. But at the same time, that puts the lie to any notion of 'secret sins' you can commit without his being there. His presence with you is persistent." [14]

In his helpful and penetrating book *How to Give Away Your Faith,* Paul Little comments on the secret life. He reminds us that throughout Scripture, God emphasizes that our real self emerges when we're all alone. God knows everything about our inner selves and He evaluates our heart. Hebrews 4:13 says, "Nothing in all creation is hidden from God's sight. Everything is uncovered and laid bare before the eyes of him to whom we must give account." God knows the whole truth. We can confide in Him because He knows us through and through. We are stripped of all pretense when we stand before Him all alone.

The truth about secret sins is that we all have them. No one is excluded (Psalm 90:8). We can't hide them (the sins) from Him. Instead, we need to acknowledge and come "clean" with our hidden sins. It is also true that our secret sin eventually will lead to outward sin. We become defiled from within. The collapse of a believer is normally not a blowout, but a slow leak. Slow leaks normally begin with a faulty inner attitude, a secret sin.

If you're not aware of your secret sins, ask God to reveal them. We can be confident that He will answer. David's prayer is a place to begin. "Search me, O God, and know my heart; test me and know my anxious thoughts. See if there is any offensive way in me, and lead me in the way everlasting" (Psalm 139:23-24). The Holy Spirit will help open our eyes. He may reveal it to us through a passage of Scripture, or he may use someone else to trigger our awareness. One way or another, he will make us aware to enhance the process of developing our character.

Once it's been revealed, it's up to us to come to grips with our particular sins. God never reveals sin to us to leave us in it. He wants us to respond to his revelation by confessing and forsaking that particular sin and by making appropriate restitution. He's always ready to hear our requests for forgiveness, cleansing and power. [15]

BENEFITS OF CHARACTER: A CLEAR CONSCIENCE

1) *We will leave a lingering legacy.* What a wonderful tribute to the Lord when we leave a picture of integrity for our families, co-workers and fellow believers. Often I try to picture myself at my own funeral. What those closest to me say on that day depends on what I'm living like today. As the old Korean proverb says, "When a tiger dies, he leaves his skin. When a man dies, he leaves his name." Our legacy is our character.

2) *We have the rare privilege of being a mentor.* We need some heroes. Older saints making an investment in younger believers. Taking people under our wing and blessing them with knowledge, wisdom and counsel. Howard Hendricks advocates that we each need a Paul and Timothy in our life—a Paul we can learn from and a Timothy we can teach.[11]

3) *We will be leaders.* We need people of God to be leaders in their homes, workplace, church and community. I'll guarantee you that character will be attractive to a watching world, and you will emerge as a leader.

4) *Our conscience is clear.* It's a tremendous relief to go to bed with your mind clear, knowing you've been true to God and others. There's indescribable freedom available to you only through Christ.

5) *A crown of glory awaits.* I can't tell you specifically what's in store, but the King will definitely have a phenomenal reward for those who lead a life of Christlike character. It will be well worth it!

CHARACTER COMMITMENT: FIRMLY PLANTED

Stephen Arterburn's book, *Winning At Work Without Losing At Home,* shares 11 signs of people who have good character: (1) They have self-confidence. (2) They live within their means. (3) They get along well with others. (4) They have positively helpful attitudes. (5) They have consideration of other people's needs. (6) They have patience. (7) They have a hunger for learning. (8) They seek growth in skills and talent. (9) They are reliable. (10) They are unselfish. (11) They are careful to love people and use things.

I once worked with a gifted athlete who had a bright future, but his major flaw was wishy-washy behavior. The voices of this world bombarded him at every turn with subtle lies. He waffled in making decisions. He had difficulty saying "yes" to the best because he couldn't say "no" to anything. His internal battles centered around the old adage, "If you don't stand for something, you'll fall for anything." Bottom line—he struggled with the character quality of firmness.

To a certain degree we are molded by society. We adapt to the ideas and habits of our peers—many of which can bring us to ruin. We are easily impressed by those who have influence. Even the strongest and most independent people often fall below their own standards which rip away at the conscience.

It takes nerves and guts to resist negative peer pressure and to be firmly planted. Listen to the warning God gives in 1 Corinthians 15:33, "Do not be deceived, 'Bad company corrupts good morals.'" The Living Bible puts it this way, "Don't be fooled by those who say such things. If you listen to them you will start acting like them." We need to build a will strong enough to resist and control forces that corrupt good morals.

CHARACTER RESTORATION: CONFESS, FORGIVE AND LEARN FROM THE PAST

Let's admit it...none of us have lived perfect lives. From firsthand experience, I've messed up. It's been said, "When wealth is lost, nothing is lost; when health is lost, something is lost; when character is lost, all is lost."[16] In my pursuit of character there have been times when I've made split-second decisions which have derailed my goal of being a person of character. Rebuilding character is a tough process. Here are some keys to restoration:

1) *Confess it to God.* 1 John 1:9 says, "If we confess our sins, he is faithful and just and will forgive us our sins and purify us from all unrighteousness." What a liberating promise from God! The great news is that failure is never fatal or final. We serve a gracious, merciful God who's eager to forgive and restore us.

2) *Make it right with people.* Just as God has forgiven us, we need to extend that same forgiveness to others (Matthew 18:21-35). Come clean with people by seeking their forgiveness. Tell the whole truth. Truth cleanses our soul.

3) *Commit to the high calling.* Ephesians 4:1, "As a prisoner for the Lord, then, I urge you to live a life worthy of the calling you have received." Don't go down that path again. Learn from your past.

SUSTAINING CHARACTER: IT'S ALL ABOUT DISCIPLINE

I'm a big believer in the basic fundamentals. There are no shortcuts or secrets to living the Christian life. If you want to retain a strong Christian walk characterized by righteousness, here are the ingredients which come only through discipline. Please know that these disciplines will never gain the favor of God. Instead, they should flow out of your life as you develop a personal relationship with Him. Ultimately, I concur with Jeff Comment who says, "When we leave this world, we should only be remembered for two things: our relationship with Christ, and our character."[17]

1) *Bible Reading.* Devour the Word of God daily. Listen closely for God's voice while reading the Scriptures. Nothing can replace intimate, timeless Truth.

2) *Prayer.* Enter your prayer closet with an expectation of hearing from God through listening and conversing with Him daily.

3) *Fasting.* With prayer, this is one of the most exciting disciplines which has helped me to focus on God and His plan for my life. I highly recommend reading *7 Habits to Successful Fasting* by Bill Bright.

4) *Solitude.* Something very special occurs when you slow down and get quiet before the Lord.

5) *Fellowship.* Hebrews 10:24 reads, "And let us consider how we may spur one another on toward love and good deeds. Let us not give up meeting together..." Plant yourself in a church and contribute within the Body of Christ.

6) *Scripture Memory.* Memorizing God's Word is one of the most powerful weapons at our disposal when feeling the tugs of the world.

7) *Accountability.* Ted Engstrom believes, "Integrity is the greatest prize of accountability. Accountability starts with yours truly—with an honest appraisal of who we are, of what makes us tick. It includes a long, hard look at our own ideals and motives. When we give an accurate account of what we think and what we do, then those around us can come to rely on us

with confidence."[18] You've heard the familiar phrase, "The burning coal removed from the embers soon grows cold." Well, here's another one, "The banana pulled from the bunch is the one that gets peeled."[15] I don't want to see any cold coals or peeled bananas. My one task in the coming pages is to help you see that accountability is the final piece of the puzzle to help you fully become the person of character God intends for you to be.

REPUTATION AND CHARACTER by Herbert Spencer [2]

The circumstances amid which you live determine your **reputation**; the truth you believe determines your **character**.

Reputation is what you are supposed to be; **character** is what you are.

Reputation is the photograph; **character** is the face.

Reputation comes over one from without; **character** grows from within.

Reputation is what you have when you come to a new community; **character** is what you have when you go away.

Your **reputation** is learned in an hour; your **character** does not come to light for a year.

Reputation is made in a moment; **character** is built in a lifetime.

Reputation grows like a mushroom; **character** grows like an oak.

A single newspaper report gives you your **reputation**; a life of toil gives you your **character**.

Reputation makes you rich or makes you poor; **character** makes you happy or makes you miserable.

Reputation is what men say about you on your tombstone; **character** is what angels say about you before the throne of God.

Notes

[1] "The War Within: The Anatomy of Lust tells the complete story of this pastor's struggle with lust. I would highly recommend reading, especially for those who desire to be freed from the bondage of lust and pornography," Name Withheld, *Leadership*, Fall 1982, pp. 30-48 and the sequel story "The War Within Continues," Name Withheld, *Leadership*, Winter 1988, pp. 24-33.

[2] Source unknown.

[3] "In Pursuit of Character," Daniel Taylor, *Christianity Today*, December 11, 1995, p. 29.

4 Much of this section is developed from information found from three sources: Warren W. Wiersbe, *The Integrity Crisis* (Nashville, TN: Oliver-Nelson Books, 1988); Ted W. Engstrom, *Integrity* (Waco, TX: Word Books, 1987); and the teachings of Tom Nelson, senior pastor at Christ Community Church in Overland Park, KS.

5 *Integrity*, p. 42.

6 "Character—A Definition" Karl Day, *Washington Watch*, November 1997, published by Family Research Council, pp. 1, 7.

7 From Dr. Graham's sermon on February 8, 1998, at Prestonwood Baptist Church in Dallas, TX.

8 *Quotes and Quips*, Covey Leadership Center, 1993, p. 13.

9 *Commitment to Character* (Warner Press, 1995), p. 79.

10 Ibid, p. 69.

11 Howard Hendricks shared these thoughts at the 1995 Promise Keepers event in Seattle, WA.

12 *Quotes and Quips*, p. 19.

13 Ibid, p. 69.

14 *The Daily Walk Bible* (Atlanta, GA: Walk Thru the Bible Ministries and Wheaton, IL: Tyndale House Publishers, 1987), June 27, p. 645.

15 Adapted from Paul Little, *How To Give Away Your Faith* (Downer's Grove, IL: InterVarsity Press, 1988), p. 176-179.

16 Author Unknown.

17 Jeffrey W. Comment, *Mission in the Marketplace* (North Kansas City, MO: MTM Publishing, 1995), p. 86.

18 *Integrity*, pp. 110-111.

Chapter Two

A CALL TO ACCOUNTABILITY

Two men were riding a sleigh during a blizzard. They were extremely cold and terrified they would not reach safety. They came upon another traveler who had fallen in the snow. He was close to death. One of the two men on the sleigh pleaded with the other that they stop and help. The other refused. The concerned one decided to stay, even though the delay could mean his death. His companion left the two of them behind. Working feverishly, the one who stayed to help massaged the unconscious man's body. After what seemed like hours of labor, the man responded and began to revive. The two men got up and walked in the snow together, the vigorous work of massage having saved them both. As they walked on, they came upon the sleigh and the man who had refused to stay and help. He was frozen to death.

The energy we spend on relationships is never wasted. Each time we stop to help a near frozen friend, we grow in our own development and character. We need each other. Together we survive. Alone, we freeze and die. Unfortunately, many people fall because they don't have to answer to anyone for their behavior. One of the best choices you can make is to intentionally pursue accountability with another person.

For years I have shared how being accountable has changed my life. Reactions I've received from a great number of people range from "What is it?" to "I'm already doing that, too!" Yet, no matter the initial reaction, once I begin sharing what my accountability group does and how we do it, I see their expressions and more than one has said, "This is something I need so badly in my life."

I became interested in accountability because of two primary reasons. The first one was personal. Though I had an impressive address and phone book listing and could mix fairly well in most social situations, I found myself longing to have someone who knew me for who I really was and who would be willing to listen, advise and challenge me to live in an upright, godly manner. John 15:13 says, "Greater love has no one than this, that he lay down his life for his friends." I did not have this type of friend. I also knew there were areas of my life where I needed greater obedience to the Lord and someone to help me follow through with my commitments. I was also dissatisfied with the surface and shallow conversations I so often found myself engaging in, even with those who were supposed to be my closest friends.

The second reason I became interested in accountability was the pattern of failures which I observed in the lives of many Christians whom I admired and followed closely. When I speak of failure, I am referring to public and private sin which seriously damaged their ministry or job, reputation, families and relationship with God. As I began to ask questions, I discovered that many of those who fell had no accountability in their lives.

Among those who had fallen was a pastor who led seminars across the country while secretly engaging in an adulterous relationship for a number of years. According to a person close to the situation, just prior to beginning this affair, he removed himself from any form of accountability because he felt he was self-sufficient; it was too time consuming and unnecessary.

Another sharp, young pastor, whom I respected greatly because of his Bible-based preaching style, was dismissed from his church when it was discovered he had inappropriate relationships with women in his congregation. A reason cited for his fall was a lack of accountability.

A business leader and deacon in a local church who had been named the "Man of the Year" in his community was recently found guilty of embezzling millions of dollars from various people and several charitable organizations. He was an investment advisor, and people placed their trust in him. Again, a lack of accountability was noted in his life.

Even the person who played a key part in my Christian faith stumbled. A victim to the temptations of the world in the areas of prosperity, career and success, he is now barely hanging on to the faith in Christ which he had vibrantly exposed to me. Apparently, there has been no one in his life to walk beside him in an accountable relationship.

In each of these cases I do not believe there was an intentional desire to fall. Genuine Christians want to live an obedient life to Jesus Christ. Yet, temptations are real and powerful. No person has the ability to always make the right decisions. Unfortunately, poor choices result in terrible consequences, no matter how innocent the initial decision might have been.

In the booklet *Accountability,* David Atchison and Billy Beacham tell about a survey of prominent Christian leaders who experienced moral failures, illustrating the need for high accountability. After an immoral relationship was revealed, Gordon MacDonald said, "I now realize I was lacking in mutual accountability through personal relationships. We need friendships where one man regularly looks another man in the eye and asks hard questions about our moral life, our lusts, our ambitions, our ego." Likewise, Jimmy Swaggert confessed, "I fasted and I prayed and I begged God for deliverance from pornography. I realize now if I had turned to my brothers in Christ for help, I would have been delivered." Chuck Swindoll stated, "When I learn of someone's spiritual defection or moral fall...I ask, 'Was the person accountable to anyone on a regular basis?'...Without exception—hear me, now—without a single exception the answer has been the same: 'NO'!" Howard Hendricks, a nationally-known speaker and professor at Dallas Theological Seminary, studied 237 instances of Christian men who experienced moral failure, and he found only one common factor—not one of the 237 had accountability relationships with other men. Those who are serious about living a pure and effective life before the Lord will find more strength when accompanied by true brothers.[1]

Examples of people who have fallen are not isolated. Unfortunately, every day people are falling away from Jesus Christ and destroying many loved ones as sin is exposed. The stark reality is that each and every one of us, including myself, is capable of falling. We are not exempt from the possibilities of stumbling, and every Christian needs some form of accountability in his or her life.

Many people are unwilling to answer to anyone! Such reasons include lack of time, a desire to maintain privacy, mistrust of others primarily due to past hurts, a fear of rejection, a secret pattern of sin and an unwillingness to change and get help, just to name a few.

But the weak spots and other areas where we are blinded usually are the places where we are attacked by temptation. Though some may fall abruptly due to one bad decision, most of those who get into trouble make a series of tiny bad decisions—even decisions which go undetected—that slowly wear down the character of a person. Song of Solomon 2:15 talks about the "little foxes that ruin the vineyard." These "foxes" may include areas where we are totally off base. At other times the "foxes" may be a slight compromise which goes unchallenged by anyone in our lives. God's Word teaches us to stand firm in the faith and to guard against falling away (Hebrews 5:14). Unfortunately, many fall away because they do not have to answer to anyone for their behavior. Is there anyone in your life asking you hard questions about the real issues which you face on a daily basis?

The dictionary defines accountability as "subject to the obligation to report, explain or justify something; being responsible or answerable to someone." It is owning up to past hurts and present shortcomings by committing to positive change. It begins with seeing the need to make changes and courage to make it happen with a "new" plan of action. Every person needs protection from himself and a safety net. Pride is the biggest enemy. We need to bring ourself to a point where we can confess our sins one to another.

Before going any further, we must be reminded that we are all sinners. Romans 3:23 says, "For all have sinned and all fall short of the glory of God." All means everyone, so whether we are a Christian or not, we all have sin in our lives. For the Christian, Jesus Christ's shed blood on the cross covers that sin, and fortunately, even when sin abounds, grace abounds even more. We are forgiven and start anew and afresh at any time because God truly forgives and restores anyone who confesses and repents. For those who have not made a decision to follow Christ yet, that same love and forgiveness is available to you at any time.

My prayer is that we would all hate sin as much as God hates sin. You have probably heard the phrase, "Hate the sin but love the sinner." I believe the definition of accountability described earlier is a practical step in staying away from the sin that so easily tempts us. Remember, accountability will not remove sin or keep you from sin, but it helps you to become aware of your sin and helps point and focus you back on Jesus Christ. Being accountable takes honesty, and if honesty doesn't exist, accountability will be a meaningless experience.

We are kidding ourselves if we think we can run the Christian race of faith alone. Scripture shows us clearly that God designed us to be in relationships with one another. Certainly there are times when we must walk alone and be a bright, shining light to the world when possibly no one else will join us. Yet, we all need a person of refuge who is committed to helping restore, equip and teach us to walk in the path God has set before us.

Though each person will face a different battle, many men and women are tempted by sexual passions. We are bombarded by television and movies; by books and magazines we read or browse; through the lust of the eyes. These lead to inappropriate behavior of sexual gratification outside of marriage. I have no idea of the percentage of men and women who seriously battle this one issue, yet it is clearly a significant one. Still, the areas of life where we need the help of another are not limited to sexual purity.

For men, other areas of struggle include power, success, a desire to accumulate wealth, job situations and ego. Women are faced with similar problems as well. The issue of a poor self-image is one which both men and women battle. Additional areas of concern include anemic living, addictions/secrets, guilt, empty/lonely lives. Even fame and fortune don't satisfy. Difficulties in any of these areas drag us away from loving and serving the Lord totally as our Christian walk becomes shallow, legalistic, meaningless and eventually non-existent.

Many Christians mistakenly believe they can live a life of integrity without help. That attitude, however, makes us more vulnerable to sin. It ignores the biblical commands to help each other (e.g., Galatians 6:2, Ecclesiastes 4:9-12, Proverbs 27:17). We're not meant to walk this journey alone.

Maintaining integrity requires the encouragement of accountability. People—especially close friends—keep us pumped up. They communicate "you can do it, you can make it" a dozen different ways. At David's low-water mark, Jonathan stepped in. Right when Elijah was ready to punt everything, along came Elisha. Paul had Timothy, Silas and Barnabas to help him.

Many people are traveling through life isolated, unconnected and unexamined. We try really hard to maintain an image that we have got it all together, when in reality we don't. Inside, we are often falling apart and desperately crying for help, but we don't have the courage to talk to someone. This is exactly the reason we need to open up our hearts to others.

Don't fall into that trap of isolation. Living the Christian life is a "we" thing not a "me" thing. There is an old African proverb that states, "If you want to go fast, go alone. If you want to go far, go together."

Isolation is the Christian's silent enemy. But don't get solitude and silence (two powerful spiritual disciplines) mixed up with isolation. Isolation is pulling away and saying, "I can live out my faith on my own, and I don't need anyone to help me." There is pride in isolation. We begin to think we can live our faith through our own power. Once we distance ourselves from those who know us best, small (and large) changes begin taking place in the absence of accountability. Isolation makes people believe that sin can be committed free of consequences. Additionally, isolation makes us think that we are the only people wrestling with a particular sin, problem, difficulty or addiction. We begin to believe that no one else will understand us, so why should we open up and seek help? We think that if we keep a lid on our problems, that we will contain it.

Accountability involves a regular check-in time to ask the hard questions and point out blind spots. Accountability also involves helping people live up to their commitments. Through involvement in each other's lives you can really help out one another, especially when temptations hit.

CHRIST, OUR PROVIDER

Certainly, Jesus Christ walks by our side on a daily basis simply because He has promised to do so. Are you aware of this promise? Robert Boyd Munger's booklet, *My Heart—Christ's Home,* gives us a beautiful picture of someone inviting Christ into his life, and Him actually entering his heart, or literally his home. It is Christ's desire to occupy every single room of our house including the secret closets. In this booklet Jesus is invited into every room of the house until one day Jesus discovers the "Hall Closet." As He does, He also volunteers to clean it out. No matter what sin or what pain there might be in the past, Jesus is ready to forgive, to heal and to make whole.[2]

Our desire to be accountable to Him and others should come as a result of desiring to be more like Him. Submitting our lives for inspection goes against our independent desires and an attitude of keeping things between "Jesus and me." But Scripture points us to a need for accountability in Ecclesiastes 4:9-10, "Two are better than one, because they have a good return for their work: If one falls down, his friend can help him up. But pity the man who falls and has no one to help him up!"

WHY DO WE NEED TO BE ACCOUNTABLE?

1. *Satan, our enemy, loves to see us stumble.*

"Be self-controlled and alert. Your enemy the devil prowls around like a roaring lion looking for someone to devour. Resist him, standing firm in the faith, because you know that your brothers throughout the world are undergoing the same kind of sufferings" (1 Peter 5:8-9).

"Put on the full armor of God so that you can take your stand against the devil's schemes" (Ephesians 6:11).

It brings great pleasure to Satan to see us fall, especially those who are in leadership positions in the Body of Christ. Yet, every believer is a target. Satan has many methods, but two of his favorite are (1) convincing us we can do it on our own, and (2) injecting distractions through our weakest areas, particularly when we have idle time on our hands. Gary Rosberg reminds us, "We need people who will 'go to war' with us. To shield yourself from Satan's poison-tipped arrows, cling to the truth of God's Word— and link up with others."[3] (For more on our enemy, see Chapter 7).

Tom Nelson, senior pastor of Christ Community Church in Overland Park, Kansas, shared in a recent sermon these three valuable points: never underestimate the deception of power; never underestimate our capacity to rationalize sin; and never underestimate the depravity of our hearts. Each of these areas needs to be recognized before a foothold is established. Micah 6:8 reminds me, "...And what does the Lord require of you? To act justly and to love mercy and to walk humbly with your God."

2. *The world is closely watching us.*

"In the same way, let your light shine before men, that they may see your good deeds and praise your Father in heaven" (Matthew 5:16).

"Be very careful, then, how you live—not as unwise but as wise, making the most of every opportunity, because the days are evil" (Ephesians 5:15-16).

"Let us not become weary in doing good, for at the proper time we will reap a harvest if we do not give up" (Galatians 6:9).

First of all, God commands us to be holy because He is holy (1 Peter 1:16). Second, it is important that we remain pure and holy because of the great example it is to a watching world. It is true that you are the only Jesus that some people may ever see. Obviously we are not perfect, but when we live in obedience to Christ, people will take notice. Perhaps they might even be attracted to a relationship with Christ by observing our actions and hearing our words.

One example is Billy Graham. Billy has been used and blessed by the Lord since he burst into the public eye over 60 years ago in the early days of the "Youth for Christ" movement. Early in his ministry he and a group of men made a commitment to one another that they would remain faithful to their spouses and have integrity in all their affairs. To a watching world, he has certainly made a difference in many lives.

3. *To remain right with the Lord.*

"But because of his great love for us, God, who is rich in mercy, made us alive with Christ even when we were dead in transgressions—it is by grace you have been saved. And God raised us up with Christ and seated us with him in the heavenly realms in Christ Jesus, in order that in the coming ages he might show the incomparable riches of his grace, expressed in his kindness to us in Christ Jesus. For it is by grace you have been saved, through faith—and this not from yourselves, it is the gift of God—not by works, so that no one can boast. For we are God's workmanship, created in Christ Jesus to do good works, which God prepared in advance for us to do" (Ephesians 2:4-10).

As these verses describe, God has done a complete work in us. Why blow it? There are many reasons to keep the relationship intact. First and foremost, He loves us. This love has been demonstrated to us time and time again, even when we fail miserably in returning that love to Him. His love for us is further demonstrated by God's willingness to send Jesus to earth to die for us (Romans 5:8). He paid a significant price for us through His shed blood, and we have the opportunity to spend eternity with Him by accepting Christ into our life. When we also consider His power and forgiveness in our life, I continue to ask: Why blow it? Living pure, holy and blameless should be a goal for every believer.

4. *Judgment is coming.*

"For God will bring every deed into judgment, including every hidden thing, whether it is good or evil" (Ecclesiastes 12:14).

Mickey Mantle, New York Yankee Hall of Famer, died several years ago. At his funeral, broadcaster Bob Costas shared these words, "Our last memories of Mickey Mantle are as heroic as the first. None of us, Mickey included, would want to be held accountable for every moment of our lives." In many ways, I wish Bob were right. I'd like to go my own independent way, never having to give an account of my actions and behaviors. But, the cold, hard reality is that God will judge. There will be a full accounting done of our lives and all will be revealed. Are you ready to face a holy, perfect and just God? Accountability will help prepare you for that day.

5. *It encourages other believers and ourselves.*

"Brothers, if someone is caught in a sin, you who are spiritual should restore him gently. But watch yourself, or you also may be tempted. Carry each other's burdens, and in this way you will fulfill the law of Christ. Therefore, as we have opportunity, let us do good to all people, especially to those who belong to the family of believers" (Galatians 6:1,2,10).

"Therefore confess your sins to each other and pray for each other so that you may be healed. The prayer of a righteous man is powerful and effective" (James 5:16).

Most people don't have close friends—they have work friends or golf partners. Our culture discourages closeness. We are taught to be autonomous, efficient, goal-oriented, disconnected from people, unemotional and self-sufficient. It is a wonderful feeling to gather with people who really love and accept you and are willing to talk to you honestly and help keep you on the "straight and narrow" path.

We need friends to encourage us in our faith. Paul on his missionary journeys took time to stop and encourage other believers, and his instructions are to encourage one another (1 Thessalonians 5:11). One of the members of our group shared that because of our group he loves Jesus Christ more than ever because the group helped him draw closer to Christ. As we laugh, cry and pray together, not only are our relationships strengthened, but we also love Jesus more. Ted Engstrom said, "We need help from each other. About the only thing we can do well by ourselves is fail."[4]

Louie Giglio has one of the best working definitions that I've seen: "An accountability group is a place where you are consistently candid, open, honest and vulnerable concerning your potential and actual shortcomings and failures in an atmosphere of mutual love, trust, acceptance and challenge, toward the goal of being conformed to the image of Christ and finishing the race."[5]

WHAT HAPPENS TO US WHEN WE ARE ACCOUNTABLE?

1. *Growth in your Christian walk.*

Opening yourself to others will result in a great time of personal growth. You will be challenged and encouraged in a multitude of ways in trusting God with your whole heart (Jeremiah 29:11-13). Knowing we do not face the battles of daily life and spiritual growth alone matters a great deal. Though your group may not have any members with a counseling degree, a willing listener and a prayer partner can be extremely comforting. Dietrich Bonhoeffer said, "Many people are looking for an ear that will listen...they do not find it among Christians because these Christians are talking where they should be listening...one who cannot listen long and patiently will presently be talking beside the point and never really speaking to others."[6] To find people who will listen long and patiently is like discovering a buried treasure.

2. *Deepening Friendships.*

Not only will the depth of friendships increase in your group, but you will find it easier to develop solid, meaningful friendships outside of the group because you will initiate conversations beyond normal surface issues (quality and quantity). Feeling love and acceptance from your group frees you up in your other friendships to be yourself.

3. *Greater Awareness.*

Discussing real issues will open your eyes to the needs of everyday life including family situations, church involvement, integrity, half-truths and a variety of other issues. The simple act of sharing the raw material of daily life with an accountability group helps us to see situations through the eyes of others. It keeps attention focused and constantly reminds us to pray. James Houston of Regent College says, "Sin always tends to make us blind to our own faults. We need a friend to stop us from deceiving ourselves that what we are doing is not so bad after all. We need a friend to help us overcome our low self-image, inflated self-importance, selfishness, pride, our deceitful nature, our dangerous fantasies and so much else."[7]

4. *Priority Setting.*

When our hectic schedules crowd out time for prayer, family relationships or exercise, we need people to remind us that the tasks that seem so urgent are not worth the compromise. These friends can help us balance competing demands and bring choices into harmony with the life taught and modeled by Scripture. An accountability relationship will also give you a place to apply action to what you are learning.

5. *Peace.*

How would you feel if Christ returned and you were in the midst of a compromising or embarrassing situation? This is a good question to ask yourself when you encounter situations which may not be appropriate. 1 John 2:28 says, "And now, dear children, continue in him, so that when he appears we may be confident and unashamed before him at his coming."

A sense of personal satisfaction, joy and peace are a few of the emotions which will begin to emerge in your private world. What a feeling to have the freedom to let other people participate with you in releasing your burdens to Christ (Matthew 11:28-30)—and the price tag is free.

6. *Support System.*

Mammoth redwood trees hundreds of feet high and several feet thick grow in the Sequoia National Park in northern California. Most trees of this size have a root system equal to what you see above the surface—but not redwoods. Although their root system is only a few feet deep, they survive the storms and wind because they grow next to other redwoods. By binding together with one another, their root systems become incredibly strong. They do not topple because of their mutual support. Being in an accountability group will provide this type of a support system.

THE DIFFERENCE BETWEEN ACCOUNTABILITY AND FELLOWSHIP

Fellowship plays a very important part in our Christian growth, but it is different from accountability. It all comes down to an openness in asking and answering the hard questions. Typically, fellowship doesn't extend beyond the routine conversations of news, sports and weather. Accountability pushes into the real issues of life. Because of a mutual commitment to one another, you may from time to time even get to the point where you have to push into areas where you may endanger your friendship. Challenging, probing discussions are invited into the conversation. Fellowship usually doesn't get this intimate.

Recently I was speaking on this subject with a group of high school students. When asked what the difference was between fellowship and accountability, one boy responded, "Accountability is what I do with other men and fellowship is when I can talk to the girls." Well said!

CHARACTER QUIZ

Before you get too smug and think that the compromising of character or the need for accountability is referencing someone else, take the following character quiz to determine how you would respond when no one's watching.[8]

1. If you found a wallet with $1,000, would you give it to the owner if no one knew you had found it?
2. If you could advance yourself unfairly, would you do it if no one would ever find out?
3. If the golf course or gym failed to collect your fee, would you voluntarily pay it?
4. If there were no locks on any house, store, or bank, would you take something if no one found out?
5. If your business partner died, would you pay his relatives their fair share, if you didn't have to?
6. If you were an employer, would you hire yourself at your salary and would you like to be working for yourself?
7. If you were a parent, would you like to be the child of a parent like you?
8. If you could watch an inappropriate movie or look at an inappropriate magazine without anyone finding out, would you do it?
9. If you had to live with someone just like you for the rest of your life, would you count it a privilege?
10. If God were to see your answers to this quiz, would He agree with you?

Notes

1 David Atchison and Billy Beacham, *Accountability* (Fort Worth, TX, Turning Point), pp. 10-11.
2 Robert Boyd Munger, *My Heart—Christ's Home* (Downers Grove, IL: Inter-Varsity Christian Fellowship, 1986 revised).
3 Adapted from "We're In This Together," Gary Rosberg, *New Man*, September/October 1995, p. 63.
4 Ted W. Engstrom, *Integrity* (Waco, TX: Word Books, 1987), p. 111.
5 *Accountability*, p. 7.
6 *Christianity Today*, March 11, 1991, page 44.
7 *Christianity Today*, March 11, 1991, page 43.
8 The character quiz was adapted from the work of Herbert V. Prochnow.

Chapter Three

A LOOK AT
OUR GROUP

In early 1990, shortly after moving to Kansas City, I met Steve
Mogensen. Through Steve I became interested in meeting in a
small group on a weekly basis. As a new believer, he was seeking
Christian fellowship. With Steve's encouragement, four of us began
meeting together at a local restaurant once a week for a time of
updates and prayer. It was a positive time, yet had little structure.
Since we were all single, it met some common needs, both social
and spiritual.

Accountability took on a new meaning and was raised to a
higher level when I began meeting with a second group of men in
the fall of 1990. Along with my roommate Steve Pelluer and Kansas
City Chiefs teammate Ken Karcher, we began getting together three
times a week. In addition to answering a set of personal questions
which had been provided by Athletes in Action director Mike
Lusardi, we also made a commitment to memorizing Scripture
together. Our goal was to memorize the entire book of 2 Timothy.
By Christmas 1990 all three of us had the book memorized and
together forged an incredible friendship.

With their help I experienced some of the most meaningful
conversations during those months. We pushed beyond the surface
areas, down to some of the nitty gritty issues about myself which
were historically off-limits to everyone in my life.

I was scared that if someone really got to know me, perhaps he
would not want to be my friend. It wasn't necessarily that I was bad
or evil, but I was afraid of people seeing my flaws and judging my
imperfections. I understand now that the fears were totally
unfounded. As I opened up to Steve and Ken, I discovered that
they accepted me and loved me more than before because of my
openness. I also found that they, too, had areas of struggles in their

lives, and they could identify with my weaknesses. No longer were we disconnected islands trying to fight this battle alone. We could help one another strive toward godly living.

When I began sharing with others about our accountability group, I learned that many people were interested not only in the topic, but also in starting a group themselves. The only problem was how to get started. I gave them our set of questions but knew this wasn't enough. Several people suggested that I write a book on accountability.

I searched through book stores for guidance and was unable to find any resource help. I visited with Jeff Comment, president of Helzberg Diamonds and past chairman of Young Life, to inquire if he knew where I could find these resources. I greatly respect Jeff because of his own experiences with accountability. He shared, "Rod, I know of nothing out there in published print to describe this type of accountability. I believe there are few, if any, who are willing to touch this subject because it is the one area of Christianity that is a little too close to the real person." In the same conversation he encouraged me to write a book.

The final confirmation for writing this book came when I heard the testimony of Minaz Abji. I first met Minaz in March 1993 at a men's weekend retreat, when the Lord arranged for the two of us to be roommates. On Saturday morning at the retreat we were visiting together prior to breakfast, and he bluntly asked me, "How can a Christian stay away from sin?" Among other things, I mentioned that my accountability group helped me. I invited him to observe our group, which he did the following week. After his first week he was quickly welcomed in as a regular participant.

Several months later Minaz was asked to give his testimony to the entire church congregation. As I sat in the audience, I was overwhelmed by his story. Minaz grew up in Uganda as a Muslim. During Idi Amin's reign, Minaz's family fled to Canada as refugees. While in Canada he married Julia, who had been raised Buddhist. After their daughter Nadia was born, they began questioning their Muslim and Buddhist heritage and sought spiritual meaning for their lives. Skeptical of "the church," they were approached by

Jehovah's Witnesses who knocked on their door one day. After attending Bible studies and the Jehovah's Witness services for five years, they still felt uneasy about the message they were hearing. On their own they attended a Christian church one day and shortly thereafter made a first-time commitment to Christ.

In Minaz's testimony I was stopped dead in my tracks when he told of the impact that our accountability group had on his life since the weekend retreat. He said, "Prior to joining this group, my faith wasn't strong. My salvation experience was real, but I was not dealing with the temptations and real issues of my life. This group has exhibited what true Christianity is all about, and now for the first time in my journey with Christ, I am seeing victories in areas where I had been defeated. And for the first time in my life I am living the Christian life." Though he had made a decision to follow Christ years before, he was truly transformed through the group's encouragement and the power of the Holy Spirit.

As he spoke, I heard the Lord saying to me, "Rod, there are people like Minaz in this world who need what you have discovered from your experiences with accountability. Write the book!"

Of course, I argued with myself that lack of time and poor writing skills were good reasons not to write a book. But along with those arguments, my mind was churning. As our pastor preached from the pulpit, I scribbled out an initial outline. When the service ended, I found Jeff Comment coming toward me. I told him about how the Lord had prompted me during the service, and he encouraged me once again to begin the writing process.

God has worked in a marvelous way through the men who have been a part of my accountability group in bringing me farther along in my journey to become more like Christ over the past ten years. Here is a brief snapshot of a few of my partners and their comments about the impact of accountability in their lives.

Ken Karcher: Ken left the Kansas City area in March 1991 and has coached at a variety of professional and college teams. He and his wife, Pauline, have four children. Ken recalls, "Those nine months together with Steve and Rod were the most meaningful times in my Christian life. Since that time, I have been seeking to be part of a group and fellowship patterned after it. Our group encouraged and challenged me to live a righteous and godly life day to day. When men hold each other accountable, Christianity becomes real!"

Steve Pelluer: Steve left Kansas City in April 1992. After getting married in 1994, he and his wife, Jennifer, now live in the Seattle area and have four children. Steve recalls, "The biggest impact was facing life honestly. It was a big step in developing quality relationships."

Dan Meers: Dan is the mascot for the Kansas City Chiefs (alias "KC Wolf"). His wife, Cam, shared that she is so excited that he is part of a group because it makes her more confident of her marriage. "Because of his commitment to our marriage, being accountable is a priority to him. It is great that he meets with other men. And because I see how it has impacted him, I'm in an accountability group with two women," she said.

While in college Dan met with two guys weekly to share and pray with one another. Once he moved to Kansas City, that was also a priority. He said, "I knew I needed the encouragement. Within our group I know I am meeting with other guys who love Jesus and have a common goal of striving to be more like Him. It is great when you are walking hand in hand together rather than by yourself.

"The accountability questions we answer each week are probing and confront areas that guys really deal with. Initially it was hard to open up and admit the weaknesses and struggles in my life. However, God has taught me that when I confess my weaknesses to the group, He uses these men to challenge and encourage me in my obedience to Christ. We constantly strive to be men of character and to live a life of purity which is a message that contradicts everything the world tells us. It has taught me to be more concerned about what God sees in my life rather than what the world says, and I'm learning to live my life for an audience of One. Accountability has also helped to challenge me to step up and be the godly father I need to be for my kids. I've always heard that someday our kids will follow our example and not our advice. Accountability challenges and encourages me to live out a godly life for my kids to see. It has also helped my marriage through the wise counsel of others, and seeing the answers to prayer week after week has also been a great encouragement." Dan and Cam are blessed with three children.

Steve Mogensen: As mentioned earlier, Steve became a friend of mine in the spring of 1990. During the previous year, he had committed his life to Christ and was looking for growth opportunities. A mutual friend encouraged the two of us to get together. Steve wanted to surround himself with as many Christian men as possible. He said, "I needed encouragement to not go back to my old friends and lifestyle. I knew without other Christian men in my life, I wouldn't make it. The group enhanced my walk with Christ. Normally men in the world, even in the church, are not asking tough questions. People in this group asked me to address tough questions because they really cared." Steve and his wife Andrea have four sons and live in Lafayette, IN.

William Hanna: I met William, an attorney, in April 1990, and he joined our breakfast group that fall. He said, "So many people go to church or Bible study, yet don't know how to apply the lessons they are taught to their lives. This group helps provide a concrete way to live out the Christian faith. Accountability serves as a barometer, and because that reading isn't always positive, accountability helps point you back in the right direction. Also, through meeting, you realize the importance of having God be in charge of all aspects of your life, not just a few of the areas. This has helped provide focus and direction to all areas of my life including my work and my marriage." William and his wife, Tanya, have three children.

Fred Olson: Fred worked with me at FCA until my departure in 2000. He said, "Accountability has helped in two primary ways: (1) the enhanced friendships with other Christian guys and the closeness we feel for one another and (2) it has strengthened and encouraged me in my faith. Seeing how God works in my partners' lives has encouraged me greatly. These kinds of deep friendships do not happen very often with guys. Also, I am much more aware of doing right and being right not only in the big things, but in the little things as well." Fred and his wife Cynthia have three children.

Mike DeBacker: Mike works for Burns & McDonnell Engineering in Kansas City, MO. He said, "The group regularly challenges me to live the pure and faithful life God desires for each of us. The group has been an anchor for me over the years including several geographic and career moves. The hour-and-a-half of sleep I lose every week to get up and meet the group is probably the best investment I've made in my adult life." Mike's wife, Darla, said, "Getting feelings out in the open with other men also results in better communication within the marriage." Mike and Darla have four children.

Bruce Rehmer: I have been part of an accountability group for the past 11 years and have been truly blessed by the times of sharpening, times of care and times of forthright challenges that have occurred during the times with my group. A group of us men were challenged by Rod at one of his speaking engagements about protecting our character though accountability. Thankfully, I found other men who desire and are striving to be more effective servants for our Lord. I have been so blessed during the times the group has lifted me and others up in prayer through times of crisis and also in times of rejoicing. My life would be shallow, empty and lonely if it wasn't for the men that have kept me accountable over the years. Bruce and his wife Sheri have two sons.

Jeff Klein: After years of investigating Christianity, Jeff (Jewish by birth) made an initial decision to follow Christ in August 1993. A friend who was instrumental in Jeff's decision called me from Seattle and asked if I could help hook him up with other believers. He joined our group, and an instant bonding occurred. He said, "Direction, guidance, friendship and fellowship are key parts of our group. Telling the guys how I reacted to and applied their input helps make me very cognizant of what I am doing with my day. I guarantee you, not one of us is a saint. We are all sinners, yet we are not judged according to our performance. As you talk about your feelings and various issues, you always come away better than when you arrived." He added, "Making real friends is very limited in our current society. These are quality relationships! You receive and give a lot. As a new Christian, I didn't feel like an outsider. I felt comfortable in sharing from the very beginning, even though I had a lack of knowledge and experience in my new faith. I have felt this way because they cared about me. Though I'm not necessarily qualified to give comments, I know God is using me, too. We all bring baggage and valuable input as well. Also, a highlight was our prayer time around the table. This was new to me at first and I really enjoyed it."

Minaz Abji: Minaz is the former general manager of the Westin Crown Center in Kansas City. In 1995 he moved to Canada to manage a number of hotel properties. Presently, Minaz lives in Washington, D.C. and he is still in the hotel management business.

In addition to what has already been covered, he added, "I was struggling with sinful thoughts, especially in my non-Christian work environment. I didn't walk the walk. Meeting with these men opened my eyes to my sin. I was shocked to see godly men opening up to these questions. The facades were broken down. I desired purity. I wanted to be obedient. Today Christ is at the center of my life. And for a long time I came and received, but now I can see how God is using me to make a difference in the lives of others. Every person needs a group like this. Christianity is more than going to church and reading the Bible; it is now in my heart. I am now experiencing real joy." Minaz also admits that his move to Toronto was a huge struggle, especially when he didn't initially seek out accountability. "I found myself reverting back to my old ways. I was like a lamb in the midst of the wolves. After experiencing some very difficult times, I returned to the Lord and accountability."

Be reminded that your personal needs and circumstances and the people you are accountable to in your lives will change, but Jesus Christ never changes. He is the one to whom you're ultimately accountable. The people you meet with are secondary to Christ. The No. 1 goal of every small group should be to bring people into encounters with God that transform them into His likeness. Radical life change, spiritual growth, Bible knowledge, fellowship, love, caring and sharing are all elements of a healthy group.

Each of the members in our group has made a commitment to follow Jesus Christ. We are confident that God has indeed

promised us salvation and eternal life because we each have personally accepted him into our lives. Have you made that decision?
Before you go any further, consider asking Jesus Christ to come
into your life. The following can guide you towards making this
happen today.

ARE YOU SURE YOU'RE A CHRISTIAN?

Here are five steps you can take to become part of God's family. If
you haven't already done these, I urge you, if you're sincerely ready,
to do them now:

1. **Admit** your spiritual need. "I am a sinner."
2. **Repent.** Be willing to turn from your sin, and with God's help,
   start living to please Him.
3. **Believe** that Jesus Christ died for you on the cross and rose again
   from the dead.
4. **Receive**, through prayer, Jesus Christ into your heart and life. Pray
   something like this from the sincerity of your heart:

*"Dear Lord Jesus, I know I am a sinner. I believe You died for my sins
and then rose from the grave. Right now I turn from my sins and open
the door of my heart and life. I receive You as my personal Lord and
Savior. Thank You for saving me. Amen."*

5. Then **tell** a believing friend and a pastor about your commitment.[1]

Notes
[1]   Adapted from Greg Laurie, *New Believer's Growth Book* (Riverside,
CA: Harvest Ministries, 1985), p.8.

Author's Note:
Due to space constraints, I was unable to include the comments
of my other accountability partners throughout the past 20 years:
Steve DeZeeuw, Vic Gamble, Will Greer and Kevin Harlan.

Chapter Four

TEAMWORK THAT WORKS

I began this project in 1990 because I was unable to find a comprehensive book devoted entirely to accountability. Some authors, like Patrick Morley in *Man in the Mirror*, dedicated portions of their writings to this subject, and I am grateful to Patrick for having the courage to approach this subject and give men a format to use. Some of the information which I am writing on accountability is adapted from Patrick's writings, and I encourage you to read his entire book. Steve Farrar, in *Point Man*, also does a great job of detailing some specific ways in which a man can better equip himself to be a godly man and leader.

Since that time, other good books to help us pursue accountability include: *Brothers!* by Geoff Gorsuch; *Raising a Modern Day Knight* by Robert Lewis and *Locking Arms* by Stu Weber.

WHAT DOES SCRIPTURE SAY?

"See to it, brothers, that none of you has a sinful, unbelieving heart that turns away from the living God. But encourage one another daily, as long as it is called Today, so that none of you may be hardened by sin's deceitfulness" (Hebrews 3:12-13).

"Instead, speaking the truth in love, we will in all things grow up into him who is the Head, that is, Christ. From him the whole body, joined and held together by every supporting ligament, grows and builds itself up in love, as each part does its work" (Ephesians 4:15-16).

"And Saul's son Jonathan went to David at Horesh and helped him find strength in God" (1 Samuel 23:16).

IS ACCOUNTABILITY A NEW DISCOVERY?

I was surprised in my research on accountability to discover that during the mid-1700s John Wesley developed an accountability model. Wesley influenced thousands of people into Christian discipleship and growth. He said, "Preaching like an apostle without joining together those that are awakened and training them in the way of God is only begetting children for the murderer." Wesley established his converts and leaders in small cell groups for mutual care and discipling. The following are some guidelines he established for these cells. Keep in mind that these were to be followed in the spirit of the law, *not* the letter of the law:

"In obedience to the command of God, by St. James and by the advice of Peter Bohler (Moravian Missionary), it is agreed by us,
1. That we will meet together once a week to confess our faults one to another, and pray one for another that we may be healed.
2. To come punctually at the hour appointed without some extraordinary reason.
3. To begin (those of us present), exactly at the hour, with singing and prayer.
4. To speak each of us in order, freely and plainly, the true state of our souls, with the faults we have committed in thought, word, or deed, and the temptations we have felt since our last meeting."

Here are some questions people were asked before being admitted to the cell groups:
1. Have you peace with God through our Lord Jesus Christ?
2. Have you the forgiveness of your sins?
3. Has no sin, inward or outward, dominion over you?
4. Do you desire to be told of your faults?
5. Do you desire to be told from time to time whatever is in our heart concerning you?
6. Consider! Do you desire that we should tell you whatsoever we think, fear, or hear concerning you?

7. Do you desire in doing this that we should come as close as possible, that we should cut to the quick and search your heart to the bottom?
8. Is it your desire and design to be on this, and all other occasions, entirely open so as to speak everything that is in your heart without exception, without disguise and without reserve?

The following five questions were asked at every meeting:
1. What sins have you committed since our last meeting?
2. What temptations have you met with?
3. How were you delivered?
4. What have you thought, said or done of which you doubt whether it be sin or not?
5. Have you nothing you desire to keep secret?

Wesley believed that every member should be responsible for every other member. The style of life they sought to share with each other was characterized by openness, transparency, a caring community and submission.[1]

What is "Submission"?

The word "submission" often is met with suspicion. Invariably the word conjures up a picture of oppression. In contrast the biblical meaning of submission is "a voluntary yielding in love, a readiness to renounce one's own will for the sake of others." A couple of words help describe submission without the negatives.

The first word is **accountability.** Accountability means I am liable to be called to account for my life. It means I am regularly answerable for key areas of my life to certain people. It means I am being held responsible for who I am and what I do. The purpose of accountability in one's life is nothing less than an attempt to become more Christlike and to grow more intimately in Him.

Because of what Jesus Christ did on the cross and our desire to serve Him totally, we are willing to submit to the scrutiny of someone else for the sole purpose of becoming more obedient and devoted to Christ. Accountability is something I *receive from* others; I ask them to *hold me* accountable. On the flip side, accountability is something I *give to* others; they ask me to *hold them* accountable. Accountability is love in action as we seek to challenge one another into growing toward wholeness. Accountability is the Body of Christ caring for each member—asking each one to demonstrate responsibility. It is a voluntary yielding in love. "To whom are you submitted?" is a loaded question in today's vocabulary, but "To whom are you accountable?" is an enabling question. "Submit yourselves to one another" (Ephesians 5:21) may not communicate well in today's setting, but "Be accountable to one another" says it clearly.

Groups like *Alcoholics Anonymous* who make "keep me honest" pacts between members definitely fit the accountability model. However, this example is usually limited to just a few specific areas, where the accountability I am referring to is designed to encompass your entire life.

Has anyone ever asked you to hold him accountable for an area of his life? Have you ever asked anyone to hold you accountable in one particular area of your life? And just exactly what is accountability, anyway?

In talking with people, it is clear that accountability is a familiar term, and everyone knows it is important, but very few people actually know how to define it. Unfortunately, most people would rather be hurt by flattery than helped by criticism (accountability). This book will outline not only the principles involved in understanding accountability but also give you a mechanism for incorporating it immediately into your life.

The second word is **interdependence**. The Body of Christ is not characterized by dependence. Dependence keeps people from wholeness. Dependence means you are unable to function as an autonomous free agent. Dependence is crippling, not freeing.

On the other hand, independence is not characteristic of the church either. We are not loners living out a private, eccentric, aloof Christian life. It is not just "God and me." Rather it is meant to be a life of interrelatedness and affirmation. We are neither dependent nor independent but interdependent. Dependence produces weak, incomplete people. Independence produces proud, pretentious people. Interdependence produces whole, loving, serving people. Interdependence is the Body using the individual's gifts for the sake of the whole. It is the Body cooperating together in love, to see men and women coming to Christian maturity in accountable, interdependent relationships. Ephesians 4:13-15 says, "Until we all reach unity in the faith and in the knowledge of the Son of God and become mature, attaining to the whole measure of the fullness of Christ, then we will no longer be infants, tossed back and forth by the waves and blown here and there by every wind of teaching and by the cunning and craftiness of men in their deceitful scheming. Instead, speaking the truth in love, we will in all things grow up into him who is the Head, that is, Christ."

Medical science has yet to discover a hand, eye, kidney or lung that can function alone. Each organ needs the other members of the body to sustain and nourish it. The only true "independent" organs are amputated, dead and useless. The same holds true in the Body of Christ. Each member of the Body needs the other members for strength, support and encouragement.

When you're interdependent, you care enough about someone else to challenge him to a higher standard of Christian living. Accountability doesn't mean you seek to control or impose your expectations on him; instead, you challenge him to respond to God's work in his life. It is having permission to point out a "blind spot" and come alongside to help change occur. The embarrassing, and sometimes painful, act of baring our soul to another can lead to growth. Gary Rosberg said, "Accountability is like building a guard rail at the top of a mountain road that protects us from going over the edge—and running an ambulance service at the bottom of the mountain just in case."[2]

THE NEED FOR TEAMWORK

As a former athlete, I participated on a number of both excellent and terrible teams. It was very easy to distinguish the difference. The poor teams were filled with individuals seeking personal gain, a lack of concern for others on the team, virtually no discipline, rampant hypocrisy and lots of backbiting and unrest. On the other hand, the good teams exhibited humility, confidence in the other members, an attitude of togetherness, a commitment to a greater cause and a belief in one another.

Teamwork is a concept which God has stressed since the beginning of time. In the Garden of Eden God saw that man needed a "suitable helper." Moses had his brother Aaron help him lead people out of Egypt toward the Promised Land. David and Jonathan had a special friendship which encouraged and challenged one another; later Nathan played an important part in David's life, as he was willing to confront him openly regarding David's sin with Bathsheba. Daniel had three close friends, Shadrach, Meschach and Abednego, to stand beside him. Paul had his special missionary companions of Barnabus, Silas and Timothy. Jesus not only had His 12 disciples but an even closer intimate friendship with Peter, John and James. In fact, examine the Bible, and look for people who lived out their faith in God alone. You will not find anyone who successfully navigated their life without a support system.

Sometimes the "supporting" person was visible and at other times they were out of the limelight. Being sent out "two by two" has always been a biblical pattern. No person can, or is meant to, live the Christian life alone. Eventually, our heart will turn towards evil. Jeremiah 17:9 says, "The heart is deceitful above all things and beyond cure. Who can understand it?"

God never intended for us to live our Christianity out as a Lone Ranger. Even the modern day Lone Ranger had his sidekick Tonto and his beloved horse Silver. "A cord of three strands is not quickly broken," says the author of Ecclesiastes. In other words, we can't walk through life solo. Today, God intends for us to not live an independent lifestyle but one of complete dependence upon Him and interdependence on others around us.

SYNERGY

Let me explain it another way through the concept of "synergy." Synergy is one of the most powerful realities in all of God's creation. And yet it appears to be little understood and seldom practiced in the hustle and bustle of daily living. For those who learn about synergy and make it a priority in all relationships—personal, work, church, etc.—the end results and rewards will be great.

Synergy is defined as "harmonious teamwork toward a common goal to the degree that the outcome is greater than the sum of the parts." With synergy two plus two equals more than four because of the bonus effect of harmonious effort. A fire of hot coals is much hotter than the individual heat of each coal when added up. In nuclear energy the key to the awesome power is fusion, or the uniting of certain elements into a chain reaction of rapid, multiple bonding or synergy.

A classic example of synergy is the two oxen of the same strength. Each one can pull four tons by itself, but together they can pull 22 tons. How can this be? Because of the extra adrenaline flow of having a partner in harmony in a task and because of the need to break the inertia of a stationary weight. It is more difficult to break the inertia of the weight than to pull it. Together the oxen can break the inertia of that much weight. That same principle was tested with two horses in Germany. One horse could pull eight tons and the other one nine, but together they could pull 30 tons.

You can observe the extraordinary benefits of synergy in nature, business, athletics, the church and marriage/family relations. Wise business leaders are learning and implementing the concepts of synergy and seeing profits rise dramatically. In athletics we see heavily favored teams lose to underdogs because one team worked well together while the other one did not. In marriage and family, synergy is critical to surviving and prospering in the pressures and trials of daily life. If a married couple is not in harmony, their prayers will be hindered, according to 1 Peter 3:7. Parents who use synergy with their children will be giving them wonderful tools for their future.

The Bible exhorts us to live in synergy with others. Exodus 18:13-27 demonstrates the benefits for Moses and the people he served. Nehemiah rebuilt the wall around Jerusalem using the synergism of many different types and ages of people who knew little or nothing about masonry. Ecclesiastes 4:9-12 illustrates the value and power of two or three together. Acts 2:22 gives a great example of synergy as the early church began to witness and minister with power and credibility. John 17 underscores the high priority for Christians to live and serve in unity, and 2 Timothy 2:2 outlines a simple plan for leadership multiplication using synergy in teaching and training.[3]

God's message is preeminently one of hope and purpose. God does have a plan for our lives. He does care about us and our circumstances. He will give us wisdom and strength when we need them. Though we may not understand His plan and purpose at every point along the way, He can be trusted. Part of the journey is recognizing that people will play a very important role in fulfilling God's plan. What is our mindset? The ultimate goal is to be obedient to the Father and help others do the same. We do this by following Jesus Christ, making Him our model. He is the one we serve!

THE DREAM TEAM

Most of the sports teams I played on in high school and college involved people who had major egos and extremely selfish behaviors. There was more emphasis made on personal accomplishments rather than care and concern for the team. Looking back, we needed to come together—to bond with one another. We may have been in the same boat, but we were all paddling in different directions.

One of the keys to a successful team is when bonding occurs. Many coaches try to create an environment where trust and acceptance occur before the season starts. It is referred to as creating the "right chemistry." If a team bonds together it can end up being a very meaningful experience; however, if positive chemistry is not achieved, it normally results in a mediocre season.

Successful teams draw from a variety of backgrounds and interests. Each player brings a unique personality and different experiences to the team. Many times, the drills, wind sprints and hours in the weight room accompanied by the sweat pouring from our bodies allow us to get to know one another. If everyone is working hard, the respect and admiration for one another deepens, and bonds forge. I have witnessed teams with sub-par talent beat teams with far superior athletes simply because there was camaraderie.

Our teammates influence us greatly. Whether it is following their inappropriate paths or allowing their positive habits rub off on us, the power of our teammates and friends on us is enormous. Proverbs 13:20 reminds us, "He who walks with the wise grows wise, but a companion of fools suffers harm." Ralph Waldo Emerson said, "...we are the architects of our own friendships." The teammates we hang out with and the friends we keep will take us one of two directions—UP or DOWN!! There is no neutrality when it comes to the people we run around with at school, church or on the job. When friendships are developed among teammates, it can cause your team to excel beyond expectations.

The Bible reminds us of the danger of living in isolation. All of us were created for "relationships" both vertically with God and horizontally with other people. In fact, I believe the whole Bible can be summarized in one word: RELATIONSHIPS. We were not designed to run the race of life alone. The New Living Translation says, "The man who is alone is in real trouble." (Ecclesiastes 4:9-10). Biblical characters like Solomon, Saul, Judas Iscariot, and many others found themselves in terrible situations because they didn't bond with people who were strong in their faith. They were not meant to live without vital life-giving relationships. In Saul's case, Samuel was a man who could have been a trusted friend. Yet, instead of allowing him access, Saul stiff-armed him and kept him at arm's length distance. As a result, Saul suffered great loss.

When you bond with someone, you can make a positive change. It begins with seeing the need to make change and having the courage to make it happen with a new plan of action. Every person needs protection from self, along with a safety net. Pride is one of the greatest enemies to this process.

NOT SUCH A SILLY GOOSE

Next fall when you see geese heading south for the winter...flying along in a V formation...you might consider what science has discovered as to why they fly that way.

As each bird flaps its wings, it creates an uplift for the bird immediately following. By flying in V formation the whole flock adds at least 71 percent greater flying range than if each bird flew on its own.

People who share a common direction and sense of community can get where they are going more quickly and easily because they are traveling on the thrust of one another.

When a goose falls out of formation, it suddenly feels the drag and resistance of trying to go it alone...and quickly gets back into formation to take advantage of the lifting power of the bird in front.

If we have as much sense as a goose, we will stay in formation with those who are headed the same way we are.

When the head goose gets tired, it rotates back in the wing, and another goose flies point.

It is sensible to take turns doing demanding jobs...with people or with geese flying south.

Geese honk from behind to encourage those up front to keep up the speed. What do we say to those around us when we honk from behind?

Finally...and this is important...when a goose gets sick or is wounded by gunshots and falls out of formation, two other geese fall out with the goose and follow it down to lend help and protection. They stay with the fallen goose until it is able to fly or until it dies; and only then do they launch out on their own or with another formation to catch up with their group.

If we have the sense of a goose, we will stand by each other like that.[4]

Notes

1   The information about John Wesley was sent to me by Craig Hamilton. The source of this is unknown, although portions were taken from "Guidelines for Groups" from Broadway Baptist Church, Kansas City, Missouri.

2   "We're In This Together," Gary Rosberg, *New Man*, September 1995, p. 67.

Chapter Five

HOW TO GET STARTED

Getting started is often the most difficult part of the entire process because it means that you see the need to enter into an accountable (submissive) relationship. You have to be willing to risk—setting aside natural, selfish attitudes and desires and come under the authority of someone who is committed to you completely. It should not be entered into lightly but with deliberate intent and mutual commitment.

WHAT DOES SCRIPTURE SAY?

"Brothers, if someone is caught in a sin, you who are spiritual should restore him gently. But watch yourself, or you also may be tempted. Carry each other's burdens, and in this way you will fulfill the law of Christ" (Galatians 6:1-2).

"Each of you should look not only to your own interests, but also to the interests of others" (Philippians 2:4).

"A new command I give you: Love one another. As I have loved you, so you must love one another. By this all men will know that you are my disciples, if you love one another" (John 13:34-35).

"Wounds from a friend can be trusted, but an enemy multiplies kisses" (Proverbs 27:6).

"You, my brothers, were called to be free. But do not use your freedom to indulge the sinful nature; rather, serve one another in love" (Galatians 5:13).

"Whoever loves discipline loves knowledge, but he who hates reproof is stupid" (Proverbs 12:1).

"As iron sharpens iron, so one man sharpens another" (Proverbs 27:17).

Reasons People Refuse Accountability

People fight accountability for many reasons. Over the past ten years as I've shared on this subject, the same excuses keep coming forward as to why they don't need accountability. Do any of the following excuses apply to you?

1. I'm the only one who struggles.
2. If they knew the truth about me, I would be rejected.
3. I can handle this on my own.
4. I've got too many problems to have someone carry those with me. No one really cares.
5. I've been burned in the past...no more.
6. I'm too busy.
7. Hey, I'm okay. Accountability is for "really" sick people.
8. What I do privately is my own business.
9. I like the sin I'm wallowing in, and I don't want to get right and change my sin patterns.
10. I can't show any weaknesses. Too many people are counting on me.
11. My sin won't impact anyone else.

Don't be deceived by believing these lies. Once again I remind you that the goal of accountability is to please God and to walk closer with Him. The apostle Paul captured the significance of this when he prayed in Ephesians 1:17, "I keep asking that the God of our Lord Jesus Christ, the glorious Father, may give you the Spirit of wisdom and revelation, so that you may know him better." The goal of spiritual friendship should never be focused on one's personality or human ingenuity but in coming to know God better. At the end of my life I want to hear Christ say, "Well done, good and faithful servant!" (Matthew 25:23).

Keys To Getting Started

Assuming you're ready to begin, here are some guidelines to help you in finding someone to walk beside you.

1) *Pray and Risk.* Talk to God about your group. Ask Him to guide you to the right person(s). Don't get frustrated if it may take time for God to reveal His person(s) for you. Supportive relationships where you discuss your weaknesses and failures are risky. Are you willing to commit yourself to others who will support and encourage you? Pray for God to show you people who desire to have a committed relationship to Jesus Christ and others.

2) *Initially find at least one person to whom you are willing to be accountable.* In the working world everyone is accountable to someone. Even the self-employed owner is accountable to customers and clients. Successful businesses challenge their employees to perform certain tasks. The employee then has the opportunity to run with the goals and make things happen. With that freedom comes the challenge for accurate reporting and a completed project (i.e., accountability). It is similar in our personal lives, too. Unless we are accountable on a regular basis, we, like sheep, will go astray (Isaiah 53:6).

The responses we communicate to one another should relate to the goals and standards we have set for ourselves, not contradicting Scripture. These goals should be set to help us accomplish our understanding of God's purpose for our lives and the priorities He has for us. We need someone to whom we can answer by giving an accurate report on how we are progressing toward these goals and standards.

Finding one or more accountability partners is not easy. The overriding qualities are people who love Christ, who want to see you succeed and who also sense a need for accountability in their own lives. Pick people who you respect, people you feel compatible with and whose judgment you trust. You do not want to end up second-guessing the person you have given authority to ask you the hard questions. Proverbs 13:20 says, "He who walks with the wise grows wise, but a companion of fools suffers harm."

You may find it more appropriate to have different people hold you accountable in different areas. For example, several of the guys in my group help monitor my weight. Another, I trust more with financial matters. This will take time to develop.

Chances are good that an existing friend is a candidate for an accountability partner. Those who share a common interest with you are ideal. Perhaps the person or persons may be someone you work with daily or serve with on a board or committee. Maybe it is someone you regularly see in your recreation routine. Someone you worship with each week may be the right person for you. I even urge you to seek out those of different ages and cultures. Stu Weber points out, "Accountability grows over time. As your relationship and confidence in one another develop and as your acceptance and affirmation take root, you earn the right to ask the hard questions."[1]

Under no circumstance should you have a person of the opposite sex be your partner other than your spouse. Spouses are particularly helpful in addressing areas of personal weakness because of the significant time spent together. We should invite accountability into our marriage and be willing to discuss all the issues with them. However, there are some things that are best shared exclusively with people of the same sex.

The Truth About Friends

Chuck Swindoll tells us that Scripture underscores the importance of friendship by making more than 100 references to it. Let's take a look at some truths about friends in general.

1. **Friends are essential, not optional.** There is no substitute for a friend—someone to care, to listen, to comfort, even to reprove (Proverbs 27:6, 17).

2. **Friends must be cultivated; they're not automatic.** "Friendship is to be purchased only by friendship. A man may have authority over others, but he can never have their heart but by giving his own."[2]

3. **Friends impact our lives; they're not neutral.** Those we are close to rub off on us, change us. Their morals and philosophies, convictions and character eventually become our own (1 Corinthians 15:33; Psalms 1:1; Proverbs 13:20).

4. **Friends come in four classifications, not one.** As we look at the different levels of friendship, notice how the number of friends we have in each of the categories *decreases* the further down the list we go. But honesty *increases* in these friendships.

a. **Acquaintances.** Acquaintances are those with whom you have infrequent contact and shallow interaction. They don't ask deep questions but skate through the relationship on the ice of superficiality.

b. **Casual friends.** With these people you have more contact, common interests, and you feel comfortable asking more specific questions.

c. **Close friends.** With close friends you share life goals, the freedom to ask personal questions, and meaningful projects.

d. **Intimate friends.** With intimate friends you have regular contact and a deep commitment to mutual character development. You share the freedom to criticize and correct, encourage and embrace. They are your sheltering trees.[3]

3) *Decide the key areas for accountability.* Patrick Morley gives us insight into this area by illustrating the "*Titanic* and the Accountability Iceberg."

The British steamer *Titanic* was considered by experts to be unsinkable. One of the largest sea disasters in history occurred when the *Titanic* struck the hidden part of an iceberg on its maiden voyage during the night of April 14, 1912. Fifteen hundred people perished as the submerged part of a mountain of ice ripped open a three-hundred-foot-long gash in the hull of what was then the greatest ocean liner in the world.

An iceberg is one of nature's most beautiful and dangerous phenomena. What we see of these masses of broken-off glaciers are beautiful—like the "best foot" each of us puts forward with our friends. But only one-eighth to one-tenth of an iceberg is visible—the rest is hidden below the surface of the water. And that is where the danger lurks.

Like an iceberg, the beautiful part of our lives is that tenth or so which people can see. What's below the surface, however, is where we live our real lives—lives often hidden from the scrutiny of other Christians. The jagged subsurface edges of our secret lives often rip open our relationships and damage our spiritual lives. What is unseen and not carefully examined can sink us when we are unaccountable for those areas of our lives.

THE ACCOUNTABILITY ICEBERG

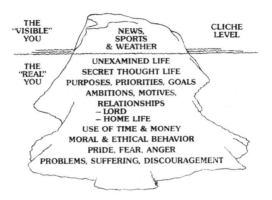

The "accountability iceberg figure" (pictured above) shows how most of our conversation revolves around the cliché level of life—news, sports and weather. But this is the tip of the iceberg—the "visible" you. The "real" you wrestles with gut-wrenching issues in the key areas of our lives every day, and we each need someone to help us navigate the submerged dangers of an unexamined life. The key areas in which all of us need accountability include our relationship with God, relationship with spouse, relationship with kids, use of money and time, moral and ethical behavior and areas of personal struggle.

What is something you really struggle with? What are your weak spots? Wouldn't you like to know your blind spots? In which areas of your secret thought life do you struggle? What are your personal areas of great temptation? These are questions an accountability partner should be asking regularly.[4]

Our accountability group has settled on 10 questions which are appropriate for our needs and are noted in Chapter 6 and the back cover of this book. A description of these questions are noted in Chapters 8-17. You should decide with your accountability partner(s) the best questions that fit your particular needs.

The composition of the group needs to be determined as well. In a closed group there are no visitors, and the more private the environment, the deeper you will converse. In an open group significant intimacy will not occur.

4) *Set a regular time and place, including a systematic method for getting through the questions.* Contact with your accountability partner(s) should be frequent. I would suggest a weekly meeting, though bi-monthly can also work. Too much happens in a month to meet less often than every two weeks. Our group gets together at 6:00 a.m. weekly in a private room at a local restaurant. The meetings go until approximately 7:30 a.m. We spend the first few minutes getting a general update from people in the group on what has transpired over the course of the past week. Usually you can get a pretty good reading on how the specific questions will play out based on this overview time. Once everyone has had time to give his update, then we proceed into the specific questions that we have decided upon. We close our time with prayer. Here are some guidelines which have helped us.

a) *Begin on time.* If someone is late, then he will miss out on the general update time. A commitment to the time parameters should be followed by all members of the group. If not, it will become a source of great frustration. From time to time we have used a variety of ice-breakers to help get started. One fun way is to describe your previous week through describing a weather forecast (i.e. partly sunny, foggy, hurricane, etc.).

b) *Limit the general time to just a couple of minutes per person.* Though this is an important time, it should not replace the core questions. If not watched closely, you can really chew up your time talking about general, non-personal issues (i.e. news, sports and weather).

c) *Have no more than five people in your group.* More than five makes it extremely difficult to get through all the questions in a timely and thorough manner. If your group is larger than five, then after the general update time, break up into smaller groups (of two or three).

d) *Have a different person begin each question, and juggle the order of the questions to meet the needs of your group.* Initially, the questions may feel awkward, unless accompanied by personal concern, compassion and friendship. They should be asked creatively. Give the person being asked the question all the "air time" needed to give an accurate report—to "give an answer." Remember, the ultimate purpose is to become more like the Lord in all our ways. Also, allowing people to initiate the questions models leadership skills and gives everyone a sense of ownership.

e) *Find your own rhythm.* Each group will be different in how its members flow together. Try to eliminate all expectations. Be careful within the small group with too much structure because it can stifle the relationships.

f) *Limit your comments until each person has had the chance to respond.* You can really disrupt the time if you pause and analyze each response. However, be sensitive to those who need specific help or instruction in working through hardships or difficult times.

g) *Keep a running list of areas where prayer requests are needed or where people make a vow to do something in the future.* Once someone makes a commitment, you have an opportunity to bring this commitment to their attention at a later time.

h) *Seek out the Word of God to discover biblical insights.* Gain wisdom and direction from the Bible not by looking for man's opinions. When direction from the Bible is not clear, refer to Chapter 6 on "gray areas."

i) *Share victories as well as defeats.* It's important to discuss progress in areas where historically you have stumbled. We have had lots of "high fives" during our accountability time together. Greg Ponchot, Indiana Pacers chaplain, helped give me insight to this area through the illustration shown below.

Quadrant #1 represents areas where we "always lose" pertaining to various sins/temptations in our life. Quadrant #2 is when we "sometimes lose." Quadrant #3 is when we "some-

	ALWAYS	SOMETIMES
WIN	4	3
LOSE	1	2

times win." Quadrant #4 is when we "always win." We need to recognize that many times there is a process of going through all four quadrants. It may be unrealistic and extremely frustrating to assume that you or people in your group can make a jump directly from Quadrant #1 to Quadrant #4. Also, if you find yourself in the first three quadrants, you can always improve. If you are in the fourth quadrant, don't become cocky and arrogant lest you find yourself becoming an easy prey for the enemy to attack.

j) *Close in prayer.* It is crucial that this be a priority for the group. Commit to pray for and encourage each other throughout the week. We also assign prayer partners on a weekly basis and encourage each person to contact our partner for a brief check-in time either by phone or in person. If you utilize prayer partners, juggle it around so that each member can build a relationship with a different person each week.

5) *Establish a covenant.* Although this can seem a bit awkward, it will give you a road map and a set of ground rules to help give some structure and boundaries. It describes our commitment level to the group, to one another, and our resolve to keeping the group a healthy and safe place. Thom Corrigan describes three types of covenants:

The first is an *assumed* covenant where each member comes to the group with an assumption of what the group should be like and what it should accomplish. Unfortunately, unless those assumptions are discussed openly, the individual group members will never be totally on the same page. This group is headed for an aimless and uncertain journey.

The second is an *oral* covenant. This is better because it is discussed with the likelihood that everyone has the opportunity to participate in the deliberation concerning the direction and make-up of the group.

Finally, there's the *written* covenant. This is the best type of group covenant because it takes the process a step further and commits your group's mission plan to paper. With this style of covenant, the wording can be edited to reflect the true heart of the group, and each member can receive a copy of it.[5]

A group covenant is a tremendous gift which needs to be nurtured and sustained. It can anchor a group for a significant period of time. I recently was with a group of men in St. Louis who believed so much in a written covenant that they had theirs notarized. At the end of this chapter there's more information on covenants. A sample of my group's written covenant is included in Appendix B and a copy of the CrossSeekers covenant is in Appendix C.

6) *Be transparent.* You will be a detriment to your accountability group if you are not honest. Richard Exley shares, "There is only one way to end the torment, only one way to escape sin's prison of pain: Renounce your sins and embrace God's forgiveness. God has forgiven your sin by faith in Christ, but experience teaches us that secret sin can seldom be overcome unless we also confess it to another person. Sin flourishes in the dark; it thrives in secret. But it withers and dies in the Light of Christ and through confession to a fellow believer. If a man continues living a double life, God will expose the sin."

He adds: "King David tried to keep his adulterous affair with Bathsheba a secret (Psalms 32:3-4), and he had great guilt (Psalms

38:4, 6-8), but only when Nathan the prophet confronted him did he get right. It was both painfully humbling and wonderfully liberating. It was humbling because David's sin became public knowledge. He could no longer pretend to be something he was not. Yet it was also liberating because he could now throw himself on the mercies of God."[6]

Gary Bauer in his January 23, 1998, "Washington Update" made reference to Dostoevsky's novel, *The Brothers Karamazov,* about lying to yourself. It says, "The important thing is to stop lying to yourself. A man who lies to himself and believes his own lies becomes unable to recognize truth, either in himself or in anyone else, and he ends up losing respect for himself as well as for others. When he has no respect for anyone, he can no longer love, and in order to divert himself, having no love in him, he yields to his impulses, indulges in the lowest forms of pleasure and behaves in the end like an animal in satisfying his vices. And it all comes from lying—lying to others and to yourself."

Your accountability group will be a safe place where you can honestly share your life. If you are not going to tell the whole truth, don't waste your time and others' as well. George Toles, a respected Seattle businessman, has been meeting with three other men since 1984. He says, "Each person has the right to be non-spiritual. After all, if you can't be honest here, can you be honest anywhere?" They have adopted the attitude of allowing each other to slide but to never drop the reins on one another. He adds, "Our group doesn't get stale because we discover new caves and caverns of undiscovered information."

7) *Stay on course.* Ted Engstrom said it this way: "Without clear, concise, measurable goals you will not be able to establish proper accountability. Accountability assumes an ability to measure performance, and without goals there is nothing against which to measure progress." He also adds, "People are much more likely to accept accountability when they participate in establishing the goals and objectives." [7] Dr. Laura Schlessinger describes it this way, "Living for yourself and believing you're accountable only to your-

self enables you to make and break the rules at whim."[8] People must take ownership of the process and embrace it.

CONFIDENTIALITY AND TRUST

The issue of confidentiality is a crucial one to consider. What is communicated in the group must stay there. Sadly, we all have been stung by leaks of confidential information. If I am going to share the real me with someone, I want to be absolutely sure I can trust him. The fear of betrayal by a friend keeps many of us from taking the risk of being accountable. Make a covenant with your partners to assure yourself and them of the commitment you have made to confidentiality.

Typically people don't open up because of fear of exposure. When we know confidentiality exists, we can take risks and experience the growth in our friendships as we honor each other. The progression is: Risk builds relationship. Relationship builds trust. Trust strengthens character.

Eventually if your group is going to last trust has to exist among the members. This trust route is what existed between Jesus and God. No matter what Jesus faced He said, "Thy will be done." Defeat itself could not daunt Him or make Him draw back. If we desire to be trustworthy, we must begin by having resolute trust in God and in God alone, just like Jesus Christ. Trust is built through the belief that God knows what is best for your life. God simply asks us to trust Him in keeping His promises. He asks us to let go of reasons, rights, and fears and simply throw our arms around Him. As our trust and dependence upon Him deepen, and as we grow in our integrity and love, we will become trustworthy in our daily lives.

One of the most radical accounts of a trust opportunity can be found in Acts 9. There, we read about a man named Saul—a powerful Jewish leader who had made it his mission to persecute all Jews who now followed the teachings of Jesus. In this story, Ananias has to trust God and Saul (eventually Paul). Re-read this story and be reminded that God says trust Me.

STAYING WITH IT

People who work out together understand the benefits of accountability. When you exercise alone, it's easier to skip a day or quit short of the mark. With a partner, there are two good reasons to finish: (1) they don't want to fall short of their verbalized goals and (2) they don't want to drag their partner down by tempting him to stop short.

I encourage you to stick it out. You will want to quit, perhaps often. Ask God to strengthen you when you want to give up. The purpose of accountability is to each day become more Christlike in all of our ways. Remember, it is Jesus who is the object of our search, our devotion, our sacrifice and our affection. Rely on Christ first and allow accountability to be a checkpoint in your daily walk with Him.

If you find that you are getting bogged down, then I encourage you to address the concerns openly and try to determine a new course of action which will meet the needs of the group. A group could improve with a new location, time, group members, different structure or a variety of other adjustments.

From time to time, you will have people leave your group both voluntarily and involuntarily. Regardless of how they leave, it is very important to maintain the confidentiality. It would be unfair to have people who left the group discover leaks of information about themselves at a later time.

ADDING NEW MEMBERS

As people move on we have found it very encouraging to bring in new members. That has proved to be extremely beneficial because it brings a new energy to the group as well as a fresh perspective. A key to success in this area is bringing new members up to speed with the rest of the group. This would include making time for each person to share their testimony with the new member apart from the regular accountability group and a willingness to share past victories and defeats with the new member. Obviously, adding someone should be done only with the consent of the entire group.

DEALING WITH CONFLICT

There may be times when you have a disagreement or a conflict within the group. I encourage you to use the principles as outlined in Matthew 18:15-17. The ultimate goal is reconciliation by following biblical principles. 1 Peter 5:2-3 reminds us, "Be shepherds of God's flock that is under your care, serving as overseers—not because you must, but because you are willing, as God wants you to be; not greedy for money, but eager to serve, not lording it over those entrusted to you, but being examples to our flock."

I'm weak in this area and am always looking for resolution models to help me. One of the best, as noted earlier, is Nathan's confrontation with David (2 Samuel 12:1-14). The keys to Nathan's success included knowing the truth, having a relationship with David based on genuine love, initiating at the right time, choosing wise words, not rushing or becoming emotional, going directly to David with the facts, having courage and desiring to affirm and reconcile. We need to be soft on the person but hard on the subject. May we all prayerfully confront these difficult, but necessary, situations.

OUTSIDE THE MEETING

Look for opportunities to support one another by getting together outside of the normal meeting time. This could be dropping by the work place, having lunch/dinner together, doing a recreational activity or attending an event together.

One of the highlights of our group is an annual weekend retreat at the Lake of the Ozarks. We schedule the event months in advance and bring along our spouses and children. It is a wonderful time to enhance our relationships.

COVENANT RELATIONSHIPS

Covenant means to agree, to be of one mind, to come together. A binding and solemn agreement to do or keep from doing. The dynamics of a covenant relationship are noted below. I encourage you to adopt these as general guidelines within your own group.

1. THE COVENANT OF **AFFIRMATION** (Unconditional love): There is nothing you have done, or will do, that will make me stop loving you. I will love you and affirm you no matter what you have said or done in your past. I may not agree with your actions, but I will love you unconditionally. I love you as you are and for what Christ wants to make of you (1 John 4:7-12).

2. THE COVENANT OF **AVAILABILITY**: Anything I have—time, energy, wisdom, myself, finances—are all at your disposal. As part of this availability I pledge regularity of time both in prayer and meeting at agreed-upon times. I consider that time to be of the highest priority on my schedule (Hebrews 10:25).

3. THE COVENANT OF **PRAYER**: I promise to pray for you, to uphold you, and to attempt to listen to the Holy Spirit concerning your needs so that I can share them with you. I believe that God desires for me to pray for you (James 5:13-16).

4. THE COVENANT OF **OPENNESS**: I will strive to be open and transparent. I need you, and I trust you with my needs. I affirm your worth to me as a person I can trust (2 Corinthians 6:11-13).

5. THE COVENANT OF **SENSITIVITY**: Even as I desire to be known and understood by you, I covenant to be sensitive to you and your needs to the best of my ability (Galatians 6:2,10).

6. THE COVENANT OF **HONESTY**: I will be honest in what I think I am hearing you say and feel. If this means risking pain for either of us, I will trust our relationship enough to take that risk, realizing that it is in "speaking the truth in love" that we grow up in every way (Ephesians 4:15-16).

7. THE COVENANT OF **CONFIDENTIALITY**: What goes on in this group stays here. I will say nothing that may be traced back or that could be injurious or embarrassing to my covenant partners. The assurance of confidentiality is vital to the success of the group (1 Corinthians 1:10).

8. THE COVENANT OF **ACCOUNTABILITY**: You have the right to expect growth from me so that I may apply the fullness of the gifts which God has given me and fulfill my God created-purposes. You have my permission to ask me about the goals I set with God, my family and my world. I expect you to lovingly not "let me off the hook." On the basis of Proverbs 27:17, "As iron sharpens iron, so one man sharpens another," I ask you to please share with me areas in my life that do not reflect Jesus because I want to grow in personal holiness (Hebrews 10:24).

9.   THE COVENANT OF FRIENDSHIP: A covenant relationship is a decision to develop friendships based on unconditional love (Proverbs 18:24).

10.   THE COVENANT OF NURTURE: It takes a conscious effort to nurture an authentic interest in others. This group forces us to do that (Philippians 2:3-8).

11.   THE COVENANT OF PATIENCE: We know that it will always take time—often a long time—to understand one another. There is no such thing as an "instant accountability group." Yet our current society, accustomed to the "instant," sometimes causes us to give up and quit before the group has time to develop (1 Corinthians 13:4-5).

12.   THE COVENANT OF EQUALITY: We will treat others as equals. The spiritual maturity, gifts and life experiences that each member brings to the group are all valid. There are no "leaders" in a covenant group (Galatians 3:28).

13.   THE COVENANT OF LISTENING: Because there are always those in a group who talk more—and those who tend to be quiet—a group requires a commitment to learn how to listen (Proverbs 18:2; 19:27).

14.   THE COVENANT OF UNANSWERED QUESTIONS: A commitment to an accountability group does not necessarily mean that if you bring a dilemma to the group, they will always provide an answer before you leave. Sometimes they are simply there to care and say, "I don't know the answer, I don't know what you should do, but I care and I will pray" (Philippians 4:6-7).

15.   THE COVENANT OF ENCOURAGEMENT: I will uplift and encourage you by believing in you (1 Thessalonians 5:11). [9]

A big part of accountability and covenant living is simply "getting together." Yet how do we really live out "iron sharpening iron" as opposed to drifting back to the old glib conversations and advice? One of the keys to this process has to do with the issue of wisdom (James 3:13-18). James makes it painfully clear that there are two sources of wisdom—man and God. Man's wisdom is "earthly, sensual and devilish" (v.15) and produces "bitter envying and strife in your hearts" (v.14) that is the cause of "confusion and every evil work." (v.16). True wisdom from God is not sought after in our culture. Wisdom from men is equated with words like "clever, ingenious, resourceful, shrewd, diplomatic, sensible, eloquent, cunning" and maybe even "tricky, crafty and sly." Man's wisdom results in answers but do those answers truly reflect God's viewpoint?

Proverbs 23:4 reminds us to "cease from your own wisdom." God's wisdom, James notes "is from above" (James 3:17). For accountability to work, God's wisdom is necessary. Yet how do we find God's wisdom? We have to open God's Word and find out what He has to say. A lawyer friend of mine told me that church members frequently approach him about legal advice. As they describe their conflict to him and the actions of the parties involved, he hears their anger, their desire to avenge themselves, and to retaliate even though they are a professing believer. In his words, "they don't come to me for godly counsel but for a big dose of 'man's wisdom.' "

How do we know when we are getting a good dose of man's wisdom as opposed to God's with our accountability partner?

1. There is little or no mention of the Bible, God or Jesus.
2. No advice to pray is given nor any attempt to pray is made.
3. The counsel gives subtle defenses of immoral actions, e.g., "Well, it's only natural you reacted like that."
4. It is suggested that you do something unscriptural or ungodly.
5. The motives and replies of the counsel appear self-serving rather than a response out of love and care.
6. The values and personal lifestyle of the counsel doesn't match his words.
7. The counsel encourages escaping responsibility rather than facing it.
8. The counsel advises that taking advantage of someone else is okay.

The key to look for in receiving input from your accountability partner(s) is to have them rely on God's Word for guidance and to be dependent upon His strength.

Former NFL players, Eric Boles and Jon Kitna, have been part of an accountability group for a number of years. They approach accountability with a combination of full transparency and not letting one another off the hook. They regularly talk about tempting situations, masturbation, personal finances, anger and pride issues—no subject is off limits. Eric states, "It is not a sin manage-ment group where we gather and console one another about the sin but don't do anything about it. Our group doesn't allow one another to get comfortable with their sin."Their covenant mindset is: "Totally understandable, but totally unacceptable." This phrase communicates that they are compassionate with one another's sin, yet they will not tolerate or excuse future behavior which does not glorify God. This is a great example of how the covenant is lived out among brothers who truly believe in one another.

Notes

1 "Someone to Lean On," Stu Weber, *Focus on the Family* magazine, June 1996, p. 4.

2 Thomas Wilson, in *Speaker's Encyclopedia of Stories, Quotations, and Anecdotes,* by Jacob M. Braude (Englewood Cliffs, NJ: Prentice-Hall, 1955), p. 155.

3 Charles R. Swindoll, *David, A Man After God's Own Heart* (Anaheim, CA: Insight for Living, 1992), pp. 129-130.

4 Patrick M. Morley, *A Man in the Mirror* (Nashville, TN: Thomas Nelson Publishers, 1992) pp. 276-277.

5 "Built to Last," Thom Corrigan, *New Man*, March/April 1997, pp. 74-76.

6 "The Silent Struggle With Secret Sin," Richard Exley, *New Man*, November/December 1996, p. 54.

7 "Accountability: An Essential Ingredient," Ted Engstrom and Ed Dayton, *Christian Management Report*, February 1997, pp. 21-22.

8 Dr. Laura Schlessinger, New York Times Special Features, *Kansas City Star*, February 16, 1997.

9 Adapted from materials provided by Dale D. Schlafer, "A Serious Call to Christian Leaders for a Devout and Holy Life," at the 1993 Promise Keepers Conference in Boulder, Colorado.

Chapter Six

DEVELOPING YOUR QUESTIONS

Every group must determine the areas where accountability needs to take place. Our group has developed 10 questions which work for us, but certainly each group should develop its own plan to address the areas of need. Over the past few years, I have seen a number of different formats and series of questions. Here are our 10 questions.

Our theme verse is, "Therefore, brethren, be all the more diligent to make certain about His calling and choosing you; for as long as you practice these things, you will never stumble" (2 Peter 1:10 NASB).

1. Have you spent daily time in Scriptures and in prayer?
2. Have you had any flirtatious or lustful attitudes, tempting thoughts, or exposed yourself to any explicit materials which would not glorify God?
3. Have you been completely above reproach in your financial dealings?
4. Have you spent quality relationship time with family and friends?
5. Have you done your 100% best in your job, school, etc.?
6. Have you told any half-truths or outright lies, putting yourself in a better light to those around you?
7. Have you shared the Gospel with an unbeliever this week?
8. Have you taken care of your body through daily physical exercise and proper eating and sleeping habits?
9. Have you allowed any person or circumstance to rob you of your joy?
10. Have you lied to us on any of your answers today?

The last question is not only a fun one, but helps remind everyone that the things shared must be done in complete honesty. If you are not going to be honest with your accountability partners, the entire commitment is meaningless.

We have taken our questions and placed them on a laminated, billfold-size card for quick and easy referencing. Each of the questions we discuss in our accountability group, along with helpful hints on specific issues are discussed in Chapters 8-17 (Section 2).

Later in this chapter I'll share with you a few different variations that may help you in developing questions that will work for you.

MAKING IT A DAILY EXPERIENCE

One of the discoveries I made from answering these questions with my group was a desire to walk in purity in my day-to-day activities. Because of my long history in maintaining a journal, I make the first part of my daily recording a summary of the following 10 questions. Due to the work of Christ in my own life and the success of our accountability group, these daily questions have really solidified my personal commitment to the goals I've established for myself.

1. Did I get up by 6:30 a.m. and have 7-8 hours of sleep? (This question really pertains to how successful I am in getting to sleep at a decent hour the night before. As a proclaimed "late night" person, my next day's performance is significantly better if I get over the urge to stay up late).
2. Did I have "quality" time with God today, through Scripture reading and prayer time?
3. Did I write at least one letter/note of encouragement? (Every day I try to write someone whom the Lord brings to mind).
4. Did I make at least one encouraging phone call to someone? (This one is similar to No. 3; it may be a local or long distance call).

5. Did I have an exercise time today? (At a minimum, I try to do some push-ups and sit-ups).

6. Did I give 100 percent best at my job, and what kinds of things occupied my work day? (This one ties directly into the setting of priorities).

7. Did I exhibit the qualities of a man or woman of God (i.e., being above reproach, purity in all matters, humility, servant, etc.)? (This ties back to leading a life of uprightness and integrity).

8. Did I do something which made me laugh or enjoy the day more fully? (I do not want to forget the value of doing something fun each and every day. Life is too short to not enjoy each day to the fullest).

9. Did I remove something on my procrastination list? What was it? (What a great feeling to remove something from this list).

10. Did I honor and encourage my wife and children? How? (These are the most important relationships the Lord has given me. I have the tremendous privilege to serve them with my best effort).

Many people have their own daily goal schedule. For instance, Joan Cronan, Women's Athletic Director at the University of Tennessee, has a daily acronym: BELLS. The "B" stands for Bible reading; "E" for Exercise; "L" for an encouraging Letter; "L" for Learning something; and "S" for doing a Special project.

VARIATIONS FROM THESE QUESTIONS

I was greatly encouraged by LPGA Hall of Famer Betsy King, who after reading this book found an accountability partner, designed her own questions and then put a Scripture reference to each one.

Feel free to adjust, add or delete questions as you deem appropriate for your own group or for you personally. My wife, Janna, met with a group of five women, and they added these questions:

Have you used your words to build up or tear down others or self? Have you exposed yourself or contributed to gossip? They have also adjusted our Question No. 6 by adding: Have you been committed to your words?

One group I know of focuses on three areas: faith, family and finances. Another group works individually in setting various goals, and then the group quizzes each other on progress of the goals at an annual retreat. Another group has an extended update time where members have the floor in answering an open question time. I have even heard of one group where periodically they will ask one of the members' spouses to come for a period of time where they can ask direct questions to the spouse to determine how things are really going from a different perspective.

Another group has a written report where all members fill in the blanks for the following four questions, prior to meeting together. This allows them to get a jump start and to be prepared to think through the week prior to arriving.

1. My pain was when_____ .
2. My growth from last week was_____ .
3. Growth I desire for next week is_____ .
4. My wins were_____ .

At the 1997 Promise Keepers Conference, one of the speakers urged men to: (1) share the Scriptures, (2) share your schedule, (3) share your relationships, (4) share where you are right now and (5) pray about all these elements.

Another group uses these questions: (1) What has been dominating your thoughts this week? (2) Have you recently put yourself in a compromising situation with another woman? (3) How are you handling the finances God has provided for you? (4) Have you been reading and studying the Scripture? What are you learning? (5) What issues are you and your wife dealing with this week? (6) How was your relationship with each of your kids this week? (7) What is happening at work that excites you? Frustrates you? Tempts you? (8) Are you having any fun? (9) And then the final question: Are you shooting straight with me or blowing smoke? [1]

One group breaks their questions into Spirit, Soul and Body. Their questions are: SPIRIT: (1) Did you seek to know His heart and as a result what did you learn from Scripture? (2) Did you seek to know His heart and allow Him to bring people to mind in your prayers? (3) Did you memorize Scripture this week? (4) Did you pray for, look for or seize any opportunities to share the Gospel? SOUL: (5) Are you continually treasuring your intimate relationships? How so? (6) What are you reading to supplement God's Word? What are you receiving from this? (7) Did you write at least two encouraging notes this week? (8) Was all of your work done heartily, as for the Lord? BODY: (9) Did your heart get five good workouts this week? (10) Did you get at least three Hans & Franz workouts this week? (11) Did you honor your body as the Temple of the Holy Spirit this week? Did you honor your body in eating and sleeping? (12) Are you feeding your spirit with LOVE versus feeding your flesh with lust?

Within the FCA ministry, accountability questions were designed with the "One Way 2 Play" program. See Page 268 for a reference to these questions.

Actually you can summarize the entire group of questions into two simple ones to save on time. These are at the heartbeat of sharing intimately. (1) What is the CLOSEST you have been to God this week? (2) What is the FARTHEST you have been from God this week?

The key is to determine areas of your life where you need immediate and specific help. Do not run from difficult questions; rather, challenge yourself to be completely above reproach in all areas of your life and be all that God wants you to be.

FROM A WOMAN'S PERSPECTIVE

Deb Shepley says, "Being involved in an accountability group has been one of the best things that I have done as a Christian. I did not need another Bible study or fellowship group. I needed to know that people cared about me, would pray for me, encourage me, and yes, keep me accountable in the areas where I struggled. Our small group of five women was targeted to female coaches. All of us have grown through the experience, and though I thought I knew them before, I have learned more about them as we have shared. One morning, one shared about her eating disorder, and it brought us closer together. I have found that in my own life a great danger is in feeling I have no needs. All around me the world emphasizes self-reliance, self-help, self-expression, self-confidence, self-sufficiency. Yet, I know I need people and more importantly, I need Jesus."

Deb, as well as other women, have discovered that accountability works for women as well as for men. In fact, it may be easier initially for women to address accountability issues.

With the help of several godly women, our ministry designed specific questions that may be more appropriate for women to answer (as opposed to the questions noted on Page 83 and the back of this book). The differences are subtle, but important.

1. What Scripture most impacted your heart this week? Why? Have you spent regular time in prayer? When?
2. Have your thoughts been pure? Have you resisted lustful, envious thoughts or exposed yourself to explicit materials?
3. How do you feel about how you've handled personal, family and/or business finances?
4. What three relationships have you nurtured most?
5. What has made it difficult to do your 100% best in the different roles in your life?
6. Have your words built up or torn down others or self? Have you exposed yourself or contributed to gossip? Have you been committed to your words? Have you put yourself in a better light to those around you?
7. Do you feel you missed any opportunities to talk to people about the Lord?
8. Have you taken care of your body through physical exercise and proper eating/sleeping habits?
9. Which fruit of the Spirit have you had the hardest time living out? Why?
10. Have you left anything hidden while answering these questions?

In addition to these questions, we also have suggested questions for teenagers and couples as noted on our web site: www.characterthatcounts.org

IT IS ALL ABOUT THE HEART

For many years, I have helped people design questions for their groups but the bottom line is found in Proverbs 4:23 which states, "Above all else guard your heart for from it flows the wellsprings of life." Another translation says it this way, "From your heart flows everything." The heart (not the questions) is what God cares about most.

Jerry Bridges said, "The word heart in Scripture is used in various ways. Sometimes it means our reason or understanding, sometimes our affections and emotions, and sometimes our will. Generally it denotes the whole soul of a man and all its faculties, not individually, but as they work together in doing good or evil. The MIND as it reasons, discerns and judges; the EMOTIONS as they like or dislike; the CONSCIENCE as it determines and warns and the WILL as it chooses or refuses—are all together called the heart."

According to John Eldridge, the subject of the heart is addressed in the Bible more than any other topic—more than works or service, more than belief or obedience, more than money, and even more than worship. Proverbs 21:2 says, "All a man's ways seem right to him, but the Lord weighs the heart." Eldridge states, "By taking out your heart, the enemy takes you out." This is why guarding your heart is critical for every believer.

There is no escaping the centrality of the heart. God knows that, and it is why He made it the central theme of the Bible, just as He placed the physical heart in the center of the human body. Our deepest thoughts are found in the heart. The heart is the source of all creativity, courage, conviction and faith, hope and love. It is the essence of our existence and the center of our being. Romans 10:9-10 says that saving faith only happens when we believe in our heart. You are not a Christian until you engage your heart—fully believing in Him with your heart.

The heart is the connection point between you and God. This goes way beyond principles, duties, programs, and accountability questions. It is not activities or information that change the way we live. The transformation and then the relationship each take place in the heart. One of the great verses of Scripture states, "You will find me when you seek me with all your heart" (Jeremiah 29:13).

Here are six keys to having a complete heart:
1) A desire to know God (Key Word: Relationship) - Psalm 37:4
2) A heart that seeks after Him (Key Word: Pursuit) - Psalm 119:10, 9:1
3) Totally trusting God (Key Word: Belief) - Proverbs 3:5-6

4) A desire to please God (Key Word: Ambition) - 2 Corinthians 5:9
5) Brokenness before God (Key Word: Humility) - Psalm 51:17;
   1 Corinthians 4:5
6) A responsiveness to God's people (Key Word: Servant) -
   2 Corinthians 4:16-18

GUIDELINES FOR GRAY AREAS
10 Key Questions To Ask Yourself

There may be some areas where concrete answers may not be easy to determine because it is not a black and white issue. I call these the "gray" areas. Here are some guidelines to consider to help you in determining the right decision to make:

1. (Desire) Do I honestly desire to know God's will? (John 5:30; 7:17)
2. (Scripture) Is there a Scripture passage or biblical principle to consider or apply? (Psalms 119:105; Mark 12:24)
3. (Prayer) Have I sincerely prayed and asked God what I should do? (Jeremiah 33:3; James 1:5; 1 John 5:14-15)
4. (Counsel) What is the counsel of others, especially from those who know and love me and God's Word? (Proverbs 11:14; 12:15; 15:22; 19:20)
5. (Loving others) Will doing this provide a loving example and build up others? (John 13:34-35; 1 Corinthians 8:9, 12; 10:24)
6. (Affect me) Will this help me to grow more like Christ, or could it potentially enslave me? (1 Corinthians 6:12; 10:23)
7. (Christ) What do I think Jesus would do about this? (1 John 2:5-6)
8. (Witness) Will doing this make me a more believable Christian and a better witness for Christ? (1 Corinthians 9:19-22;10:32-33)
9. (Glorify) Will doing this bring greater glory to God? (1 Corinthians 10:31)
10. (Peace) Do I honestly have a peace about doing this? (1 Corinthians 14:33; Philippians 4:7; Colossians 3:15)[2]

Notes
[1] "We're In This Together," Gary Rosberg, *New Man*, September/October 1995, p. 64.
[2] Author Unknown.

Chapter Seven

SATAN AND HIS STRATEGY

When I played college football, our team spent many hours watching films of our opponents, reading scouting reports, looking for patterns and tendencies and determining strengths and weaknesses. Before we stepped onto the battlefield each Saturday, we had a pretty good idea of who we were up against. Ultimately, preparing ahead of time resulted in developing a game plan which we felt would result in victory.

In the game of life our opponent, Satan, is our enemy. In this battle Satan will be defeated by God in the end. However, along the way Satan will do everything in his power to defeat us. As believers we can be successful against this opponent if we know his strategies and how to call upon the weapons of warfare to defeat him.

WHO IS HE?

Satan is first identified in Genesis 3:1 as a serpent, "more crafty than any of the wild animals." He distorts God's truth and leads Adam and Eve into the first sin. In Genesis 3:15 Satan receives his punishment from God as the first mention of Christ is made: "He (Jesus) will crush your head, and you (Satan) will strike his heel." Right then Satan's doom was assured, but that did not stop his destructive nature. Perhaps his stubbornness, anger, evil nature and pursuit of self was all part of the reason he decided to take as many people down with him as possible.

Isaiah 14:12-15 and Ezekiel 28:12-19 give a vivid picture of Satan's fall from heaven. Pride was in his heart. He wanted to be God. He is even described as a "marvelous creation," and, though powerful, he remains in subjection to God's power, and there is absolutely nothing he can do about it. He goes by many titles including Prince of Darkness, Beast, Destruction, Anti-Christ, Devil, Serpent, Tempter. I believe one of his greatest weaknesses is that he can't foresee the future. That is probably another reason why he is so persistent, and until Christ defeated him directly by overcoming death on the cross, he might have thought he could win. Even when Jesus showed up in the flesh, Satan was present, trying to twist God's Word (yes, Satan knows the Bible well).

One of the greatest "con" jobs of all-time is a perception that exists even among Christians that Satan is not real. The Bible extensively addresses him throughout the Old and New Testament. Jesus warned us repeatedly about him as written by all the Gospel writers. Moses, David, Peter and Paul all knew of his existence and covered him in their writings. We see a firsthand account of his presence in the life of Job and Zechariah. Yet, in spite of these many references, there are many who do not believe he exists. In a recent Barna poll of people who claimed to be a Christian, only 25 percent endorsed the belief that Satan is real. The Barna findings stated, "Many believers claim to trust what the Bible teaches, but they reject the notion of a real spiritual adversary." We are in a dangerous situation when we do not understand that there is a spiritual war raging with a real enemy who comes to "steal, kill and destroy."

WHAT IS SATAN LIKE?

1. *A murderer and a liar.* He is the father of all lies. He distorts and twists the truth. He lies about God and His love for you. He is the author of conflict. He is the opposite of God in every character quality. There is nothing good in him. He rejoices in death (John 8:44).

2. *He masquerades himself as an angel of light.* He tries to convince you that his ways are best (i.e., by promoting self first, seeking anger/revenge instead of forgiveness, murder instead of life, addictions instead of submission). He camouflages his true identity and purpose by making his ways seem appealing. Sin is Satan's agent (2 Corinthians 11:14).

3. *A sinner from the beginning.* The author of all sin. He will do anything to remove people from God's love and fellowship with other believers (1 John 3:8).

What Are His Strategies?

1. *At times he is blunt.* Newspaper accounts and media reports tell us that satanists, sorcerers, witches and all types of people are roaming the world under the influence of Satan and his power. First Peter 5:8-9 says, "Be self-controlled and alert. Your enemy the devil prowls around like a roaring lion looking for someone to devour. Resist him, standing firm in the faith, because you know that your brothers throughout the world are undergoing the same kind of sufferings."

2. *More times he is subtle.* He is coy, attractive and very deceitful. He convinces us to compromise just a little bit as he begins to wedge his way in. He will distract us by attempting to remove God from every part of our life. He attacks areas of weakness by throwing temptations our way. He also attacks areas of strength, especially areas where we feel self-confident and where we feel we can do something alone without God's help. He will also try to cause us to doubt that God exists, and he is the king of procrastination. He will always try to get you to begin something tomorrow that should be started today.

Regardless of his method, his goal is to deceive, destroy, rule and accuse. He will do whatever is necessary to accomplish his goals. Throughout the ages, Satan has tried to either destroy the Bible or to destroy people's confidence in God's Word. That will never happen because God's Word is eternal. The present day attack of Satan is rigorous and even intensifying as we approach Christ's return. Satan's strategy is well planned, but the Christian's weapons are more powerful. We can resolve to stand for what is right and true, no matter what the cost because we have an eternal reward that will never fade.

WHAT ARE WE TO DO?

1. *Put on the full armor of God.* We have been equipped with offensive and defensive weapons which will help us extinguish his fiery darts. Prayer and knowing God's Word minimize his effectiveness. We can call upon His power to aid us in the battles we face (Ephesians 6:10-18). Our enemy knows we grow in spiritual power as we spend time with God. The devil will try anything, even misdirecting our desires, to attack the source of our spiritual power. It is true that Satan trembles when we are on our knees and in His Word.

This divine armor, the armor of God, has been prepared for us, but we must choose to put it on. It is noteworthy that there is no armor for the back. If we turn our back on the enemy, we are exposed. This armor is compared to the offensive and defensive tools of first century military armor. Each piece of armor details a different aspect of being spiritually secure. The process of Christian maturity involves an ever-increasing understanding of who we are in Christ. The enemy constantly bombards us with negative messages that distort our identity in Christ. We need protection from these destructive forces. Just as our troops put on armor each day before going out in warfare, visualize yourself putting on each piece of the armor. Daily prayer is a time to "put on the full armor of God." See Appendix K "Putting on the Armor of God."

2. *Trust God.* Believe that God will be true to His Word. He has promised He will never leave us, nor forsake us. No matter what you face, stay close to Jesus Christ. He will provide a way out when temptation knocks at the door (1 Corinthians 10:13).

3. *Don't get isolated.* Former FCA Senior Vice-President Ralph Stewart uses a soccer illustration. He says, "One tactic of an offensive-minded soccer team is to get a player isolated one-on-one against the goalie. At this point he has an excellent chance to score. Satan tries a similar attack on God's people. If he can get the Christian separated from the encouragement of fellow believers, the Christian is weakened. Satan makes us feel alone in the battle when we become isolated from other believers."

REMEMBER, WE WIN!

1. *God is still in total control.* First John 4:4 says, "You, dear children, are from God and have overcome them, because the one who is in you is greater than the one who is in the world." No matter how bad things may appear, Satan is in subjection to Almighty God. My good friend Eric Boles reminds me, "We aren't fighting for victory, we are fighting from victory!" We are the victors and the battle has already been won by Jesus Christ when He rose from the dead.

2. *Satan and his faithful will receive their due.* Matthew 13:49-50 predicts, "This is how it will be at the end of the age. The angels will come and separate the wicked from the righteous and throw them into the fiery furnace, where there will be weeping and gnashing of teeth." Revelation 20:10 elaborates, "And the devil, who deceived them, was thrown into the lake of burning sulfur, where the beast and the false prophet had been thrown. They will be tormented day and night forever and ever." I want a front row seat at this event. The turmoil and pain he has caused so many will finally be poured out upon him for eternity.

IF I WERE THE DEVIL

If I were the Prince of Darkness...I'd want to engulf the whole world in darkness, and I'd have a third of its real estate and four-fifths of its population...but I wouldn't be happy until I had seized the ripest apple on the tree; so I'd set out however necessary to take over the United States.

I'd subvert the churches first; I'd begin with a campaign of whispers; with the wisdom of a serpent I would whisper to you as I whispered to Eve, "Do as you please." To the young I would whisper that the Bible is myth. I would convince them that man created God instead of the other way around; I would confide that what's bad is good and what's good is square...the old I would teach to pray after me, "Our Father which art in Washington."

And then I'd get organized. I'd educate authors in how to make lurid literature exciting so that anything else would appear dull and uninteresting; I'd threaten TV with dirtier movies and vice-versa; I'd peddle narcotics to whom I could; I'd sell alcohol to ladies and gentlemen of distinction...I'd tranquilize the rest with pills, if I were the devil.

I'd soon have families at war with themselves, churches at war with themselves, and nations at war with themselves until each in its turn was consumed; and with promises of higher ratings, I'd have mesmerizing media...fanning the flames.

If I were the devil, I'd encourage schools to refine young intellects but neglect to discipline emotions, just let those run wild, until before you knew it, you'd have to have drug-sniffing dogs and metal detectors at every schoolhouse door. Within a decade I'd have prisons overflowing, I'd have judges promoting pornography; soon I could evict God from the courthouse, then from the schoolhouse, and then from the houses of Congress, and in His own churches I would substitute psychology for religion and deify science. I would lure priests and pastors into misusing boys and girls and church money. If I were the devil, I'd make the symbol of Easter an egg and the symbol of Christmas a bottle.

If I were the devil, I'd take from those who have and give to those who want it until I had killed the incentive of the ambitious. And what'll you bet I couldn't get the whole United States to promote gambling as the way to get rich. I would caution against extremes in hard work, in patriotism, in moral conduct. I would convince the young that marriage is old-fashioned...that swinging is more fun, that what you see on TV is the way to be, and thus I could undress you in public...and I could lure you into bed with diseases for which there is no cure.

In other words, if I were the devil, I would just keep right on doing what he's doing. Paul Harvey....good day (from his broadcast on March 8, 1993).

Chapter Eight

DAILY TIME WITH CHRIST

Have you spent daily time in Scriptures and in prayer?

Experiencing true accountability takes a conscious daily effort. What better place to begin than by making sure you have daily time with Christ. In fact, all the areas which we will address in the following chapters will be more achievable when this one discipline is carried out.

When I was 17 years old, I was introduced to a "Quiet Time." Though I had grown up going to church, I thought Sunday morning was the time you took your dusty Bible off the shelf (if you could find it) and went to church. There were better things to do during the week than spend daily time with God.

It took the example of a former college football quarterback to convince me of my need for a "Quiet Time." I saw in him excitement and enthusiasm about scheduling time with God every day. He also had an uncompromising lifestyle. He said the strength to live the Christian life was directly tied to his time with God. He told me that this was a critical part of his day, and he encouraged me to make it a daily discipline. I remember that first day I felt a sense of great accomplishment after reading the Bible for three minutes and then closing with probably a 30-second prayer. But after years of making this a regular practice, I too have discovered the importance and the excitement of spending time with Jesus Christ.

A George Barna released survey noted that more than 90 percent of Americans own a Bible. In fact, those households have an average of three Bibles. However, many of them are gathering dust on coffee tables or bookshelves as less than one-third read their Bible weekly. When asked why they don't read the Bible, respondents to the survey gave as their most common reasons a lack of time, difficulty in understanding Scripture and irrelevance to their lives.[1]

In the context of accountability, I have discovered that when I am actively reading and praying, all the other areas of my life more effectively fall into place. Irregular time with Christ produces a multitude of problems.

WHAT DOES SCRIPTURE SAY?

Jeremiah 29:12-13 promises, "Then you will call upon me and come and pray to me, and I will listen to you. You will seek me and find me when you seek me with all your heart." Jesus' life was characterized by earnest devotion to the Father as evidenced by His commitment to arise early in the morning to pray (Mark 1:35). The Son of God realized that even He needed daily fellowship alone with God, and it was a top priority. Now if Jesus Christ needed this time with God, isn't it obvious that we need it as well?

"All Scripture is God-breathed and is useful for teaching, rebuking, correcting and training in righteousness, so that the man of God may be thoroughly equipped for every good work" (2 Timothy 3:16-17).

"For the word of God is living and active. Sharper than any double-edged sword, it penetrates even to dividing soul and spirit, joints and marrow; it judges the thoughts and attitudes of the heart. Nothing in all creation is hidden from God's sight. Everything is uncovered and laid bare before the eyes of him to whom we must give account" (Hebrews 4:12-13).

"How can a young man keep his way pure? By living according to your word. I seek you with all my heart; do not let me stray from your commands. I have hidden your word in my heart that I might not sin against you...Your word is a lamp to my feet and a light for my path" (Psalm 119:9-11,105).

"And when you pray, do not be like the hypocrites, for they love to pray standing in the synagogues and on the street corners to be seen by men. I tell you the truth, they have received their reward in full. But when you pray, go into your room, close the door and pray to your Father, who is unseen. Then your Father, who sees what is done in secret, will reward you" (Matthew 6:5-6).

"Devote yourselves to prayer, being watchful and thankful" (Colossians 4:2).

"Do not be anxious about anything, but in everything, by prayer and petition, with thanksgiving, present your requests to God. And the peace of God, which transcends all understanding, will guard your hearts and your minds in Christ Jesus" (Philippians 4:6-7).

"This is the confidence we have in approaching God; that if we ask anything according to his will, he hears us. And if we know that he hears us—whatever we ask—we know that we have what we asked of him" (1 John 5:14-15).

THE TRUTH ABOUT OUR TIME

Imagine every day your bank account was credited $86,400 and every night all the unspent money was taken away. What would you try and do? Spend every cent—of course! Well, we each have such a bank account—it is called time. Every day we are given 86,400 seconds. At the end of each 24-hour period, whatever we failed to use is lost. A balance is not carried over to the next day, and we're not allowed overdrafts. Each day the bank named "Time" opens a new account with us. Each night it burns the records of the day. If we fail to use the day's deposits, the loss is ours.

Time lost is gone forever. Some of us tell ourselves that we will work twice as hard tomorrow to make up for what we did not do today. Each of us should always do our best with the time we have been given.

We can't be efficient with our time if we spend time on frivolous activities and outright sin. Paul wrote about the problem of being drunk with wine (Ephesians 5:18), but he could have added drugs, porn, food and online chat rooms to his list of detrimental time wasters. How many hours do you spend each day on these or other unhealthy behaviors?

God's Word urges us to be filled with the Spirit, making the most of every opportunity. Having God's power helps us say no the bad stuff and yes to God's will. To make each day productive, we must first understand the Lord's will. If we are going to grasp His plan, then we need to know what it is, so a good way to start each day is with a quiet time and Bible reading. How will you spend your 86,400 seconds today?

WHAT IS A "QUIET TIME"?

I define it as time alone with God and allowing Him to speak to me through the Bible and communicating with Him through prayer. This intimate time alone with God is the key to deep Christian growth and maturity. Every committed Christian has this discipline as a core priority!

The amount of time you spend is not the most important factor. Invest the first few minutes in preparing your heart in prayer. Then read your Bible. Pick a place to start, and then read consecutively—verse after verse, chapter after chapter. Don't race! Read for the pure joy of reading and allowing God to speak. You may want to also use a devotional book or a Bible study. The last few minutes should be set aside for prayer. Establish, renew or enliven your personal prayer time by giving God quality time before anything else calls for your attention each day. An easy way to remember a good prayer model is by using the word ACTS.

A - *Adoration.* A time of worshiping Him. Tell the Lord you love Him. Reflect on His greatness, His power, His majesty and sovereignty. You are simply adoring our awesome God.
C - *Confession.* After entering His presence and confronting His holiness, it is evident how unclean we are. Therefore, confess and be cleansed from the sin in your life. Confession comes from a root word meaning "to agree together with." It means you are agreeing with God on specific sin that you have encountered (1 John 1:9).
T - *Thanksgiving.* An expression of gratitude to God. Think of specific things to thank Him for: family, job, church, ministry,

health, answered prayer and even the hardships (1 Thessalonians 5:18).

S - *Supplication*. This means to "ask for, earnestly and humbly." This part of your prayer time focuses on making your petitions known to Him. Ask for others, then for yourself.

Another effective prayer model that I regularly use is one developed by Bob Beltz. He designed this after *The Lord's Prayer*. What a beautiful way to pray in accordance with the way Jesus taught His disciples. I encourage you to review Appendix D and take an extended time to pray through this model.

ACTIVATE THE POWER

In the life of every believer is the power of prayer. Does prayer really make a difference? There is a recurring theme throughout Scripture: *Prayer on earth results in action in heaven*. Need an example? One of the best is found in the book of Revelation. In the first seven chapters, John hears the noises of heaven, glorious and loud. The angels speak. The thunder booms. The earth quakes. The stars fall. Trumpets blast. The living creatures chant, "Holy, Holy, Holy," and the elders worship. From the first word of the angel there is constant activity and nonstop noise until Revelation 8:1, and suddenly all of heaven is hushed. It reads, "When he opened the seventh seal, there was silence in heaven for about half an hour."

Why the silence? Why were the angels quieted? You're going to love this answer. Because someone was praying (see verses 2-5). All of heaven became quiet because of a prayer. When someone prays, God listens. What an incredible honor to know that God is attentively and carefully listening to our every word. Yes, prayer on earth results in action in heaven.

I'm more convinced than ever that God hears the prayers of the penitent, contrite soul. Psalm 51:17 says, "The sacrifices of God are a broken spirit; a broken and contrite heart, O God, you will not despise." He embraces those who come to Him broken of selfish desires and agendas. Our own merit will never commend us to God. It is the worthiness of Jesus that will save us, His blood that will cleanse us. Yes, God wants us to present our needs and cares before Him, but He also wants purity and brokenness. Psalm 66:18-20 reminds us that if we cherish sins in our hearts, clinging to any known practice, the Lord will not hear us.

For this very reason it is imperative that we enter His presence clean. God is ready and willing to hear the sincere prayer of the humblest of His children. In love, our Heavenly Father will answer our prayers by giving us that which will be best for us—that which we ourselves would want if we could see, as God does, all things as they really are. It would be presumptuous to claim that prayer will always be answered in the very way and for the particular thing that we desire. God is both too wise to err and too good to withhold any beneficial thing from those who follow His will.

William Carey said, "Prayer—secret, fervent, believing prayer—lies at the root of all personal godliness." Real prayer is life-creating and life-changing. Prayer is the central avenue that God uses to transform us. It is impossible to flourish spiritually while neglecting individual prayer. Pray someplace where you can be alone. And as you go about your daily labor, lift your heart to God frequently. Prayer rises like precious incense before the throne of grace.

SUGGESTIONS IN DEVELOPING YOUR "QUIET TIME"

1. *Use a Bible with a readable translation.* There are many translations which are effective. The key is finding one which you understand.

2. *Set a regular time and place.* Determine when and where you can have the best uninterrupted time with God. For me, early morning works best. The key is, once the time and place is set, continue to make every effort to not allow anything to disrupt this valuable time with God.

3. *Ask God to reveal Himself to you and grant you wisdom from above.* James 1:5 says, "If any of you lacks wisdom, he should ask God, who gives generously to all..." Before beginning your time

with God, take time to realize you are in God's presence, and ask Him for wisdom to understand the Scripture you are about to read. Claim this promise and ask, "Lord, what do you want me to learn today? Teach me what you want me to know from your Word."

4. *Have a plan in mind.* Haphazard reading develops haphazard results. There are a number of devotional guides which are extremely effective including *Walk through the Bible, Our Daily Bread, Growing Strong in the Seasons of Life, Cross Training Workout, Campus Journal, Drawing Near,* etc. A good selection of Old and New Testament passages is recommended.

5. *Use your pen, and mark up your Bible.* Underline special passages, and make notes in your Bible. Ask, "How does this Scripture apply to me? How can I put this into practice today?" Keep a notebook with "Quiet Time" notes of lessons which God is teaching you, and incorporate this into your journal time (more on journaling below).

6. *Maintain a regular journal.* A journal is much more than a diary of events summarizing the day. Here you can record insights that you are learning and what God is teaching you through these experiences. I have kept a journal since age 17. Spiritual growth and maturity are documented as the Lord has worked in my life. One day my plan is to pass on these journals to my children and hopefully to their children so they can know God and me in a better and unique way.

7. *Make prayer a major part of your "Quiet Time" and day.* I use a number of different methods as noted earlier. Another way of praying for others and yourself is to group certain people or situations into certain days. For example, Sundays you may want to pray for your church and pastor; Mondays for national and local government; Tuesdays for family members; Wednesdays for co-workers or schoolmates; etc.

Perhaps you have had a regular "Quiet Time" in the past, but it has grown old and/or ineffective. Here are some suggestions to help invigorate:

1. *Read for inspiration.* It is not necessarily designed to be an in-depth study of a passage or book. It is meant to be an inspiration in your walk with Christ for that particular day.

2. *Don't take copious notes.* Save this for specific study sessions. Try to record one or two insights or promises that God gives you daily. You will soon have a bundle of precious jewels from God. These can be valuable in times of need and spiritual dryness.

3. *Have variety.* It is not necessary to do it exactly the same way every day. Have a plan, but feel free to vary.

4. *Be consistent.* Some days you may not feel like having a "Quiet Time." Do your best to have just a short one, even if it is just reviewing underlined passages that God impressed on you in weeks and months before.

5. *Read with your mind open to God.* He will surprise you with insights and keen ideas and lead you to do some things you never thought you could or would do. Just give Him a chance.

6. *Expect a blessing.* You will receive this blessing if it is not just a legalistic ritual, but a personal, intimate fellowship with Almighty God. God desires your fellowship; He longs for it. He will honor your willingness to spend time with Him.

7. *Pray before you read.* Ask God to give you wisdom and concentration in your reading. Then read and pray through the Scripture.

8. *Get it on your schedule.* If your regular time is early in the morning, then be committed to it. Satan would love to squeeze it out of your day with numerous other activities. When you do blow it, confess it, forget it and renew your commitment to get back on track the next day.

9. *Make notes about passages or topics you want to study more in depth at a later date.* Then go back to these lists and do it!

10. *Meditate on what you read.* A good way to keep in mind what you read is to check up on yourself throughout the day. I often ask myself, "What did I read in my 'Quiet Time' today?" If you have difficulty recalling it, then you are not retaining any of it.

11. *Remember the importance of spiritual food.* Through the nourishing of our souls, we literally "eat God's Word." Spiritual strength is directly related to intake of the Word.

12. *Enjoy it.* Your "Quiet Time" should not be legalistic or drudgery.

Listen to the experience of Paul Little describing his personal time with the Lord: "In studying the Bible many people seek to discover facts about the Bible, even facts within the Bible. But information about the written Word is not an end in itself. If you've ever tried to produce spiritual life and power simply by reading verses, organizing information and making outlines, you know it's a futile effort. Benjamin Franklin wrote commentaries on the Bible, but as far as we know he never became a Christian.

Basically, the Bible's purpose is to bring us into contact with the living God in Jesus Christ. A telescope helps to point us to the star. Of course we should know how the telescope works to use it, but what a tragedy when we get engrossed in its operation and forget to look at the star. Failure to distinguish between the means and the end may be the problem a lot of us have in our personal devotions.

Maybe we're thinking, "I've tried a regular quiet time, but it was dry as dust. I couldn't get anything out of it." Have you ever felt as though you were cranking out ten verses a day and it didn't mean a thing to you? You began to feel discouraged: What's the use? Why bother?" Very similar feelings hit most of us at times. There's no sense in acting out empty rituals. Maybe we've failed to recognize that the purpose of our quiet times is to come face to face with the living God himself in the Lord Jesus Christ. Or maybe we've failed to realize that he is a living person who wants to meet us. We should always come to the Scripture expecting to meet the living Lord, for essentially his Word is not a textbook but a revelation of himself.

Another problem we may experience in our personal Bible study arises from lack of direction. It's been said, "He who aims at nothing is sure to hit it." If we enter our quiet times with the purpose of getting something to remember, it will help to have a notebook and pen to write down new thoughts. I always keep a column of specific ways I can apply a truth. Sometimes I write down a prayer so that I can ask the Lord how to apply it. I've found that written prayers have fewer requests and far more worship in them. Lack of purpose will soon depress the appetite for Bible study."[2]

FROM A FRIEND

Dear Friend,

How are you? I just had to send a note to tell you how much I care about you.

I saw you yesterday as you were talking with your friends. I waited all day, hoping you would want to talk with me, too. I gave you a sunset to close your day and a cool breeze to rest you—but I still love you because I am your friend.

I saw you sleeping last night and longed to touch your brow, so I spilled moonlight upon your face. Again I waited, wanting to rush down so we could talk. I have so many gifts for you! You awoke and rushed off to work. My tears were in the rain.

If you would only listen to me! I love you! I try to tell you in blue skies and in the quiet green grass. I whisper it in leaves on the trees and breathe it in colors of flowers, shout it to you in mountain streams, give the birds love songs to sing. I clothe you with warm sunshine and perfume the air with nature scents. My love for you is deeper than the ocean and bigger than the biggest need in your heart!

Ask me! Talk with me! Please don't forget me. I have so much to share with you! I won't hassle you any further. It is your decision. I have chosen you and I will wait—because I love you.

Your Friend,
Jesus[3]

Notes

[1] Adapted from article written by David Briggs, AP Religion Writer, *Kansas City Star*, Aug. 24, 1996, p. E-13.

[2] Paul Little, *How to Give Away Your Faith* (Downers Grove, IL: InterVarsity Press, 1988), p. 182-183.

[3] Source unknown.

Chapter Nine

SEXUAL TEMPTATIONS AND LUST

Have you had any flirtatious or lustful attitudes, tempting thoughts, or exposed yourself to any explicit materials which would not glorify God?

Why does this area continue to be such a problem, especially for men? Unfortunately, many reported incidents have been covered by local and national media involving people of faith who have fallen in this area of sexual temptation. It is not surprising that God's Word deals directly with this issue and the perils involved when we do not rely on Christ's power and His promises. Within the context of accountability this is one area which needs to be continually addressed by all accountability groups. WHY? Because it can jump up and attack you at any time. It is one of Satan's strongest and most effective weapons.

Jerry Kirk says, "Choosing to let Jesus be in control of your sex life will shape every other area of your life because sexuality is at the center of our being. This decision will influence your current and future ability as a husband, father and Christian. Choosing purity is difficult, but for those who put in the hard work and prayer, living by Christ's standard is a road to deep joy and real sexual satisfaction." He adds, "This matters to God because it goes to the very heart of our witness, our understanding of God's faithfulness and the vital issue of whether we really believe God when He tells us a given course of action is better for us. It matters to God because He deeply loves us and wants us to enjoy that which is most fulfilling and meaningful. Practicing sexual purity, even though it's hard, is also one of the most accurate reflections of the depth of our relationship with Christ."[1]

WHAT DOES SCRIPTURE SAY?

"But I tell you that anyone who looks at a woman lustfully has already committed adultery with her in his heart" (Matthew 5:28).

"Rather, clothe yourselves with the Lord Jesus Christ, and do not think about how to gratify the desires of the sinful nature" (Romans 13:14).

"Do not love the world or anything in the world. If anyone loves the world, the love of the Father is not in him. For everything in the world—the cravings of sinful man, the lust of his eyes and the boasting of what he has and does—comes not from the Father but from the world. The world and its desires pass away, but the man who does the will of God lives forever" (1 John 2:15-17).

"Flee from sexual immorality. All other sins a man commits are outside his body, but he who sins sexually sins against his own body" (1 Corinthians 6:18).

"Flee the evil desires of youth, and pursue righteousness, faith, love and peace, along with those who call on the Lord out of a pure heart" (2 Timothy 2:22).

"Because he himself suffered when he was tempted, he is able to help those who are being tempted" (Hebrews 2:18).

"It is God's will that you should be sanctified: that you should avoid sexual immorality; that each of you should learn to control his own body in a way that is holy and honorable, not passionate lust like the heathen, who do not know God; and that in this matter no one should wrong his brother or take advantage of him. The Lord will punish men for all such sins, as we have already told you and warned you. For God did not call us to be impure, but to live a holy life" (1 Thessalonians 4:3-7).

"So, if you think you are standing firm, be careful that you don't fall! No temptation has seized you except what is common to man. And God is faithful; he will not let you be tempted beyond what you can bear. But when you are tempted, he will also provide a way out so that you can stand up under it" (1 Corinthians 10:12-13).

"Finally, brothers, whatever is true, whatever is noble, whatever is right, whatever is pure, whatever is lovely, whatever is admirable—if anything is excellent or praiseworthy—think about such things" (Philippians 4:8).

"But each one is tempted when, by his own evil desire, he is dragged away and enticed. Then, after desire has conceived, it gives birth to sin; and sin, when it is full-grown, gives birth to death" (James 1:14-15). Dr. Bruce Wilkinson breaks down this verse into the seven stages of every temptation: (1) the look, (2) your lust, (3) the lure, (4) the conception (biting the hook), (5) the birth (the taste), (6) the growth (drowning in it) and (7) the death.[2] If you don't kill "the look" immediately, it will eventually lead to death, as this verse describes.

Scripture tells us that Jesus has encountered every temptation, yet He was without sin (Hebrews 4:15-16), so it is an encouragement to know we can approach him with confidence to help us in our time of need.

WHAT ARE PEOPLE SAYING?

Every time I talk about our accountability questions, this particular question frequently receives the same reaction from men. One common response has been, "This is an area I really need to talk about." In fact, in passing along these questions to hundreds of men, I have only met one person who said he had no problems or temptations with lust—I didn't believe him.

In my own life I battled these temptations for years. My secret was an addiction to pornography beginning as an early teen. No one, including my parents or other Christian friends, had a clue. I was able to hide my secret while leading Bible studies and sharing my faith with others. Ironically, I even helped mount a successful charge to rid my college campus of showing x-rated movies at our Student Union Building.

In my 20's, I joined the staff of the Fellowship of Christian Athletes and also was part of the ministerial team for a large church on the University of Washington campus. In the late 1980's, I was the co-chaplain for the NBA's Seattle SuperSonics basketball team before moving to Kansas City in 1989. I ministered to many coaches and athletes (high school, college and professionals) during those years, and yet I maintained my secret. As my responsibilities grew, my secret drove me to a place where I would silently utter, "God, will today be the day people find out who I really am?" I prayed for authenticity but I felt like I was incapable of transparency and honesty.

Because of my position as a Christian leader, I did not feel I could confess this to anyone. I thought it would damage my relationships with those around me, so I silently hid them. Though I remained a virgin until I married, I had been exposed to inappropriate materials (via television, magazines and books) as well as my own desires of the flesh. My mind was stained with pictures. I would be victorious for a season or two, but then during times of loneliness or despair, Satan would strike quickly, and the garbage would return. Because I believe that God judges our thought life equally with the actual act, I knew my sin and God knew it as well (Matthew 5:28).

My breakthrough happened when I got caught looking at pornography while in the Dallas airport by a dear friend from Seattle who just happened to be in the same gift shop as me as I was grabbing a Playboy magazine off the rack. He came up from behind me, tapped me three times on the shoulder and asked, "Rod, what are you doing here?" As I scrambled for an answer, I never forgot the look of disappointment in his eyes. Just about a month prior to this Dallas incident, I had entered into an accountable relationship with two other men. Upon my return home after this trip, I got in front of these two guys and I told them, "I have been a phony, a fraud and a hypocrite. I have a secret and my problem is pornography." For the first time, I became real with someone about my struggle. It was an admission to God, others and self that I needed help to find victory. This disclosure began the process of healing and restoration for me. No more hidden closets or secrets.

Imagine my surprise to find men who were willing to verbalize their battle with lusts and temptations and discover I was not alone. Up to that point I thought I was the only one who battled these issues. I also began to share my sin with the group and soon found I was able to release, for the first time in my life, some of the garbage that had consumed my life. We encouraged one another to remove the junk. Incredible freedom began to occur, and Christ became alive in this area of my life, enabling me and others to see positive, victorious results for the first time.

Rather than continually being overwhelmed by our lack of success, we began telling stories of how we had remained pure, unstained when faced with areas where we had historically stumbled. Even today, it is exciting to see men in our group standing strong. Having been married for many years, I can honestly say that my accountability group helped me to recover from the past, and prepared me to be the kind of spouse who would be completely faithful to my wife. I do know, however, that being married does not necessarily make it easier to overcome lustful temptations (compared to when I was single). In fact, I am bombarded continually in my marriage by all types of temptations. I know Satan's attacks have only become stronger since he loves to throw destruction in my path, hoping I, too, will fall, as so many others have in the past.

FORGIVENESS IS AVAILABLE

If you have fallen in the past, today you can start anew. Jesus Christ's shed blood provides forgiveness and will put you back on a life of purity. Scripture reminds us that complete forgiveness is available in our journey of seeking God and His will.

Titus 3:3-5 says, "At one time we too were foolish, disobedient, deceived and enslaved by all kinds of passions and pleasures. We lived in malice and envy, being hated and hating one another. But when the kindness and love of God our Savior appeared, he saved us, not because of righteous things we had done, but because of his mercy. He saved us through the washing of rebirth and renewal by the Holy Spirit." First John 1:9 reports, "If we confess our sins, he is faithful and just and will forgive us our sins and purify us from all unrighteousness." Philippians 3:12-14 reminds us of Paul's outlook to press on towards the goal as opposed to wallowing in your sins which have been fully forgiven through Christ.

Let's be honest! Being sexually pure is not easy whether you're a seasoned believer or a new follower of Christ. I want to encourage each of you to remain pure at all costs. God commands us to live upright and pure, saving ourselves completely for our marriage partner. With the strength of the Almighty God and the help of people around you, you can do it. Let me share with you some ways that you can minimize sexual temptations.

TELEVISION

What we see on television today is absolutely disgusting. We see all the flesh we want, not only on cable channels such as HBO, Showtime, Cinemax (I call it "Sin to the Max"), Playboy, MTV, etc., but also regular network stations, too. Every person who desires purity ought to evaluate every single station and program to determine whether or not it is appropriate viewing material.

I would also encourage you not to "channel surf" by using your remote to flip through the channels continually. No matter how innocent you think it is, you will eventually get to a channel you should not be watching, and it is difficult to keep the remote going when a sexy scene is unfolding before your eyes. Though we have cable in our home, we have made decisions about what we are going to watch, and we do not stray from these. An easy guideline in evaluating what is inappropriate viewing is to ask the following question: "How would Jesus, your spouse or children react to this particular show?" There was a period of time during my single years when I placed a picture of Christ directly above my television set. That really helped keep me on track!

When traveling away from home and in a hotel, here are several suggestions to help remain on the straight and narrow:

1. Take pictures of your family, children, spouse or girlfriend, and place them all around the television set.
2. Before checking into your room, ask the hotel to turn off the premium channels on your set.
3. Specifically ask one of your accountability partners to quiz you on the amount of television and the specific shows you watched while away from home.

4. Do not even turn on the set. Instead, spend concentrated time studying Scripture and praying.
5. Whenever possible, arrange to stay with friends either in your hotel room or in their home.

MOVIES AND MAGAZINE RACKS

Once again, evaluate beforehand the movies you will be watching by reviewing the rating, using common sense and listening to the comments of people you trust who have seen the show. And if something becomes steamy, feel free to leave the theater entirely or at least leave to get some popcorn.

Believe me, after being in hundreds of airports, gas stations and grocery stores, magazine racks have a way of catching your eye. My advice is to just turn and walk away. This is one more tool of Satan to lure you into sexual temptation.

INTERNET PORNOGRAPHY

Today, men and women can access pornography with a few key strokes on the computer, and many times this occurs mysteriously on your screen with little warning. Sadly, I have spent a significant amount of time with men over the past several years counseling them through this addictive pattern.

One man who had worked a substantial number of years in full-time Christian work began accessing the internet privately. His browsing escalated over the years until ultimately he was caught in an internet sting operation which involved a teenager. This man lost his ministry, his reputation, and spent time in jail paying the consequences of his behavior. Today, he is trying to rebuild his family and his credibility in the community.

In another situation, a pastor had removed himself from accountability and within a few weeks of doing so, he had his first encounter at home with internet pornography. He told me that he remembered the day it first popped up on his computer screen, "I was curious and just wanted to see what was there." That initial gaze resulted in multiple looks and eventually he began staring at the material from his office at the church. One day, the church secretary found him observing sexually provocative sites. His secret pattern became public knowledge as he ended up going before his young family and the entire congregation confessing his sin.

The internet is a dangerous place filled with numerous potential land mines for those who are tempted. Establish boundaries and safeguards for yourself and your family members. There are a number of filtering programs and other proactive steps you can take to protect yourself and others from the seductive lures of the web.

THE BEACH/PARK/MALL OR VIRTUALLY ANYWHERE

There is nothing I can do about the first look at an attractive woman, but the second-third-fourth look I can control. Appreciate God's handiwork, but do not take the additional looks. When you do, you could be treading on dangerous ground. No matter where you go, you are bound to see attractive people. Be aware that the additional looks are where trouble begins. If you have to, just drop your head or deliberately focus on something else.

SOME THOUGHTS FOR SINGLES

I was extremely pleased with the response that the "True Love Waits" campaign received across America beginning in 1994. Hundreds of thousands of teens pledged to remain sexually pure until marriage. What a wonderful statement. When I was growing up, you were not cool if you were a virgin. I am glad to see that so many have now decided to remove themselves from safe sex techniques and return to what the Bible says about sex: Wait until you are married.

When I married Janna, I was a 32-year-old virgin, and I admit it was not easy to remain pure, but I did it! It was thrilling that Janna was a virgin as well. It was well worth the wait, and we believe God blessed our obedience. In today's society, it's rare to see couples wait on sex until their wedding day.

I'll admit there were times of frustration and discontentment, wondering if God was going to bless me with a mate. At times while dating, my conduct was not at a level which pleased God or myself, but He protected me in a powerful way. Know your boundaries before you get yourself into a compromising situation. Part of this can be controlled through your surroundings, such as not going back to your apartment after dinner, knowing full well that your roommates will not be there. This is extremely tempting. Some positive guidelines from a family I know are: (1) no touching below the chin or above the elbow, (2) never lie down beside someone and (3) no extended kissing (obviously there are other "no touch" areas as well). Believe me, going beyond these limits can and will lead to compromise.

Here are some pointers to help you stay focused as a single:
1. *Be thankful for your singleness.* Singleness isn't a form of punishment by God. There are many benefits to being single, such as having the freedom to travel without excessive responsibilities, an ability to spend significant time with friends and family, great opportunities to serve others in the community, etc.
2. *Nurture your relationship with Christ.* Focus on becoming the person God wants you to be rather than expending a significant portion of energy trying to catch a mate. Don't think that a spouse is going to take care of your every need...only Christ can do this.
3. *Build friendships with members of the opposite sex for the sake of friendship and nothing more.* This will allow you to meet people without applying pressure.
4. *Be selective about the materials you read, watch and listen.* What you let yourself be exposed to will strongly affect your actions and attitude. Psalm 101:3 says, "I will set before my eyes no vile thing. The deeds of faithless men I hate; they will not cling to me."
5. *Remember that sex is a wonderful gift from God, yet it is reserved solely for marriage.* No matter how strong the temptation, wait until your wedding day. It is well worth the wait!

6. *Trust Jesus.* He is faithful and will provide the right person at the right time, if it is part of His plan.

WHAT ABOUT IF YOU'RE MARRIED?

Many couples vow to God, their family and friends on their wedding day their complete commitment to one another. Yet so often we see unfaithfulness to the partners by entering into inappropriate relations with people from the opposite sex. The surveys tell us that over a third of all men cheat on their spouses. The Bible clearly tells us this is wrong. One area which should be off-limits is to share intimate conversation or even counsel people of the opposite sex in a private setting. Even the most innocent situation should be avoided.

LIVING A LIFE OF SEXUAL PURITY

God has set a high standard, albeit one that will bless us and those we love. Here are some key principles from Jerry Kirk which many have found helpful:

1. *Past mistakes don't mean future failure!* Few if any Christians are without some sexual sin. But a mistake in the past is no reason to give up practicing sexual purity. Confession and forgiveness can cleanse.

2. *Sexual purity is as much a matter of the mind as it is of the body.* Romans 12:1-2 refers to "being transformed by the renewing of your mind." Allowing sinful thoughts to take root in our minds and hearts is the first sign of an actual physical sex sin. Nourishing thoughts of sexual unfaithfulness will later be difficult to resist.

3. *Practicing sexual purity is a process as well as a commitment.* This must be cultivated like any other godly habit, or it will not be there when temptation comes. Joseph fled without his cloak rather than sin against God with Potiphar's wife (see Genesis 39).

4. *Don't pretend your desires don't exist.* Denial doesn't work. God created us as sexual beings, and our desires are normal. We need to channel them in productive, God-given directions.

5. *No substitute exists for personal accountability with other godly people.* Secret sins have much more power and usually last much longer than those we acknowledge to our Christian brothers and sisters.

6. *Understand the importance of sexual purity to our marriages, families and heritage.* Our faithfulness gives strength to our spouse and children.

7. *Understand the importance of sexual purity to our Christian witness.* Nothing undermines our influence more than sexual failure. We must work on purity not only for our own well-being and joy but also for the health of the church.

8. *Understand the importance of sexual purity to our own sexual fulfillment within marriage.* In God's design we become one spiritually and emotionally when we become "one flesh." Thus, a man brings to his marriage bed every woman with whom he has ever had intercourse. Each can affect his ability to wholeheartedly and single-mindedly love his wife and enjoy true and unique intimacy with her. Men and women who have premarital sexual encounters will regret it.[3]

PRACTICAL TIPS FROM ONE WHO STUMBLED

I received a letter from a pastor who had an extramarital relationship and was removed from his church. After an extended time of recovery from his compulsive sexual behavior he offered advice to our FCA staff. He wanted to encourage people who were challenged by sex videos, masturbation, obsessive ogling of women, inappropriate sexual fantasies, flirting, etc.

He believes the following guidelines should be considered seriously to achieve victory in sexual areas:

1. *Be honest with yourself, God and significant others.* Call it what it is—a sin—which, if not checked, can lead to obsessions, family breakup, ministry complications and shame to you and all who look to you for Biblical leadership. This is serious business and must not be minimized.

2. *Practice the three-second rule.* Do not let your mind run unchecked in sexual areas for more than three seconds. 1, 2, 3—

stop looking, stop fantasizing, stop remembering, stop holding another's hand, stop pretending this is harmless. Say to yourself when tempted, "STOP, RIGHT NOW." Say, "In the name of Jesus I want to stop." Then move to think about something else that is good and positive (Philippians 4:8-9).

3. *Don't put yourself in the place of temptation.* You know the magazine stores you can't frequent. Don't buy the racy magazines. Don't let anything questionable enter your brain which might stay there. Be careful about what TV movies or programs you watch. It is so easy to "surf" the stations late at night when your spouse has gone to bed or is watching something else in the other room. Stay out of areas known for prostitution. Don't stay in any hotels or motels where "adult movies" are available.

4. *Share your "challenge" with trusted friends who love you.* Choose wisely people of the same sex who you know you can trust and be safe with. You know they will not pass it on to others. They are eager to share their stories with you, and all are responsible to hold each other accountable. That is, don't let anyone in the group minimize, intellectualize, rationalize, spiritualize, evade or deny boundaries of acceptable Christian behavior that they may be overstepping. Full disclosure to someone or some group can be your way out of a dangerous "fog."

5. *Develop a healthy sexual life with your spouse.* Don't blame her for your misconduct. Think of creative ways of loving her. Talk openly with her about your challenge. Keep no secrets from her from here on out. Be a lover again. Do whatever it takes to jump start your marriage.

6. *Along with other needs, bring this little spark of sexual misconduct, which can easily become a roaring fire of out-of-control behavior, before the Lord in prayer.* Don't play games with God—it doesn't work or pay off. Let Him in on your struggle. Be specific in prayer. Don't treat God like a "benevolent grandpa." He who will forgive us also demands holy living. The payoff for holy, obedient living is joy and peace. Don't miss it.[4]

CLOSING THOUGHTS

When sexual temptations confront us we can either stand firm or fall flat. James 4:7 is the key, "Submit yourselves to God. Resist the devil and he will flee from you." One minister recently admitted to an eight-year affair. When asked if he heard alarm bells warning of danger he responded, "Oh yes, I heard the alarms, but then I decided to disconnect the wires." We need to make a commitment that when the alarm bells go off, we will not disconnect the wires. Those who do not heed these warnings will ultimately "crash and burn."

In the biblical account of Joseph, we see him resisting the seductive advances of his master's wife, while King David gave into temptation and had an adulterous affair with Bathsheba. Both of these men had human limitations, but Joseph recognized his weaknesses and knew the proper response, while David overestimated his strengths. Dr. David Jeremiah points out, "If sexual purity isn't a problem, you are more godly than David; stronger than Samson; and wiser than Solomon." All three of these biblical giants struggled in their relationships with women.

Do you know your weaknesses? Do you allow impure thoughts about sex to stay in your mind? Are you engaging in any flirtatious activity with anyone who is not your spouse? Have you set your boundaries? Answering these types of questions will help you establish protective safeguards when the temptations hit. Becoming accountable to trusted friends in this area will help put a guard around your heart and protect you from the destruction that could await you.

In addition to strong accountability, I encourage you to actively and diligently "put on the Lord Jesus Christ, and make no provision for the flesh in regards to its lusts" (Romans 13:14). How do we put this verse into action? It literally means "giving thought to" so we need to give Jesus greater priority than our own flesh desires.

HOW TO AVOID SEXUAL TEMPTATION
by John Maxwell
(Presented at the 1994 Promise Keepers Conference)

1. Run!
2. Accept responsibility for your failures.
3. Be accountable.
4. Listen to your wife.
5. Be on your guard. Some safeguards include:
     *Don't travel alone (if possible).
     *Call your wife nightly (when traveling).
     *Don't be alone with a woman.
     *Talk positively about your wife.
     *Carefully pick your close friends.
6. Determine to live a pure life.
7. Realize that sexual sin prostitutes Christ's Lordship.
8. Recognize the consequences of sexual sin.
9. Think about your children.
10. Get a new definition of success.

Notes

[1] Jerry Kirk, *Seven Promises of a Promise Keeper* (Colorado Springs, CO: Focus on the Family, 1994), pp. 92-93.

[2] Dr. Bruce W. Wilkinson, *Personal Holiness in Times of Temptation,* Course Workbook (Walk Thru the Bible, 1997), p. 23. (Author's Note: These materials and corresponding video are outstanding in understanding sexual sin and our need for holiness. To order, call 1-800-763-5433).

[3] Adapted from Jerry Kirk, *Seven Promises of a Promise Keeper,* pp. 94-97.

[4] Source unidentified.

FINANCIAL DEALINGS

Have you been completely above reproach in your financial dealings?

During my college years at Central Washington University I earned a degree in accounting and later received my Certified Public Accountant's license while working for Ernst & Whinney, a public accounting firm. However, what I want to tell you in the following section has little to do with what I learned in the education system. It has much more to do with the application of biblical principles and common sense. In fact, the Bible has more to say about money than any other topic—over 2,000 verses worth.

WHAT DOES SCRIPTURE SAY?

While many Christians think responsibility to God amounts to 10 percent, in reality all money belongs to God and we are simply caretakers of it (Matthew 24:45-51 and Luke 16:10-13). As stewards of these funds, we are responsible for properly managing this property while we have it in our possession. God can decide to entrust us with as much or as little as He chooses. As a steward (not owners) of God's finances, it is our responsibility to be a faithful manager. If we are faithful in our stewardship, God makes certain promises to us including peace (John 14:27), provision (Matthew 6:31-33) and prosperity (Matthew 19:29).

First Chronicles 29:11-13 tells us that God owns everything. You've got to believe this, and once you do, you must change your spending habits and be willing to live within your income. In simple terms, total income has to exceed total expenditures. Also, anything of material value which takes priority over God and carries with it symptoms of worry, greed, resentment, self indulgence, poor record-keeping, anger and *debt* creates "financial bondage." This usually occurs for three reasons:

1. *Financial ignorance.* There is a vast number of people in the world today who are not aware of financial matters or the responsibilities associated therewith, nor are they interested in understanding numbers (Proverbs 24:3-4).
2. *Wrong attitudes.* Greed is a primary reason (James 3:16).
3. *Poor planning.* This includes a lack of budget preparation, using debt financing and not properly utilizing advisors around you (Proverbs 16:9).

The Christian community has just as many problems with money as non-believers. I encourage you to look at Appendix E for a biblical approach to finances. Anyone can improve and enhance his financial situation by applying the following principles.

STEWARDSHIP

It has been said, "You can't store up treasures in heaven if you're holding on to the treasures of earth." This is illustrated by hunters in North Africa catching monkeys. A hunter hollows out a gourd and makes a hole in its side just large enough for a monkey to insert his open hand. The gourd is then filled with nuts and tied to a tree. The curious monkey is attracted to the smell of the nuts and reaches inside to grasp them. The hole in the gourd is too small, however, for the animal to withdraw his fist as long as it is tightly closed around the nuts. Because he refuses to release his prize, the unsuspecting monkey is easy prey to his captor. Unwilling to relax his grasp, he actually traps himself!

Satan uses a similar method to ensnare us. He tempts us to grasp more and more material possessions, which we think will bring us security. As long as we tenaciously hold on to them, we are enslaved. The biblical warning in 1 John 2:15 is true, and in verse 17 we are reminded, "the world is passing away, and the lust of it; but he who does the will of God abides forever." Remember what happened to the monkey. Don't be fooled by the devil's bait! Each one of us is a steward of something which God has given us. James 1:17 tells us, "Every good and perfect gift is from above, coming down from the Father of the heavenly lights, who does not change like shifting shadows." Our talents, abilities and possessions are gifts from God, and it is our responsibility to be good stewards of these gifts.

Jesus commended those who took their talents and as good stewards multiplied their influence through wise investing. He chastised those who received their talents and did nothing with them (see Matthew 25:14-30). The issue of stewardship reveals who is really in charge of our life. If Jesus Christ is truly calling the shots, then we will be faithful and obedient to His call. If we are just giving lip service to Jesus Christ, our tendency will be unfaithfulness and disobedience. Jesus told us that it is impossible to serve both God and man. Who are you serving today?

TITHING

The Bible clearly instructs us to tithe to the church and God's work here on earth. There are many opinions as to what the correct percentage should be. Because I believe that God owns everything, the pressure to determine a set percentage is relieved. As a suggestion, a minimum of 10 percent of your gross (pre-tax) wages should be a starting point. Freely give, and you will discover the joy of participating in God's grace in ways you never dreamed possible. In our own personal finances we have discovered that giving above and beyond 10 percent of our income has been a great blessing and joy. If you want to be free from financial bondage, this is the first area I would address (Malachi 3:8).

Frankly, it was discouraging for me as a CPA to prepare income tax returns several years ago for my Christian friends and to discover they were giving practically nothing to their church and charities. One couple was making in excess of $50,000 and very vocal about their Christian faith and church involvement, yet had given less than $50 annually. I confronted them on their lack of giving, and they told me they were too poor to give and had nothing to spare. In later years as their income mounted, they were in financial bondage because I believe God's blessing was not on their life primarily due to their stance on tithing. This couple had difficulty accepting the fact that all money belongs to God.

On the flip side, I have seen people give who had literally nothing and watched God bless them financially because their priorities were in order.

ELIMINATE DEBT

The Bible is specific about debt in that it is not a normal situation, yet it is permitted in certain cases (Psalms 37:21). We are not to accumulate long-term debt, to avoid surety (which is borrowing without the ability to repay), to make an absolute commitment to repay everything we do owe (Ecclesiastes 5:5), and to realize that while in debt, we are in servitude to our lender (Proverbs 22:7).

The only debt I find acceptable is for home financing, and if necessary, student loans to get through college. Even with this debt I encourage you to pay off the balance as quickly as possible. For example, if you make one additional full payment on a 30-year home mortgage every year, you will completely repay the entire debt in about 19 years. Outside of home financing and a minimum amount of student loans, I believe you should not have any other debt. I realize this may sound unorthodox. However, no matter how persuasive the arguments to borrow may be, it just works out better not to become the borrower.

If you are currently facing large debts, then begin the process immediately of ridding yourself of this burden by determining exactly how much you owe and developing a repayment plan to remove the debt completely. If you need help, then seek counsel and begin to develop a pay-back plan. One of the members of our group became debt-free several years ago, primarily because the group helped him develop a plan to do so.

CREDIT CARDS

For some it may be wiser to completely eliminate all credit card activity. I know some who have elected this alternative, primarily because of a bad credit experience or an inability to monitor such activity. If you do need a card, my advice is simple. Find one credit card which meets your needs and get rid of all others. Then make a commitment to repay the entire balance every single month. By making minimum payments, you will suffer from extraordinary interest charges in just a short period of time. This is unwise (Proverbs 20:16).

If possible, look for a card that will benefit you. For instance, some will give you frequent-flier miles or credits toward major purchases such as cars or refrigerators or even cash rebates.

DISTINGUISH WANTS VERSUS NEEDS

It has been said, "We spend money we don't have, to get things we don't need, to impress people we don't even know or like." Evaluate every single purchase you make by two categories: "wants" versus "needs." Virtually every "want" is not necessary if you take the time to consider why you desire it. Each time you feel tempted to buy something not planned, wait and pray about it for a few days. And with "needs," do your homework. I am a stickler for finding sales or bargains, and many times I will hold off purchasing something initially until I find it on sale. Sometimes neighborhood garage sales offer many of the items on the need list. Also, do not forget to use coupons. I enjoy looking for this source of free money which is available to us every day through the mail, newspapers and books.

BUDGETING

One financial expert said, "If you aren't budgeting, chances are you're flying by the seat of your financial pants." Though I realize this can be a painful process, I encourage you to keep close track of all your incoming and outgoing funds through the use of a budget plan. Initially, maintain records of all funds spent, including cash, over a three- to six-month basis, to determine average spending levels. Then set maximum spending levels on a variety of matters. Include in your plan items such as tithe, savings and investments as well as your housing, utilities, food, recreation, clothing, medical/dental, school/child care, insurance, transportation, emergency car and/or house repairs, etc.

Once your plan is set, stick to it. There are a number of books and computer programs available in your local Christian bookstore to help guide you in this process. A budget will help set guidelines to relieve the tension associated with spending. This is extremely important for everyone but particularly for families. Commit your plan to prayer, and ask God to give you wisdom and direction (Proverbs 16:3).

GOOD RECORD-KEEPING

No matter how unorganized you claim to be, there is no excuse for sloppy financial record-keeping. Reconcile your checkbook on a timely basis, keep your files of financial records up-to-date, keep your will and beneficiary information current, maintain all prior year income tax information and other key financial data in a safe, secure place. Important and irreplaceable documents such as deeds, marriage certificates and original insurance policies should be placed in a bank safe-deposit box. As a steward of what God has given you, you have a great responsibility to keep track of it.

RENDER UNTO CAESAR WHAT IS CAESAR'S

Have honesty and integrity in dealing with all your taxes and bills (Matthew 22:17-21). Completely repay all your debts in their entirety, and do not cheat on your taxes.

Here is an example that I related to my group years ago. We were preparing to sell our house when I discovered a termite problem. When the exterminator showed up, I was told I could spend $130 to partially fix the problem in order to meet the minimum standards for selling the house or spend $500 and be sure the problem was resolved. It crossed my mind to go for the lower option, but I did not feel it would be honest. Therefore, I went for the $500 job, much to the terminator's surprise. Upon completion of the work, I was told my response was rare, and he was curious as to what I did for a living. It gave me a great opportunity to tell him about my work with the FCA and my faith in Christ. Later that night we received a full-price offer on our home. I am confident that because we made the right decision, God blessed us. God desires for us to be upright in all our financial dealings.

IDENTIFY SCAMS AND GET-RICH SCHEMES

We have made it our policy to not buy or commit to anything over the telephone. I cannot tell you how many times we have been called by a variety of people wanting our money for some worthy cause or telling us over the phone how we can get rich quick. Our response is always for people to send us information in the mail, and we will be glad to review and read their material for ourselves. Most of the time, the materials are never sent, and if they are, you can discover the small print very quickly. If I have questions that I cannot answer, I have the freedom to take these materials to outsiders whom I trust for valuable counsel.

At other times, you will be approached in person by people who will make strong sales calls, and you will feel unable to say "NO." I urge you to not feel compelled to agree to something until you are totally sure. I have walked away from many opportunities until I have had a chance to review and pray through situations using the wisdom of my wife, family and friends to help me determine the right course of action. The times I have acted alone and have reacted quickly, primarily out of greed, are the times when I have been burned financially.

DIVERSIFYING YOUR ASSETS

In current economic times it is important that your eggs are not all in one basket. Spread out your funds into several different banks and institutions and possibly across national boundaries. Obtain a combination of cash and other high liquid accounts to go alongside other investment options such as stocks, bonds, real estate, insurance contracts, etc. I would also have several trustworthy investment advisors helping you manage your funds appropriately and minimize your overall risk.

SAVING FOR THE FUTURE

It is very important that you have funds ready to meet your future needs and those of your family. Set aside a portion of your monthly income to help you meet your medium and long-range financial goals. This includes the needs you have for life insurance, retirement and children's college education fund. I also believe you should have a cash disaster fund to help offset major unexpected bills such as car repairs, medical expenses, etc.

FAMILY FINANCES

It is sad to report that today's church families are some of the most negligent when it comes to financial issues. Larry Burkett reported the following for "church families" from his seminar, "Your Finances in Changing Times":

- 40% are overspending every month.
- 20% are on the verge of divorce.
- 50% of all these marriages end in divorce.
- 90% of the divorces point to financial difficulties.

It is crucial within a marriage to decide who will handle paying the bills, balancing the checkbook, doing the research and making the investment decisions. Once this is decided, it is important that both have input and full knowledge about financial matters. Periodically, take an inventory of everything that relates to money (savings and checking accounts; credit cards; life, health and auto insurance policies; stocks, bonds, mutual funds and other investments; and real estate holdings) so there are no surprises for either of you. Also, make sure you have a valid will and that your estate planning is in order in case of an untimely death.

One of Satan's primary methods for destroying families is through financial matters. First Timothy 6:10, 11, 17 says, "For the love of money is a root of all kinds of evil. Some people, eager for money, have wandered from the faith and pierced themselves with many griefs. But you, man of God, flee from all this, and pursue righteousness, godliness, faith, love, endurance and gentleness. Command those who are rich in this present world not to be arrogant nor to put their hope in wealth, which is so uncertain, but to put their hope in God, who richly provides us with everything for our enjoyment."

Keep your lives free from the love of money, and be content with what you have because God has said in Hebrews 13:5, "Never will I leave you; never will I forsake you." Matthew 6:19-21 says, "Do not store up for yourselves treasures on earth, where moth and rust destroy, and where thieves break in and steal. But store up for yourselves treasures in heaven, where moth and rust do not destroy, and where thieves do not break in and steal. For where your treasure is, there your heart will be also."

How do we know when the love money more than God? Here are eight signs of financial discontentment:

1. Thoughts of money consume my day.
2. The financial success of others makes me jealous.
3. I define success in terms of what I have rather than who I am in Christ.
4. My family is neglected in my pursuit of money.
5. I close my eyes to the genuine needs of others.
6. I live in the paralyzing fear of losing my money.
7. I'm prepared to borrow myself into bondage.
8. God receives my leftovers rather than my first fruits.

28 MONEY-SAVING TIPS FOR YOU AND YOUR FAMILY

1. Have a specific and realistic savings goal in writing with deadline dates. Even saving small amounts can add up to large sums of money over time.

2. Keep track of all your expenses (including cash), and review them at the end of each month so you know where your money is going.

3. Learn the difference between wants and needs. Focus your spending on the needs.

4. Build an emergency fund equal to three to six months' living expenses or more if you can, and keep it in a safe and liquid investment.

5. Insure yourself and your loved ones adequately against loss of property, job or income and against legal liability and major medical expenses.

6. Pay off all your credit card debt every month. You should never make an interest payment on your credit card. Look for a "no-fee" card or one that has incentives for airline, automobile or cash credits.

7. Do not buy or rent more house than you can afford. Do not let your mortgage or rent make it impossible for you to save.

8. If you have a mortgage and have no other higher-interest debt, pay the mortgage off as quickly as you can by making extra payments toward the principal.

9. Look for quality and comfort, not excessive display, in your home's furnishings.

10. Drop expensive "add-on" services you can easily do without, such as extra features on your telephone or cable television.

11. Take full advantage of coupon and refund offers, but do not buy anything you do not need just because you have a coupon or will get a rebate.

12. Shop the grocery stores and wholesale clubs that save you the most money and time. Prepare a weekly menu and shop only from a list. Avoid expensive, ready-to-eat items and paper products. Carry a lunch to work.

13. Look at your car only as a contraption to take you from point A to point B, not as a status symbol.

14. Buy sufficient liability coverage for your car, but refuse to pay for excessive collision or comprehensive insurance.

15. Buy the best quality clothes you can find at reasonable prices, and take care of them so they will last a long time. Also, color-coordinate your wardrobe so items can be worn in combination with others to save on shoes and other accessories.

16. Do not buy something which will require two incomes to pay for.

17. Learn to see, read and listen to ads and to extract the useful information from among all the hype.

18. Do not shop on impulse or because you are bored, but make a list of the things you need and stick to it. Do not feel obligated to buy everything on your list immediately, but take time to research.

19. Learn to enjoy life's simple pleasures, many of which are free. With vacations, go off-season to avoid peak prices and consider places that are close to home.

20. Shop around for the best deal among banks and savings and loans, and refuse to keep your money in low-interest, high-fee bank checking accounts.

21. Learn about mutual funds, and then use them to diversify your investments.

22. Educate yourself about taxes and tax rates. The Internal Revenue Service will answer your questions (1-800-829-1040) and send you dozens of publications for free (1-800-829-3676).

23. Estimate at the beginning of each year how much your income from all sources is going to be, then adjust your withholding at work so you come as close to a zero refund or payment at tax preparation time.

24. Contribute the maximum allowed to your employer's 401(k) salary deferral plan and to your Individual Retirement Account or a tax-sheltered annuity vehicle. Look for employer matching fund incentives.

25. Educate yourself about investing. With so many excellent magazines and books available, there is no excuse not to do so. Invest wisely with investments that will let you sleep at night. Greed will lead to destruction.

26. Take care of yourself. Keep in good health so you can enjoy the fruits of all your labor and savings and share that enjoyment with your loved ones.

27. Share a portion of your fortune with your local church and favorite charity. Feel the joy of helping others less fortunate than yourself.

28. Make sure your will and estate planning issues are in proper order.

KEYS TO LEADING A PROSPEROUS LIFE

1. *Be a Worker.* Numerous times in Scripture we are told that the prudent and diligent increased, the foolish and the lazy decreased. Those who base their economic actions on truth will prosper, while those who violate truth will not (Matthew 25:29).

2. *Be a Giver.* Proverbs 11:24-25 "One man gives freely, yet gains even more; another withholds unduly, but comes to poverty. A generous man will prosper; he who refreshes others will himself be refreshed." You cannot out give God!!

3. *Be an Asker.* Luke 11:5-13 reminds us about this principle in the parent/child relationship. Here's some other great scripture on "asking": 1 John 3:22, 5:14-15; Matthew 7:7-11, 21:22; John 11:22,14:13-14, 15:7; James 1:5-6, 4:2-3; Zechariah 10:1.

4. *Be Attentive.* 1 Timothy 6:17-18 "God....richly provides us with everything for our enjoyment." Keep your eyes and ears open. It's not based on luck or good fortune. Be quick to give God the credit.

5. *Stay Connected to God and His Word.* Joshua 1:8 and 2 Chronicles 31:21—Hezekiah who "in everything he undertook...sought his God and worked wholeheartedly. And so he prospered."

6. *Remain Humble.* James 1:9-11. The rich need to recognize their humanity and the fleeting nature of life. This is in no way a condemnation of the rich, but is a warning against pride.

7. *Don't Be Anxious.* Matthew 6:25-34 and Philippians 4:6, 19. Dependence on God frees us from worry and anxiety. It does not free us from being responsible stewards.

As the Scriptures state so clearly, there are great dangers associated with the accumulation of riches and how it impacts our lives and those around us. I believe the key is to *surrender total control to God.* Only when you allow God to be in total control of this area will you experience peace in your financial matters.

When you believe God owns it all, there is no fear of loss. In summary, try this simple plan based on a percentage of income: *tithe* 10 percent, *save* 20 percent and *live off* the remaining 70 percent.

Chapter Eleven

QUALITY RELATIONSHIPS

Have you spent quality relationship time with family and friends?

God has charged men to provide leadership in their homes and families. This includes leadership in the form of loving authority (honoring his wife with respect), leadership in the form of spiritual training, and leadership in helping to maintain the marital relationship. As part of this role, developing and maintaining quality relationships is vitally important. The Bible urges us to embrace one another's pains and triumphs.

When I was single, the subject of "quality time" came up every now and then. Frankly, I had no clue what it meant. My accountability partners and my wife have helped me begin to understand. It is not just spending time together, but time when you focus your attention on the one you are with, whether it be your spouse, child or friend.

It is extremely rude to be in the midst of a conversation and have your attention diverted by things happening around you. I try to put myself in the position of those whom I'm talking to during conversations. After all, if I am talking to someone, it is annoying to have people casually listening. Therefore, I have tried (I'm still learning!) to implement the following when talking to people:

1. *Eye contact.* Get your focus off the newspaper, TV and others nearby and make a deliberate effort to truly hear them. Face them squarely. This communicates, "I'm available; I'm choosing to listen to you." Adopt an open posture—crossed legs and arms often suggest, "I'm not interested." Watch for nonverbal behavior such as posture, body movements and gestures. Notice frowns, smiles, raised eyebrows and twisted lips.

2. *Ask questions.* There are times when you will need to be quiet and just listen, but many times you can help carry the conversation by knowing how and when to ask questions. Give nonverbal answers—nod, smile, raise your eyebrows. These signal that you are listening.

3. *Avoid clock watching.* If you have another appointment or things to do, let the person know up front what time constraints you have. If you have unlimited time, remove your watch so complete attention can be given.

4. *Mix in your experiences, if appropriate.* Do not dominate the conversation, but find a way to add your own thoughts without disrupting the flow of the conversation.

There are many people I'd love to contact regularly, but with limited time and resources, I've had to make relational priorities. Specifically determine how you intend to spend time with people around you. And in your relationships, give love without expectations, just as God demonstrates love to each one of us.

WHAT DOES SCRIPTURE SAY?

"A new command I give you: Love one another. As I have loved you, so you must love one another. By this all men will know that you are my disciples, if you love one another" (John 13:34-35).

"My command is this: Love each other as I have loved you. Greater love has no one than this, that he lay down his life for his friends" (John 15:12-13).

"Let us therefore make every effort to do what leads to peace and to mutual edification" (Romans 14:19).

"Therefore encourage one another and build each other up, just as in fact you are doing" (1 Thessalonians 5:11).

PUTTING OTHERS BEFORE SELF

There is a wedding prayer that says, "Now our joys are doubled, because the happiness of one is also the happiness of the other. Now our burdens are cut in half, since when we share them we divide the load." In our relationship with God and others, we double our joys and cut our burdens in half. Meaningful time with others is not the whole solution for living a life of integrity, but a life of integrity wouldn't be possible without them. God made us to be interdependent—not independent. We are part of a group striving toward reality with God—not isolated individuals. We need each other.

Every important relationship in life must be built on loyalty. Building loyalty in others is done by demonstrating loyalty to them. Marriages must be built on this habit or they do not survive. Leaders look for this quality with those they serve. Jesus Christ required loyalty from his disciples and in the lives of Christians today. One teenager told me, "Loyalty is not just a 'cool' characteristic to have—it is a requirement for survival." True friends are of utmost importance and loyalty is one of the key character qualities. It creates a feeling of deep trust in authentic friendships.

Loyalty is a key component one should address when sharpening one's character. Loyalty is required on a daily basis, and it is a necessity for every successful relationship. In a real sense, "we are all each other's bodyguard." Loyalty involves protecting those in our sphere of relationships. We want the best for each other. We have a stake in the life of each person. We value each other. We look after each other. We strengthen and inspire each other. Our fellowship becomes our family, our fortress, and our energizer.

One way to demonstrate our loyalty is through being a servant. Servanthood isn't reserved for those who are skilled or gifted for service—servanthood is a duty for all Christians. Our role model is Christ himself who came "not to be served, but to serve" (Matthew 20:28).

Rick Warren said, "We serve God by serving others. The world defines greatness in terms of power, possessions, prestige, and position. In our self-serving culture with its 'me first' mentality acting like a servant is not a popular concept." FCA Vice-President Dan Britton states, "In the athletic world, everyone struggles to some degree with the "me first" mentality. We buy into the lie that we are better than others because of our giftedness in athletics. So are we consumed with self or with serving? When serving, we need to have intentionality (Plan it!), intensity (Seize it!) and intimacy (Feel it!). The passion for serving must come from the heart."

GOD

In the midst of maintaining quality relationships, again, spending daily time with the Almighty God is the most important of all. See Chapter 8 on maintaining this as a key part of your day and life. Your other friendships will be enhanced when this is your top priority.

SPOUSE

After God, the next most important relationship you have is with your spouse. Usually during courtship it is easy to focus your energies on your future mate, but many men stop the romance within hours of saying, "I do." To maintain a successful marriage, it is important to continue the dating process. This means setting aside specific date nights just for the two of you to get away and enjoy each other's company. This becomes even more critical when you have children. Frequently, Janna and I escape on date nights, overnights and even entire weekends by ourselves, so we can focus on our relationship.

A great habit is to spend time praying together on a regular basis. Be specific in your requests and open about your needs and concerns. One of my accountability partners prays every single night with his spouse and the results are incredible. He says that it brings a special closeness and unity to their marriage. I'm talking about the open kind of prayer where both the husband and wife pray honestly from their hearts. They confess their own shortcomings, and demonstrate their sensitivity by praying for the needs in each others' lives. This kind of prayer will bring intimacy into a relationship. Some people even say that praying together and sexual intimacy are interrelated. "Christians find that the more their spirits are refreshed in prayer and informed by sharing, the more glorious the act of sex becomes," say authors John and Paula

Sandford. If you are having difficulty in praying with your spouse, here are some suggestions:

1. *Start small and keep it simple.* Have brief, informal prayers at naturally convenient times.

2. *Pray about everyday matters.* Don't try to be religious or overly spiritual. Pray through areas of concerns that the family is involved with.

3. *Openly tell God—with your spouse present—about your relationship with Him.* Thank God for His gifts, blessings and answers to prayer. Be honest and vulnerable as you ask for God's help.

We've learned much from Gary Chapman's book, *Five Languages of Love*, discovering one another's primary love language. They include (1) words of affirmation, (2) gifts, (3) acts of service, (4) quality time and (5) physical touch. Each person has one love language which means more to him than all the others. You may appreciate them all, but one will speak to you more deeply.[1]

As spouses, we are called to love, respect and submit to one another. Each and every one of us have specific needs. For many women, this includes affection, communication, financial support, respect, validation, devotion, reassurance, and the need to be cared for and understood. Men need sexual fulfillment, recreational companionship, domestic support, trust, acceptance, appreciation, admiration, approval and encouragement.

Gary Smalley has many solid messages for couples. His "five secrets of a happy marriage" are:

1. *Healthy couples have a clearly defined menu of expectations.* They have made certain decisions relating to how they are going to interact together (i.e., how they will honor one another, a plan for dealing with unresolved anger, activities that foster emotional bonding, etc.).

2. *Healthy couples understand and practice meaningful communication.* The goal is to feel safe in sharing honestly and intimately with one another.

3. *Healthy couples are associated with a small, healthy support group.* Regular time with three or four couples can make an incredible difference in your own marriage.

4. *Healthy couples are aware of unhealthy or offensive behavior stemming from their heritage.* Make a conscious decision to overcome past mistakes and look to gain support for the changes.

5. *Healthy couples have a vibrant relationship with Jesus Christ.* Be totally dependent upon Him as your primary source of abundant life. Your spouse will let you down at some point—Christ doesn't.[2]

There are many resources and ideas available for enhancing your relationship with your spouse. Here are 10 brief tips which might help you in making a decision about getting married or in reinforcing some of the basic principles involved in every successful marriage.

1. *Lifelong Commitment.* When a man and a woman decide to marry, they are committing themselves to remain together forever, until death. "What God has joined together, let man not separate" (Matthew 19:6).

2. *Shared Identity.* In marriage a man and woman are brought together into union—"they will become one flesh" (Genesis 2:24). They become one as they blend their lives together. It's once-and-for-all, yet it's a process that needs time, love, patience and forgiveness (Genesis 2:23-24).

3. *Absolute Faithfulness.* Marital faithfulness is the fulfillment of the vow made before God during the wedding ceremony. The Bible demands sexual fidelity. "You shall not commit adultery" (Exodus 20:14).

4. *Unreserved Love.* This is genuine, heartfelt, through-thick-and-thin, till-death-do-us-part love. A husband and a wife are to love each other with an unreserved love that leads them to honor one another, to esteem one another, to consider one another's welfare above their own and to stay by one another's side through the highs and lows of marriage. "Love never fails" (1 Corinthians 13:8).

5. *Mutual Submission.* Submission and love go together. We know that God is love, but how do we know He loves us? Because with great humility and submission, Christ went to the cross (Philippians 2:5-8). Marriage is give and take. It is overcoming selfishness. It is being a servant.

6. *Well-defined Roles.* Marriage works best when both husband and wife accept their roles. It's a functional necessity exemplified by Jesus. He came to earth to carry out the will and plan of God. Although He was equal to the Father, He submitted to the Father's leading. When the Bible says that the husband is the head of the wife (Ephesians 5:23), it simply means that the husband is to provide responsible leadership without being dictatorial or self-serving.

7. *Sexual Fulfillment.* Sexuality is not evil. Inside marriage sex is not sinful. But it must not be made more important than it is, nor should it be minimized. It's part of the overall picture—an intimate part of the shared identity of husband and wife (1 Corinthians 7:3-4).

8. *Open Communication.* For a marriage to work, communication barriers must be broken down. These four suggestions might help:

(a) Tell of your need to communicate.

(b) Don't rehash old conversations.

(c) Start on the fact level.

(d) Move on to the feeling and conviction level.

9. *Tender Respect.* This is generally more of a problem for men. Therefore, a husband must make it his goal to give his wife special honor and respect, making sure he doesn't rob her of the joy of life.

10. *Spiritual Companionship.* What a difference it makes when a marriage has a godly husband and a dedicated wife! Love and sacrifice will set this marriage apart and make possible a true spiritual companionship. As a man and wife draw closer to God, they will draw closer to each other.[3]

Dave Gibson, associate pastor of Grace Church in Edina, Minnesota, says there are 12 words which will save your marriage. "I am sorry. I was wrong. Please forgive me. I love you." Recently I found a card that I gave my wife after one of my blunders. It read, "Being humble and apologetic does not come easily for me...unfortunately, being stupid does." That pretty much sums it up for me.

CHILDREN

Your kids also need concentrated time with you. No matter how old or young, this is a top priority. Too often, children get our leftover time instead of the best. Jeff Kemp, executive director of Washington Family Council and former NFL quarterback, says, "Children, our next generation, gain their sense of value, their identity and their character from the intimacy and quality of parental relationship."[4]

In a study conducted during the 1970s a team of researchers wanted to learn how much time middle-class fathers spent playing and interacting with their small children. First, they asked a group of fathers to estimate the time spent with their one-year-old youngsters each day and received an average reply of 15 to 20 minutes. To verify these claims, the investigators attached microphones to the shirts of small children for the purpose of recording actual parental verbalization. The results of the study were shocking. The average amount of time these middle-class fathers spent with their small children was 37 seconds per day! Their direct interaction was limited to 2.7 encounters daily, lasting 10 to 15 seconds each! That amount of time represented fatherhood for millions of America's children in the 1970s, and I believe the findings would be even more depressing today.[5]

It is an unfortunate situation when children do not have the opportunity to spend quality time with their parents. No wonder kids of this generation are bombarded by negative peer pressure due to spending a majority of time with their peers.

Here are some timely tips from Walt Mueller to consider in helping your children respond positively to negative peer pressure:

1. *Teach your children about the powerful role that friends play in our lives.* An old proverb says, "He who walks with the wise grows wise, but a companion of fools suffers harm." Discuss examples of this principle that you see in the media and everyday life.

2. *Actively build your child's self-image from day one.* Kids who experience ignorance, absence or cutting remarks from their parents are significantly more likely to go to their peers for the accep-

tance and approval that they so desperately need. Find something to appreciate daily and encourage and bless them through praise.

3. *Examine yourself.* A positive example is the greatest educational tool at a parent's fingertips. Do you give in to negative peer pressure in your life?

4. *Encourage involvement in a positive peer group.* Positive peer pressure can be a powerful tool to help our kids make wise choices. There are church groups, scouts and other volunteer organizations where your children will be surrounded with others their age who are living responsibly and wisely, and learning how to reach out to others with compassion and sensitivity.

5. *Pray, pray, pray.* Ask God for wisdom, courage and strength as you lead your children.[6]

Let me also add a few other words of encouragement in dealing with your family, particularly children:

1. Pray and read the Bible together as a family. This will establish a legacy.

2. Cultivate creativity. Help your children identify their unique gifts, talents and interests. Plug yourself into these areas. Be careful to not overprotect. Look for teachable moments as you discuss life.

3. Encourage interdependence. The values of teamwork, sharing and caring should be taught and modeled.

4. Maintain a sense of humor. Humor breaks tension, relieves stress and helps maintain our perspective about what's really important.

5. Express anger responsibly. While anger is a normal part of a family life, it's important to express anger without indicating that the child is not loved. Avoid attacking statements like "You are so stupid; can't you ever do anything right? I can't wait for you to get back to school." Communicate your anger in a way your children know right from wrong and know your motive is love.

6. Put your family on your calendar. Date nights with your spouse and kids; mark important events on the calendar—birthdays, anniversaries, school programs, sporting events, concerts, family vacations and so on.

7. Introduce accountability to your kids. Our ministry has designed a set of accountability questions for teenagers as noted on our web site: www.characterthatcounts.org. These questions can be modified based on the age and maturity of your children. I have met a number of parents who are intentionally pursuing a formal accountability time with their children with remarkable success.

After one of my seminars, a mom and her 15-year old son approached me and shared that they had read my book and had been accountable to one another over the past year. The genuine smile on their faces revealed that they were having a dynamite experience. This was later confirmed when I privately pulled the young man aside and heard him say how impactful and freeing this time had been. Though this type of accountability with one another is not the norm, it has worked positively for this family.

Another family has adopted a weekly check-in time called "PIT Stop." PIT represents the following acronym for their time together—"P" for Prayer; "I" for Inspiration (a devotional thought); and "T" for Talk Time (this is where they go through a series of accountability questions which have been designed for each family member to answer).

PARENTS, SIBLINGS AND OTHER RELATIVES

Whether you live in the same home, city or across the globe, these relationships need specific attention. Maintaining communication, even when living far away, has to be a priority even if it is through the mail or by phone.

FRIENDS

As a single person, I used to dread my friends' weddings because it meant they would most likely drift totally out of my life. When Janna and I got married, we made a commitment to each other that we would continue to interact with friends from our single years. It has been positive for us to continue to make these relationships important.

I also encourage you to determine if your relationships are "draining" or "replenishing." By "draining" I am referring to those friends who are demanding in the effort to maintain (we give significantly more than we gain). On the flip side, "replenishing" relationships are when you are greatly encouraged and strengthened when spending time with these people. It is important to have a proportionate number of each, especially if you have a high number of "drainers" in your life.

You've probably heard the old saying, "If you want to have a friend, you must first be a friend." The bottom line is that true friendship takes hard work. We all need friends. Find friends who will say, "I'm with you. Count on me. I'm here."

PASTORS/MINISTERS/PRIESTS

Some of the most needy people may be those who are in full-time Christian service. Dr. Gary Oliver polled pastors and discovered that many were weary, wounded and discouraged. We may need to take an active part in replenishing and encouraging them. The statistics (among many others shared by Dr. Oliver at the 1993 Promise Keepers conference in Boulder) show the following:

- 90% are not properly trained for ministry.
- 70% do not have a close friend.
- 40% wanted to leave the ministry within the last three months.
- 50% feel incapable of doing their job.
- 37% have inappropriate sexual behavior.

Bill Hallstead, pastor of the Church of Christ in Truman, Minnesota, wrote an article titled, "Perils of the Professionally Holy." In this piece he stated that a high number of pastors had failed sexually primarily due to three reasons:

1. *Over-familiarity with God.* Many are so accustomed to the reality of God that they no longer stand in awe of Him. Because careers and all other aspects of life are wrapped around the church, some pastors begin to lose the awe that keeps them in profound respect of the holy and righteous God who will judge His people.

2. *Sin saturation.* Pastors confront a numbing array of people's sins. Week after week, a torrent of sins needing forgiveness flows past them until they lose sense of the awfulness of sin. In dealing with so many gross sins, a pastor's temptation seems so minor. They preach forgiveness, which covers them as well as those they minister to.

3. *Job overload.* Even our pastors need time away from work. After all, everyone else has a break from time to time. These times of break away should not violate the holiness of God, but instead keep the relationship with God fresh, new and exciting.

Too many ministers are living with tremendous burdens of isolation, loneliness and discouragement. We need to be supporting our pastors daily through prayer and simple encouragement, both in their professional and personal lives. Spend time getting to know your pastors, serving and loving them.

I would urge you to commit yourself to a congregation. God has ordained the church as the primary means of helping believers mature in Christ (Ephesians 4:12-13). If you intend to grow, be an active participant in a body of believers. Be a resource and refuge for your pastor and other members of the church.

NEIGHBORS

We believe that God strategically places us in living situations where we are called to befriend those who live close by. One Easter my wife and I made homemade bread and delivered the loaves to our neighbors. Block parties are also important. These provide a basis for building a community and letting your light shine to those you see regularly.

CO-WORKERS AND EMPLOYEES

This is a great place to develop tremendous friendships both in secular and Christian work places. Keep your eyes and ears open, and you will be blessed. When I was at Ernst & Whinney, I was surrounded by people who were extremely successful, as defined by the world's standards. Yet, as relationships formed, I discovered they too had many significant needs and were receptive to sharing those with me as we spent more time together. Don't let the appearance of "having it all together" stop you from developing relationships with those who you will spend time with on a regular basis.

The key is meeting them at their point of need. Often this means listening—not giving advice or admonitions, just listening. Strive to take relationships seriously. Superficial relationships will remain shallow and will not flourish.

KEEPING UP WITH THOSE WHO LIVE FAR AWAY

Obviously, there are some people who live too far away to see on a regular basis, and thus it becomes important to communicate either by letter or phone. The goal of these instructions is to develop long, lasting friendships. Here are ways to keep in touch:

1. *Personal letters.* Mike Rohrbach taught me many years ago the value of writing at least one letter a day to someone as a source of encouragement. It is extremely uplifting to go to my mailbox and find a note from someone, so for years I have made it my goal to write a letter to someone every day.
2. *Form letters.* If personal notes won't work, use a form letter to stay in touch with your friends and acquaintances; even these letters serve as an information source. Often, I will add a personal note or two to a form letter to personalize it.
3. *Phone calls.* Just like letters, I try to make one encouraging phone call a day to someone whom the Lord puts on my mind. Whether it be a local or long distance call, it is good to talk to someone every day.

THE BUILDER AND THE WRECKER

I watched them tearing a building down,
A gang of men in a busy town.
With a yo heave ho and lusty yell
they swung a beam, a side wall fell.
I asked the foreman, "Are those men skilled,
the kind you would hire if you wanted to build?"
He laughed and said, "Why, no indeed,
just common labor is all I need.
They can easily wreck in a day or two
what builders have taken years to do."
So, I asked myself as I went my way,
which of those roles have I tried today?
Am I the builder who works with care,
measuring life by the rule and square,
patiently following a well-made plan,
carefully doing the best I can?
Or am I the wrecker who walks the town,
content with the labor of tearing down?[7]

Notes

1 Adapted from Gary D. Chapman, *The Five Love Languages* (Chicago: Northfield Publishing, 1995). For the two-session video about the five love languages, call 1-800-458-2772.

2 Adapted from Gary Smalley, *Seven Promises of a Promise Keeper* (Colorado Springs, CO: Focus on the Family, 1994), pp. 107-113.

3 Adapted from "What Will Make My Marriage Work?" by David Egner (*Sports Spectrum Magazine*, January/February 1992), p. 24.

4 *Washington Citizen*, published by Family Research Council, September 1994, p.2.

5 James Dobson, *What Wives Wish Their Husbands Knew About Women* (Wheaton, IL: Tyndale, 1975), pp. 157-158.

6 *Today's Father*, published by National Center for Fathering, Vol. 2, No. 3.

7 Author unknown.

Chapter Twelve

OUR 100% BEST

Have you done your 100% best in your job, school, etc.?

In my job with FCA there are times when I am asked what kind of athlete Jesus Christ would be. My response has always been, "He would be the best, not only in terms of performance, but also in terms of His attitude and work ethic." With this in mind I believe we are also called to that same type of effort in whatever environment we are placed.

WHAT DOES SCRIPTURE SAY?

Colossians 3:17 instructs, "And whatever you do, whether in word or deed, do it all in the name of the Lord Jesus, giving thanks to God the Father through him." Colossians 3:23-24 adds, "Whatever you do, work at it with all your heart, as working for the Lord, not for men, since you know that you will receive an inheritance from the Lord as a reward. It is the Lord Christ you are serving."

God expects our best effort in all of our endeavors. Whether on the job, in the classroom, on the athletic field, within our church or with our spouse, children and family, we are supposed to do our best for God's glory. God is our audience, not our employer, teacher, coach, pastor or spouse. When we remember that He is the one whom we serve, our performance can be centered solely on Him.

According to 1 Thessalonians 4:11-12, "Make it your ambition to lead a quiet life, to mind your own business and to work with your hands, just as we told you, so that your daily life may win the respect of outsiders and so that you will not be dependent on anybody." First Corinthians 10:31 is the bottom line, "So whether you eat or drink or whatever you do, do it all for the glory of God." Both of these passages point to a strong work ethic and excellence in all matters.

SHOWING DETERMINATION

After one to four years at sea, the king salmon determines to head home—back to the stream where it hatched. Swimming against the fierce currents and leaping up waterfalls, the mighty salmon increases its daily speed as it covers the hundreds of miles home. Determination gives us resolve to keep going in spite of roadblocks. No matter how daunting the task, to be determined is to see it through despite the obstacles facing us.

God's Word stresses the importance of personal determination. The Lord assures us His glory is the goal (1 Corinthians 10:31), not man's approval. Furthermore, when He tells us to love, He tells us to do it fervently (1 Peter 4:8). When maintaining a friendship, it is to be devoted (Romans 12:10). When steering clear of evil, we are told to stay away from even the appearance of it (1 Thessalonians 5:22). When seeing a brother or sister in need, we are to bear the burden sacrificially (Galatians 6:1-2), not stay at a safe distance. When it comes to my sport, I am to be disciplined (2 Thessalonians 3:7-8) and diligent (1 Thessalonians 2:9). The Scriptures abound with exhortations to go above and beyond the required call of duty—to a dedication which persists against opposition, doing my tasks with excellence.

Paul's words in Philippians 3:12-14 say press on for the goal and the prize found in Christ Jesus. God calls us to never go backward. Attempt something great for God, and do it with all your might. Few things are more rewarding than the exhilaration of achievement after wholehearted effort. The stronger the current opposing us, the sweeter the victory will be. We are never finished until the race is done. Our adversary, the Devil, tries to discourage us constantly, but through determination, we can accomplish our goals in spite of opposition.

PLAYING TO AN AUDIENCE OF ONE

When I was a high school senior, we had a great football team with a perfect 9-0 record and a No. 1 rating in the state. However, one of the greatest lessons and memories of that season was learned from a scrawny sophomore during an early-season practice. Tim Tontz was a speedy 135-pounder who specialized in punt returns. On our senior-dominated squad he made a mark.

At the end of each practice our coaches had the entire team do extra running drills to help us in our conditioning. As seniors we knew the routine and the effort needed to make it through this time. At best, we were giving a 75 percent effort, but since we all went at the same pace, no one got in trouble. The problem was Tim. While the rest of the team coasted, Tim would sprint the entire distance. He consistently beat everyone by a wide margin, and because of Tim we ended up running more than we wanted.

As one of the leaders of our team and a friend of Tim, I finally decided to approach him and explain that he was making us look bad. "Tim, slow down and go our speed," I pleaded. His reply knocked me over: "Rod, I am disappointed in you as a fellow Christian. You see, when I play or practice, I picture Jesus Christ in the stands cheering me on to do my best. You and the other seniors can jog if you want; I am going to play for Him."

I learned a valuable lesson that day that I have never forgotten, and it changed my whole perspective on athletics. I pushed myself in those practices to stay up with Tim, and our whole team responded to his leadership. I know this contributed to our team's success. This new attitude also carried over to other areas of my life. Jesus became my audience, and no longer do I perform for anyone but Him.

One professional athlete who has applied the principle of playing to an audience of One is Kansas City Royals All-Star Mike Sweeney. Going into the 1999 baseball season, Sweeney was told by his coach that he had a zero percent chance of making the squad. Trade rumors were swirling throughout the off-season. During spring training Mike committed himself to not listen to the voices of other people but instead perform solely for the Lord.

Much to the surprise of his coaches and teammates, Sweeney not only made the team, but he had a breakthrough year. He followed up the 1999 season by making the All-Star team five different times in his career.

One of Mike's secrets is that he doesn't read the daily newspaper anymore because it became too big of a distraction. Mike has tremendous humility and great insight. He says, "I don't try to live up anybody's expectations except the Lord. I've heard nice things about me before…yet all of us have to learn. Even when you're a success, everything is a learning process."

We all have been given unique talents and abilities which God wants us to use completely. In all you do, do it for Him, and allow Him to use you to the fullest. Many times I hear people establishing different standards at work or various daily activities from other aspects of their lives. Does this bring glory to God? Let me give you some specifics.

ON THE JOB

As employees, we are called to give our employer our best possible effort. Do you work diligently, or do you hang out at the coffee pot? Do you give a minimal effort, or do you strive for excellence? Do you try to keep learning, or have you stagnated? Do you maintain a positive spirit with your peers, or do you spend time gossiping and tearing down others? Do you complain and even become embittered about your salary situation, especially when you compare yourself to others in the organization? Do you think of others, or do you always think of yourself? Do you accurately compute your travel expenses? Does Jesus Christ shine through you in your job?

In answering these questions can you stand before God and your employer and honestly say you have done your best? When I worked in Seattle for Ernst & Whinney, I answered to some very demanding people. When I realized that I was working for the Lord and not for them, I began to excel in the work place. I could have easily cut corners or been slightly dishonest or just done enough to get by. But does that please God?

Measure your performance against a standard of working for Jesus Christ. It takes having a teachable spirit and self-discipline. Successful professionals make the fine art of self-criticism as natural and frequent as handing out business cards. It takes hard work to develop a discipline of reflection and then put it to work. Employment success often boils down to one word—ATTITUDE. No company can tell you what kind of attitude you're supposed to have, but attitude translates into performance. Employers take note and often reward those who have a positive, engaging attitude.

In addition, Romans 13:1-7 reminds us also that all authority has been granted by God and that we are given no other options but to submit to that authority. These Scriptures also tell us that we will find favor with God if we willingly place ourselves under the authority.

All employees must guard against workaholism. In the rush to put in longer and longer hours, what often gets neglected is the personal side: family, friends, church, hobbies. Too much driving to achieve, succeed and control can lead to over-reliance on the job for satisfaction. The key is finding a balance to lead a personal and professional life where both are equally gratifying.

I believe long hours at the office aren't necessarily wrong, but it is the attitude that often comes with it. Workaholics often feel safer in the office because they know their hard work and a tough attitude will lead to success and approval whereas the emotional relationships at home may be more tenuous and stressful. At the office the workaholic is a corporate hero by being available around the clock, demanding of self and others to succeed at all costs. Harder work yields even more success and recognition. The imbalance begins to feed on itself. The final results are a domination of work on the individual's time and energy with neglected personal relationships.

If you are a workaholic or close to becoming one, I challenge you to evaluate the way you schedule your time and set priorities. Ask God for wisdom and direction. Talk to your spouse and your accountability partners on how to better balance your life. Learn to say "no" to after-hours work commitments when they conflict with personal life. Take real vacations and enjoy the benefits of a week-end away from work to not only relax but also restore yourself when you return to the job.

WHAT IF YOU ARE THE BOSS?

Are you fair when supervising people? Do you set a Christian example for your co-workers? Do you encourage and bless those you work with? Do you empower others to do their best? Do you effectively communicate your vision for the organization and then place people in the right positions to carry it out? When you are the boss, it is important to communicate and be sensitive to those who work with you. When situations are not working out right, you need to assist them in improving their performance, if possible, or help them get into an environment where they can succeed.

As a supervisor if you find yourself constantly out of time, buried in trivia, unable to get the important things done while helping everyone else, you're probably suffering from one of leader-ship's most common diseases: the failure to delegate and empower others. Moses faced the same problem. After leading his people out of Egypt, he insisted on ruling personally. His "micro-leadership" kept him so involved, in fact, that the Scriptures report that he was busy from morning until evening. Fortunately, Moses' father-in-law, Jethro, gave Moses some great advice in Exodus 18:18-27: "You and these people who come to you will only wear yourselves out. The work is too heavy for you; you cannot handle it alone...that will make your load lighter because they will share it with you. If you do this and God so commands, you will be able to stand the strain, and all these people will go home satisfied" (v. 18, 22b, 23).

Jethro was right! No one person can do it all. Furthermore, there are probably people in your organization who can do certain jobs better than you. You must learn to delegate. Though some are reluctant to do so, there are far more reasons to delegate than to do everything yourself.

Christian leaders possess many important qualities, which include dependence on Christ; an ability to understand problems and offer solutions; setting priorities; juggling multiple tasks; taking the initiative; having mastery and knowledge of the profession; strong interpersonal skills with a genuine interest in those you work with; a persistent drive to succeed; able to learn and change continuously; consistency and transparency; and they create a spirit of openness.

An effective resource to help you in monitoring employees you supervise is found in Appendix F (Weekly Tune-Up Report). It can also be helpful in the development of healthy communication between the boss and the employee.

SCHOOL

Grades are not necessarily an indication of your effort. Even during my school years cheating on exams was commonplace. During my sophomore year of college I had a golden opportunity to cheat on a final. A buddy of mine had stolen the test and had it "aced." Though I needed a good grade, I just could not participate with him, so I spent many hours preparing for this exam while he lounged in the student center. On test day he finished the exam within 30 minutes while I labored for over two hours along with the rest of the class. Imagine our surprise when the final grades were posted; I got an A for the semester, while he settled for a B. Again the Lord receives the glory for this happening, and I learned another lesson.

My advice when it comes to schooling is to not miss classes, do all your homework and truly make an attempt to learn the material, not just get your grade. Remember, honor the Lord and make Him your audience.

TIME MANAGEMENT

An area of great frustration for many people, especially as they try to do their best in their day-to-day lives, is the issue of having limited time. If you are like me, I somehow believe that if we had 30-hour days (or at least an extra five or 10 hours each week), my problems would be solved. Surely this extra time would relieve the tremendous pressure. Unfortunately, our lives leave a trail of unfinished tasks, unanswered letters, unvisited friends, unread books and neglected family relations. But would a longer day solve our problem? Wouldn't we soon be as frustrated as we are now with our 24-hour allotment?

Each of us is given the same 24 hours a day. How we use our time depends on our priorities and goals. We make the hours count for what we think is important. I am an advocate of working smart, not just long. At the end of life you've never heard someone say, "I wish I had spent more time at the office." Therefore, the important commodity called time requires attention to details and a specific plan of action, or your time can quickly begin to slip away. It is also crucial that you not become a workaholic or a loaf. Either label would be inappropriate for someone who claims to be a Christian.

In his book *Tyranny of the Urgent*, Charles Hummel tells us about how Jesus Christ managed and controlled His time while He was on earth. Though He was God, He was also human, and He experienced many of the same pressures and strains that a shortage of time brings. Yet at the end of His brief three years of ministry, John 17:4 says, "I have brought you glory on earth by completing the work you gave me to do." With so many unmet physical and spiritual needs around Him, He had peace because He knew that He had finished the work God had given Him.

The key to Christ's success was that He received His daily instructions in quiet moments with the Father. Consistently, you see that nothing came in the way of His intimate time with God. If Jesus needed this time with God, how much more do you and I need to seek it out? Jesus, though His ministry could have easily extended another 5-50 years, knew God in a way where He experienced tremendous peace. Hummel says, "The path to freedom is continuing day by day to meditate on the Scriptures and gain our Lord's perspective."[1]

I strongly encourage you to read *Tyranny of the Urgent*. It will give you great insights on how to distinguish between the important and urgent needs that come up daily. Here are a few other points to consider in getting a handle of your time:

1. *Learn to delegate.* Find people who are skilled (or teach them) to perform the task. There are people who can perform them as well as you can. We tend to cling to the jobs we can do well. When we do give a task to another, we need to acknowledge, praise and thank them for the final product.

2. *Control your time.* Do not let strong-willed people dominate your schedule. You are in charge of your time...if you are not, someone will take advantage of it. Ephesians 5:15-17 says, "Be very careful, then, how you live—not as unwise but as wise, making the most of every opportunity, because the days are evil. Therefore do not be foolish, but understand what the Lord's will is."

3. *Do not be governed by every emergency.* Set your priorities and goals. Constantly evaluate to make sure you are on track. As Matthew 6:33 recommends, "But seek first his kingdom and his righteousness, and all these things will be given to you as well."

4. *Determine when certain tasks should be performed based on when you are at your best.* Some tasks are better performed at certain times and under certain conditions. For instance, I'm better when I spend the early mornings doing my quiet time. I'm better at reading books in the summer when the job pressures ease off. We should all know our rhythms and be in touch with how to maximize our time under the appropriate conditions. Ecclesiastes 3:1-11 tells us there is a time for "everything under heaven."

5. *Learn to say "no" to good things, so you can say "yes" to the best.* Many worthy causes and events are available every day, but there is no way to do them all. Through prayer, establish criteria to help you make right decisions. Psalm 130:5 confesses, "I wait for the Lord, my soul waits, and in His word I put my hope."

6. *Budget time far in advance (even months ahead).* Put into your schedule all the non-negotiables such as work and family responsibilities. Then identify days of rest, personal time with immediate and extended family, date nights, play days...even your quiet time. After these are scheduled, then you can drop other items into your schedule. Psalm 31:14-15a stresses, "But I trust in you, O Lord; I say, 'You are my God.' My times are in your hands..."

7. *Make a list of all unfinished projects, and attempt to do the most difficult one first.* Making a list gives you perspective. Do not put

off something that can be done now. Ideally, make it your goal to never pick up something twice. Another helpful hint is to make sure that everything you have has a home. If you can't find a place for something, perhaps it is something you shouldn't keep. Organize everything into four piles: To Do, To Pay, To File and To Read. Then when the daily deluge of paper starts, you can find an appropriate place for everything. You'll always know where things are, and you can stop spending your valuable time looking all over the house for that bill you need to pay. Proverbs 14:23 says, "All hard work brings a profit, but mere talk leads only to poverty."

8.   *Use a daytimer or calendar that works for you.* Carry it with you, and maintain a simple, useable system. If you are married, review what is on your schedule on a regular basis with your spouse.

9.   *Do an accounting of your current daily routine through monitoring time by half-hour increments.* How do you currently spend your time? Through this exercise you will find out what things are chewing up major blocks of time. Specifically, I encourage you to drastically cut down on your TV viewing. This one alone can steal valuable time. Count the hours you and your family spend watching the tube. No doubt you will find major amounts of time buried there.

OUR WALK NEEDS TO MATCH OUR TALK

Actions speak louder than words, and people follow our actions, not our words. People watch what we do on the job or at school, and if it differs from what we say, we lose credibility. We need to model the values that we speak. Here are just a few areas we should examine:

- Time and Money: We may talk about being committed to God, our family, the church, or something else, but our real values are revealed in our checkbook and daily schedule. The ways we spend our money and our time tells others what is important to us.
- Selection of Friends: There is no neutrality in friends. They will either bring you up or they will bring you down. Be careful about who you choose to spend time with.

- Language and Humor: Paul encouraged the Christians in Ephesus to refrain from obscenity, foolish talk, and coarse jokes, and to focus instead on giving thanks (Ephesians 5:14). Foul language, dirty jokes, racial slurs, and sarcastic statements can elicit a laugh or intimidate others. Either way, it is inappropriate to talk and joke in this way.
- "Little" Decisions: Our lives are filled with countless decisions that reflect our commitments, values and disciplines. By virtue of the daily choices we make such as watching television programs or movies that suggest that violence and premarital or extramarital sex are acceptable, we send a signal to those watching that we believe this is okay in real life situations.

Peer pressure, no matter how young or old, can be the difference between doing our best and not. The pressure may start off like an innocent invitation but progressively, the heat is turned up. Knowing how to respond calmly and with confidence takes an alert mind. Here are several suggestions to help you stay sharp:
- Ignore the pressure completely or change the subject. Sometimes the best response is to not respond at all.
- Clearly and confidently share that you are not interested. A strong response has a way of "drawing a line in the sand." Once you make your stand, be consistent. If you waver, you're likely to fall and the likelihood of you being tempted again will occur and then the peer pressure will intensify.
- Remember that those who pressure us are many times feeling insecure about themselves and want us to participate to validate their own behavior. The truth of the matter is they don't care about us—they only care about themselves.
- Establish a covenant or contract with a friend, coach, minister or your parents. My parents use to tell me that I should transfer the "heat" on to them.
- Always be ready!! If you are prepared and know what you are going to do in advance, you are much more likely to successfully follow through with an appropriate response.

HAVE YOU HEARD OF THE 7 HABITS?

One of the most poignant books of our time is Stephen Covey's *The 7 Habits of Highly Effective People* (Simon & Schuster; 1990). (Though not a "Christian book," it contains many insightful, helpful principles.) Here are the seven habits:

1. **Be Proactive.** Take responsibility for your own effectiveness, happiness and circumstances.
2. **Begin with the End in Mind.** Identify your various roles, then think about the long-term goals you want to accomplish in each of those roles.
3. **Put First Things First.** Having identified roles and goals, now schedule and adapt as necessary to accomplish your goals and "the end" (Habit 2).
4. **Think Win/Win.** Constantly seek mutual benefit in all human interactions.
5. **Seek First to Understand, Then to Be Understood.** Listen to get inside the other person's frame of reference, then present your own ideas contextually.
6. **Synergize.** As "the whole is greater than the sum of its parts," so a group working together can accomplish more than an individual.
7. **Sharpen the Saw.** This focuses on personal renewal. In short, attend to your personal physical, mental, social/emotional and spiritual needs.

Notes

[1] Charles E. Hummel, *Tyranny of the Urgent* (Downers Grove, IL: Inter-Varsity Christian Fellowship, 1994 revised).

Chapter Thirteen

HALF-TRUTHS AND OUTRIGHT LIES

Have you told any half-truths or outright lies, putting yourself in a better light to those around you?

This was added to our list of weekly questions because we realized how many times we tend to be dishonest. Often half-truths are spoken out of convenience rather than taking the needed time to be absolutely correct. The irony of a half-truth is that it is actually a 100-percent lie. That is what we try to address and eliminate as part of our regular conversations with others.

"Be more concerned with your character than your reputation because your character is what you really are while your reputation is merely what others think you are," states John Wooden, former UCLA head basketball coach.[1] I have known people whose character is questioned because their reputation has scarred them. Neither their words nor actions are trusted. What a terrible predicament it is when your character is in jeopardy.

It has been said there are three kinds of people: those who say they are great, those who say they are not and those who forget who they are. The first two are subject to pride—one openly, the other through false humility. The last is the person whose eyes are so fixed on Jesus Christ he finds no reason to exalt any other than Him (Ephesians 2:8-10).

WHAT DOES SCRIPTURE SAY?

"Do your best to present yourself to God as one approved, a workman who does not need to be ashamed and who correctly handles the word of truth. Avoid godless chatter, because those who indulge in it will become more and more ungodly" (2 Timothy 2:15-16).

"Likewise the tongue is a small part of the body, but it makes great boasts. Consider what a great forest is set on fire by a small spark. The tongue also is a fire, a world of evil among the parts of the body. It corrupts the whole person, sets the whole course of his life on fire, and is itself set on fire by hell...but no man can tame the tongue. It is a restless evil, full of deadly poison" (James 3:5,6,8).

"The Lord does not look at the things man looks at. Man looks at the outward appearance, but the Lord looks at the heart" (1 Samuel 16:7b).

"But I tell you that men will have to give an account on the day of judgment for every careless word they have spoken. For by your words you will be acquitted, and by your words you will be condemned" (Matthew 12:36-37).

"For whoever exalts himself will be humbled, and whoever humbles himself will be exalted" (Matthew 23:12).

THE IMPORTANCE OF TRUTHFULNESS

John 8:32 says, "Then you will know the truth, and the truth will set you free." Someone once said, "Tell the truth, and you can forget about it. Tell a lie, and you will have to remember it forever." Telling the truth brings freedom, but lies always entangle.

We sometimes whitewash our lies by calling them "unimportant" or by saying "everyone does it," but every lie leads directly and indirectly to more lies. In addition, there are the everyday exaggerations that eat away at a person's credibility. Words like always, never, best, most, and biggest often aren't true. Exaggerations erode a person's future trustworthiness.

The primary consequence of deception is the loss of trust. Living falsely betrays our friends, family, co-workers, teammates, and anyone else who discovers our lie. When individuals are not trustworthy, they will find themselves becoming more and more isolated. Trust is a vital part of any lasting and meaningful relationship. Conversely, damaged trust is one of the most difficult things to restore.

Can you honestly say that you practice truthfulness in your words, attitudes, and actions? Would those who know you best say you are a truthful person? When you fail, do you correct the matter as quickly as possible? Make it your goal to clear your record with others. Commit yourself to speaking the truth, even if it means going against popular opinion. Be willing to say what the world needs to hear, even when it doesn't want to hear it. Remember, the trail of truthfulness leads to true success, and it does set you free.

Too many people believe "truthfulness" is a relative thing. They say, "Isn't being close good enough?" Well, not really. Finding truth can be very difficult in today's culture. For example, students are bombarded with many different "truths." They are told that sex is safe, drugs are fun and won't hurt you, drinking too much won't do anything to you, and the lies go on. Everybody's doing it, so it must be okay. WRONG!!

You see, Jesus Christ is truth. He is the only Man who lived 100 percent truth. Throughout history, many men and religious groups have claimed to be the truth, but only Jesus Christ has proven to be true time and time again. Many people will try to say their way is the truth, but to the believer, truth is only found in God's Word and the life of Christ.

Searching for truth in your life? Start with Jesus first. I guarantee you will find no match. The truth--our truth--can be found at the cross.

How About a Little Humility?

We often brag to exalt ourselves in the eyes of others. First Peter 5:6 says, "Humble yourselves, therefore, under God's mighty hand, that he may lift you up in due time." James 4:6b adds, "God opposes the proud but gives grace to the humble." Why is it so easy to stretch our stories to a point where they become untruth?

It was recently reported that a prominent Christian comedian had been living a lie about his past. When discovered, it sent shock waves through the Christian circles. People were dismayed by discovering the truth behind this person's ministry. He had exaggerated his past by stretching the truth. He said, "I feel that, in some cases, I have stepped over the line between honest ministry and good entertainment. I was not trying to lie. I just wanted to be good at my job, and I forgot to be entirely true to my calling." This led to an investigation by the IRS into the organization's tax-exempt status as well as put on hold all ministry efforts in a determination to find out the truth.[2]

I believe that most of us do not deliberately want to lie. Yet it can be very easy to stretch the truth, and this is lying. Many of the guys in our group have been challenged by this question during their conversations on a day-to-day basis. Several have admitted being in the midst of a half-truth and then retracting words right on the spot to make it truthful. More than once, we have had to swallow our ego and pride and admit to this being a part of our week.

This issue boils down to integrity. It is complicated when you begin to carry on a lie. Soon you cannot keep straight who even knows the truth. Furthermore, a lie shared over and over can eventually start sounding like the truth. God commands us to tell the truth.

Several years ago I met a man who claimed to be a baseball star. After watching him play, I suspected something was not quite right, but I just thought that perhaps his skills had deteriorated quickly. Yet he persisted in telling me and others about his collegiate and professional background. One day I telephoned the sports information department at his university to find out about his career. As I suspected, he had never played at all. When I confronted him with the truth, it stung him deeply, and he ran from me for years. Later I became aware that this was only one incident in a series of self-promoting lies. In his case I believe he became so convinced of the lies that eventually they began to sound like the truth. His is a sad story.

Charles Edward Jefferson summarizes humility this way, "Much of the so-called Christian humility isn't humility at all. It is a slimy, crawling, despicable, snaky thing, a compound of vanity and falsehood. People who say they do not amount to anything, they cannot do anything, they have no talent, they do not know anything—never speak the truth. Their ego is masquerading under the form of humility. The humility that Jesus wants, and which he exemplified in his life, is a form of strength. Only the strong man can be really humble. It is a willingness to lay aside one's rights, it's a refusal to use one's power, and it's a readiness to come down and to make one's self of no reputation."[3]

SEEKING FORGIVENESS

When you become aware or convicted of a half-truth or outright lie, you need to quickly confess your sin to God and to the person or persons to whom you lied, seek forgiveness and reconcile with them, realizing they might be hurt and offended. Several times in the past few years I have had to plead for forgiveness with a number of people including my wife. Here is a simple forgiveness process for the parties involved.

The one who offended or lied must: (1) admit he has done something wrong before God and man and (2) then he must specifically and sincerely ask God and the person he offended or hurt for forgiveness.

The one who has been offended must: (1) specifically forgive the person involved and (2) then should do everything possible to not only forgive but also to forget the incident. Though this is difficult, to say you are forgiven and then to bring it up and re-hash it again and again is not forgiveness at all.

LIVING A LIFE OF INTEGRITY

Dr. Gary Oliver gives us tremendous insights into the area of personal integrity. Integrity by definition is "a strict adherence to a moral set of values." This includes utter sincerity, honesty, candor, not being artificial or shallow and not making empty promises. Those with integrity are committed to the absolute, unchanging directives as stated in the Bible. Jesus is our model.

Every day we're influenced by the philosophy and values of those around us. In a famous experiment some students put a frog in a container of water and began to heat the water slowly. The water finally reached the boiling point, yet the frog never attempted to jump out. Why? Because the changes in the environment were so subtle that the frog didn't notice them until it was too late.

As Christian men and women, it's easier than we think to end up like the frog. Many godly people—pastors, seminary professors, respected and beloved Christian leaders—have yielded to the world's value system because they failed to discern the subtle changes occurring around them. Before they knew it, they were in hot water. They didn't want that. They didn't intend to get there. They didn't think it could happen to them. But it did.

The Bible says, "For he chose us in him before the creation of the world to be holy and blameless in his sight" (Ephesians 1:4), to "live a life worthy of the calling you have received" (Ephesians 4:1), to be "mature" (Ephesians 4:13) and be "imitators of God" (Ephesians 5:1). When we hear the word "holy," we often think of someone else, not ourselves. The word "holy" refers to someone separated and set apart for God. That can include all believers in Christ Jesus.

Here are seven ways that God can help you move beyond good intentions and down the path of integrity:

1. *Make a decision.* In the Old Testament, Daniel chose not to compromise and defile himself (Daniel 1:8). Almost every day you come to some kind of fork in the road. Like Daniel you will face tough choices. What you decide at that fork is greatly influenced by the choices you made earlier.

2. *Choose to put first things first.* Truth must be planted in our hearts daily. It isn't merely reading but allowing the Holy Spirit to plant the truths of Scripture deep into our hearts and minds through consistent Bible reading and memorization, meditation and prayer.

3. *Determine where the line is, and then stay a safe distance behind it.* Determine what kinds of things are healthy and unhealthy. Whatever distracts or weakens us will put us at risk. Determine where the line is, and if it's not something that is clear in Scripture, then pray about it and seek the wisdom of God and the counsel of

several wise friends. Once you've decided where the line is, walk 10 yards back, and make that your line! Always leave yourself a margin.

4. *Guard your heart.* We can't serve two masters (Matthew 6:21).

5. *Guard your mind.* The mind is the place where decisions are made for or against the truth. What we choose to read, watch and think about will determine, to a great degree, whether we will be victims or victors, conquered or conquerors.

6. *Guard your eyes.* Joseph was smart (Genesis 39), and Job knew the importance of guarding his eyes (Job 31:1), but David lingered too long, stared a bit too much and unwisely entertained an unhealthy fantasy. He didn't guard his eyes and ended up committing adultery with Bathsheba and murdering her husband, Uriah.

7. *Guard the little things.* Luke 16:10 says, "Whoever can be trusted with very little can also be trusted with much." How we handle the seemingly little things determines, over time, our response to big things. Be on guard against rationalization, little lies, itsy-bitsy temptations and trying to justify your actions.[4]

Proverbs 10:9 says, "The man of integrity walks securely, but he who takes crooked paths will be found out." With this in mind, Jeff Comment sums it up: "A man of integrity is secure. The one who lacks integrity will be exposed. We may hide our lack of integrity for a while, but never from God and never for long."[5]

THE RESOLUTION - FROM THE MOVIE "COURAGEOUS"

THE RESOLUTION is a bold declaration of commitments that men are making to be faithful to God as the spiritual leader of their home. As read in the movie, this 14-point statement should be printed, framed and mounted to mark the moment and celebrate the commitment being made to God and family.

THE RESOLUTION

• I DO solemnly resolve before God to take full responsibility for myself, my wife, and my children.

• I WILL love them, protect them, serve them, and teach them the Word of God as the spiritual leader of my home.

- I WILL be faithful to my wife, to love and honor her, and be willing to lay down my life for her as Jesus Christ did for me.
- I WILL bless my children and teach them to love God with all of their hearts, all of their minds, and all of their strength.
- I WILL train them to honor authority and live responsibly.
- I WILL confront evil, pursue justice, and love mercy.
- I WILL pray for others and treat them with kindness, respect, and compassion.
- I WILL work diligently to provide for the needs of my family.
- I WILL forgive those who have wronged me and reconcile with those I have wronged.
- I WILL learn from my mistakes, repent of my sins, and walk with integrity as a man answerable to God.
- I WILL seek to honor God, be faithful to His church, obey His Word, and do His will.
- I WILL courageously work with the strength God provides to fulfill this resolution for the rest of my life and for His glory.

As for me and my house, we will serve the Lord. ---Joshua 24:15

For additional information, see: www.courageousresources.com

Notes
1 Coach Wooden shared this quote while attending the 1992 FCA Camp at Thousand Oaks, California.
2 *Contemporary Christian Music* magazine, May 1993, p. 28.
3 Charles Edward Jefferson, *The Character of Jesus* (New York, NY: Grosset & Dunlap, 1908), p. 265.
4 Adapted from Dr. Gary Oliver, *Seven Promises of a Promise Keeper* (Colorado Springs, CO: Focus on the Family, 1994), pp. 84-90.
5 Jeffrey W. Comment, *Mission in the Marketplace* (North Kansas City, MO: MTM Publishing, 1995), p. 48.

Chapter Fourteen

SHARING THE GOSPEL

Have you shared the Gospel with an unbeliever this week?

God could have planned from the very beginning of time to use anything to tell the world about Himself. For some reason He chose the human race. While on this earth, we have a responsibility to share the truths of God, His Son Jesus Christ and the plan of salvation with the people who are placed in our lives. It is important to remember it is the Holy Spirit who convicts and changes the heart of an unbeliever. We are not called to coerce people into accepting Christ. We are called to be used by God as He sees fit to help bring people to the point of making a decision to accept or reject Christ.

It has been said, "Success in witnessing is simply taking the initiative to share Christ in the power of the Holy Spirit, leaving the results up to God." Let the presence of Christ so radiate in your life at all times that others are attracted to the Christ in you. I'm convinced when our character and our conduct are Christlike, people will be converted.

Regardless of how bold you may be, we are called to live out Matthew 5:13-16: "You are the salt of the earth. But if the salt loses its saltiness, how can it be made salty again? It is no longer good for anything, except to be thrown out and trampled by men. You are the light of the world. A city on the hill cannot be hidden. Neither do people light a lamp and put it under a bowl. Instead they put it on its stand, and it gives light to everyone in the house. In the same way, let your light shine before men, that they may see your good deeds and praise your Father in heaven."

Why does Christ use salt and light as illustrations in this passage? By its nature, salt prevents corruption in the preservation of goods. It enhances and improves taste. By its nature, light illuminates and shows the way through darkness. As salt and light, we play an important role in God's salvation plan.

At the 1993 Promise Keepers Leadership Conference, Dr. Glenn Wagner said, "You could easily define the meaning of the world as relationships, and even these fit a 10/10/80 principle: 10% will change if you give them good information; 10% will never change no matter what information you give them; 80% will change if a relationship is involved." Seek out relationships with unbelievers, not only inviting them to church, but giving them your time.

WHAT DOES SCRIPTURE SAY?

"The goal of this command is love, which comes from a pure heart and a good conscience and a sincere faith" (1 Timothy 1:5).

"But in your hearts set apart Christ as Lord. Always be prepared to give an answer to everyone who asks you to give the reason for the hope you have. But do this with gentleness and respect" (1 Peter 3:15).

"For God did not give us a spirit of timidity, but a spirit of power, of love and of self-discipline. So do not be ashamed to testify about our Lord" (2 Timothy 1:7-8).

"No one who denies the Son has the Father; whoever acknowledges the Son has the Father also" (1 John 2:23).

"Whoever acknowledges me before men, I will also acknowledge him before my Father in heaven. But whoever disowns me before men, I will disown him before my Father in heaven" (Matthew 10:32-33).

PEOPLE ARE WATCHING

Those who watch you closely or from afar should be able to see the light and taste the salt that pours out from you. Don't be surprised by how much people are watching you. As the song says, "You're the only Jesus that some people may ever see." First Peter 2:12 says it this way, "Live such good lives among the pagans that, though they accuse you of doing wrong, they may see your good deeds and glorify God on the day he visits us."

In Matthew 13:1-23, we read the parable of the Sower and the Four Soils. All of us have a responsibility to plant seeds of faith to a watching world. Others are called to water the seeds and eventually collect the harvest. Only God can take credit for the final acceptance, yet we play an important role in living out and communicating our faith to others.

I believe the first step in presenting the Gospel to someone is by initiating and establishing a relationship. Within that relationship if you get the opportunity to share the Gospel, that is wonderful. In addition to forging a friendship, keep your eyes and ears open to sharing what God has done in your life. Perhaps you will have fertile soil with an opportunity to plunge right into the Gospel. In other cases there may be a long season of planting seeds, awaiting the right moment to share your faith. There may not be a perfect time to witness. Yet as a relationship is developed, ask God to give you a natural opportunity.

I admit that I get nervous and a bit tongue-tied when I try to articulate my faith, but God faithfully provides the right words. What joy there is when someone hears the truth of God and responds by making a decision to follow Him. And because of this reason, I have made 2 Timothy 4:2 my prayer that I would "be prepared in season and out of season." This means that I am prepared when called upon or prompted by God to testify for Jesus Christ and His wonderful work within me. Are you ready at a moment's notice to tell someone your story of coming to a faith in Christ? If not, I challenge you today to write out your personal testimony that can be shared in 3-5 minutes stating what you were like before receiving Christ, how you met Christ and what He has done to change your life since accepting Him.

Obviously, I don't get the opportunity to witness every single day, but I'm ready. Also, don't get hung up on feeling like you need to know every single theological argument and biblical reference before you communicate your faith. I love the story of the blind man in John 9. When questioned by the authorities, the blind man did not know all the answers, but one thing he did know from verse 25, "I was blind, but now I see!" In simple terms his life was changed, and he was telling people about it.

In my work with Character That Counts, I have a tremendous platform to share my faith with adults and students. Telling the good news of Christ is an incredible experience. We don't have to look far to find people who need Christ. This includes neighbors, co-workers and others you may meet in the course of day-to-day life. In many ways, the most difficult people to share our faith with may be family members because they know us best.

Several members in our accountability group get numerous chances to share their faith to others. As the Kansas City Chiefs mascot, Dan Meers gets multiple opportunities to testify to thousands of young people through school assembly programs. Mike DeBacker, within his engineering firm, is not shy about spreading his enthusiasm for Christ with his co-workers. When my wife, Janna, worked, she had many chances to share her faith with fellow nurses and patients. Several years ago, I had the chance to play softball on a team of non-Christians, and it was a fun opportunity to let the Lord use me to be "salt and light" in that environment. We have discovered that so many people are eager to know God and are responsive to find out why we are different.

Even in interacting with people who may only cross your path for a few minutes, you still have a chance to live out God's love before them. Many times simply displaying a servant attitude will create opportunities to share your faith. In these cases I encourage you to keep your antenna up and look and listen for natural ways you can share the good news. Regardless of what you say, do, or the time involved, let your light shine.

A THREE-LEGGED STOOL

John 15 shows us that Jesus gave instructions regarding three key relationships: with Jesus, with fellow believers and with the world. Do you have these three key relationships? Are all three connected and in sync? If a three-legged stool is missing one leg, it isn't complete; therefore, it topples over. How would you measure yourself if these relationships were each a leg on a three-legged stool?

Some people have a great relationship with God, but they can't get along with Christians, or they easily slip back in the ways of the world from time to time. Others have great relationships with believers but hardly spend any time (if at all) with God, or the pressures of the world pull them down. Some enjoy the world so much that no one even knows they are a Christian.

To maximize each of these relationships, first deepen your walk with Christ, and then pray for a change in heart in order to positively interact with the believers and the world. And while you are in the world, do not get seduced by its temptations, but instead be a witness for Christ. We are called to go into the world and spread the Gospel in our community.

EVERYONE IS A HIGH PRIEST

When I was a member at University Presbyterian Church in Seattle, its motto was "every member a high priest." It communicated a message that every person in the congregation played an important part in the kingdom of God, in touching and serving the needs of others. Hebrews 5:1-3 tells us, "Every high priest is selected from among men and is appointed to represent them in matters related to God, to offer gifts and sacrifices for sins. He is able to deal gently with those who are ignorant and are going astray, since he himself is subject to weakness. This is why he has to offer sacrifices for his own sins, as well as for the sins of the people." These Scriptures point out so well that the high priest was a weak person, yet played an important part in reaching and touching others.

After all, the only perfect high priest was Jesus Christ. Hebrews 7:26-28 says, "Such a high priest meets our need—one who is holy, blameless, pure, set apart from sinners, exalted above the heavens. Unlike the other high priests, he does not need to offer sacrifices day after day, first for his own sins, and then for the sins of the people. He sacrificed for their sins once for all when he offered himself. For the law appoints as high priests men who are weak, but the oath, which came after the law, appointed the Son, who has been made perfect forever."

KEYS TO SHARING YOUR TESTIMONY

The purpose of a testimony is to introduce others to Jesus Christ. Your audience may be in a one-on-one setting or a large group of people. The goal, through the power of the Holy Spirit, is to move people either toward the point of conversion or into maturing obedience in Christ. Regardless of the opportunity, be ready to give an accurate account and clearly communicate who Jesus Christ is in your life.

An outline for building your testimony should include:

1. How you came to know Christ personally.
2. Identify the specific steps of salvation including:
   Recognition of the need for Christ in your life, turning away from the sinfulness of your life, accepting Christ's forgiveness for your sin and receiving Jesus Christ as Savior and Lord.
3. Scripture is crucial to illustrate and document what has happened.
4. Cover the basics of the Gospel including: Man's sinfulness, which separates us from God; the life, teachings, death and resurrection of Jesus Christ as the payment (atonement) for man's sins; and through faith in Jesus we are redeemed into "new life" as outlined in 1 Corinthians 15:1-4.
5. Your new life in Christ. Speak of the changes Christ has brought into your life and what He means to you. Talk about things that will cause others to want to know Him as well. (Note: Be real, not pie in the sky. Include challenging and specific times of growth.)
6. In your conclusion use an illustration (if appropriate) to capture the theme of your testimony.
7. Tell how they can become a Christian by reviewing the meaning of salvation, presenting Scripture and if appropriate, be ready to issue a call to commitment.
8. Close in prayer.

If you can do all of the above in less than five minutes, it is ideal. Obviously, if you have more time, you can expand. By having the basics down to five minutes, you can quickly determine what are the most important parts and remove the extraneous thoughts. Determine the time frame you have before you start. Use wisdom in selecting Scripture references. Too many or too few can work against you.

Be conscious of not using religious terminology, clichés or phrases which the unchurched may not be familiar with or cause them to be uncomfortable. Also, be careful using particular denominational dogmas or doctrines which could sidetrack the overall purpose. Negative comments about people, churches, denominations or issues will be counterproductive.

Finally, and most importantly, rely on the power of the Holy Spirit. There is no salvation without the work of the Spirit. He is the one who convinces men and women of their sin and of their need for Christ (John 16:8). He causes a change in life, the new birth (John 3:5-6). He is the author of maturity in the Christian life (Galatians 5:22-25). He is the link between truth and transformation, between knowledge and action. Without obedient, active dependence on the Holy Spirit, our efforts in sharing Christ will fall woefully short.

Christians often speak of being a "good testimony." The word testimony usually makes us think of verbal witness, but being a good testimony for Christ means much more than just talking about Him. If actions speak as loudly as words, how we live is more important than what we say in influencing people for Christ. A testimony for Christ mandates that we live lives of obedience to Him.

KEYS TO WITNESSING

Paul Little writes, "If we are genuinely enthusiastic about our Lord and are comfortable in making friends, we may naively assume that all our witnessing problems will disappear. However, our real-life experiences will show us otherwise. There are times when we try to witness, eagerly expecting a great response, and plunk, we fall flat on our faces....our message comes off as clumsy and awkward."

Mr. Little suggests that we consider the example of Jesus as illustrated in his conversation with the woman at the well as told in John 4.

1. *Contact Others Socially.* Initiate face-to-face contact with non-Christians. Jesus moved beyond the barriers and actually went out of his way to associate with people from all backgrounds.
2. *Establish Common Ground.* Take time to establish communication bridges. Most Christians want to skip the "nonessentials" and get right to the point. This type of one-way conversation will only bring resentment as you drone on and on. Jesus was a master at relating to others. Take the time to listen and build rapport. Asking a lot of questions will help draw people out. As instruments in God's hands, we can positively and patiently begin where their interests lie. Later on we can profitably discuss spiritual matters together.
3. *Arouse Interest.* At the well, the woman's curiosity began to burn as Jesus drew her along. His treatment of her contributed to her very positive response. In following the Lord's example, you can turn small events in conversations toward spiritual things. Christians can be assertive and bold, without being obnoxious. Listen to the Holy Spirit to know how far to go with them.
4. *Get the Ball Rolling.* Statements or leading questions often precede the formal witnessing process. As you listen to their response, be ready to speak briefly, emphasizing the reality of Christ to us today and eliminating boring and probably irrelevant details. Focus on simply saying what Christ means to you now.
5. *Don't Go Too Far.* Give people only as much of the message as they are ready. Despite the woman's obvious interest and curiosity, Jesus didn't give her the whole story at once. Gradually, as she was ready for more, he revealed more about himself. Allow them to verbalize what they are thinking as you exchange ideas and thoughts.

6. *Don't Condemn.* Jesus didn't bypass the questions about her husbands, but he did no finger pointing or head-wagging in judgment. Her sin itself condemned her, not Jesus. A good rule to follow is the simple quip: "You catch more flies with honey than vinegar." Find a way of making a legitimate compliment rather than a stinging criticism. Criticism sometimes can be far more natural to our lips than praise, but praise can make others more open to the gospel.

7. *Stick With the Main Issue.* Late in this chapter, Jesus steered the discussion back to himself by shifting the emphasis from *where* to *how* one worships. Though their questions may be valid, stay away from tangents. Any legitimate question can be a tangent if it sidetracks us from the main issue.

8. *Confront the Person Directly.* Eventually after the bridge of friendship is developed, you will need to cross the bridge and bring the non-Christian into a direct confrontation with the Lord Jesus so they can realize their personal responsibility to decide for or against him.

Once we begin to grasp these principles and move out in faith, witnessing becomes a regular part of our day. Watch with anticipation to see how God will give you opportunities to work in the lives of others.[1]

Notes

1 Adapted from Paul Little, *How To Give Away Your Faith* (Downer's Grove, IL: InterVarsity Press, 1988), p. 49-70.

JESUS!

Have you spent time with the PRINCE OF PEACE?
Does your life reflect the MORNING STAR?
Are you trusting in the ADVOCATE?
Do you live, move and have your being in the LORD OF ALL?
Are you adoring the ROOT OF DAVID?
Are you pure before the LAMB OF GOD?
Have you given up the rights to yourself to the SHEPHERD AND BISHOP OF YOUR SOUL?

Are you yielding to the HEAD OF THE CHURCH?
Have you separated yourself to the HOLY ONE?
Are you worshiping the KING OF KINGS?
Are you consumed with the SON Of GOD?
Have you thrown the world away and embraced the LORD GOD ALMIGHTY?
Are you passionately in love with the MESSIAH?
Are you in prayer with the GREAT INTERCESSOR?
Are you communing with the TRUTH?
Do you hear the voice of the WONDERFUL COUNSELOR?
Are you walking with the CHIEF CORNERSTONE to the corners of the earth?
Are you ready to stand before the RIGHTEOUS JUDGE?
Are your eyes fixed on the AUTHOR and FINISHER OF YOUR FAITH?
Are you intimate with the SAVIOR?
Is your only aim to please the CHIEF SHEPHERD?
Are you holy before the MIGHTY GOD?
Are you beholding the LIGHT OF THE WORLD?
Are you sitting at the feet of the LION of the TRIBE OF JUDAH?
Are you on fire for the SON OF RIGHTEOUSNESS?
Is your great passion for the RESURRECTION AND LIFE?
Are you seeking the face of the ALPHA AND OMEGA?
Are you devoted to the LORD JESUS CHRIST?
Is your daily life preparing you for the bride of the GREAT I AM?

What is your Christianity?
Is Jesus your life? Are you His, completely His for His Good Pleasure? He loves you, He gave Himself for you. Come to Him and love Him.

HE IS WORTHY!

AUTHOR'S NOTE: This was developed by Wade Salem, former FCA Area Director in Erie, PA. Are you ready to tell people about Him?

_____

Chapter Fifteen

EXERCISE, EATING AND SLEEPING

Have you taken care of your body through daily physical exercise and proper eating and sleeping habits?

These three areas represent my favorite activities, yet they also are the areas that are the most greatly abused and neglected. Amazingly, when these disciplines are in good working order, I feel fresh, confident and balanced—ready to take on any challenge. When ignored, I feel lethargic and frustrated.

WHAT DOES SCRIPTURE SAY?

We only receive one earthly body from God; therefore, we need to take good care of it. First Corinthians 6:19-20 warns, "Do you not know that your body is a temple of the Holy Spirit, who is in you, whom you have received from God? You are not your own; you were bought at a price. Therefore honor God with your body."

Psalms 139 talks about how intricately we were made and developed in the womb. Developed from 23 chromosomes from each parent, we become one uniquely-created person. We also have 206 bones, muscles, joints, ligaments and tendons making up our bodies. We have a responsibility to properly care for what God has created.

PHYSICAL EXERCISE

Much has been said in our society about the need for regular exercise, and we are all aware of its importance for healthy living. All exercise requires discipline, yet if we choose types of exercise that are enjoyable to us and fit our lifestyle, we'll more likely stick with it.

Not only do I feel much better when I am on a regular work-out schedule, but I also believe it improves all the other areas of my life including greater productivity, broader creativity, higher concentration and enhanced relationships. Depending on your age and previous exercise history, you may want to get a check-up before embarking on a new exercise program.

If possible, I encourage you to work out at least three days a week. It can range from a hard 10-mile run, a racquetball game or a walk through the neighborhood. Bicycling, aerobics, weight lifting programs, basketball, golfing (carry your clubs), softball, etc., are options available to you among many others.

Conditioning Programs: The key is doing something which will elevate your heart rate to 60% to 85% of your maximum heart rate (see chart on the following page), and sustaining it for an appropriate period of time (normally 20 to 60 minutes). Sit-ups and pushups every morning or evening are excellent.

Exercise increases your body's need for oxygen. In order to deliver more oxygen to working muscles, your heart must work harder to pump blood throughout your body. Continued throughout your life, exercise ultimately makes your heart stronger and decreases your chance of developing heart disease. Physical exercise will boost the strength and readiness of your immune system. Even a moderate program will help you fight off colds and other health conditions. In addition, regular exercise improves the tone and efficiency of your muscles and enhances your lung function.

Before you start your fitness journey, it's a good idea to know what you want to accomplish. Do you want to lose weight, or are you headed toward cardio-respiratory fitness? Your goal will determine the intensity of your workout.

High intensity exercise for shorter periods of time promotes cardio-respiratory improvement, and burns mostly muscle glycogen as fuel. This helps reduce the possibility of heart disease and improves endurance. A low-intensity workout for longer periods of time burns more calories from stored fat.

Regardless of your fitness goals, remember to warm up and cool down by stretching for at least 15 minutes before and after you exercise, using gradual, non-bouncing movements. You'll increase your muscle elasticity and help decrease the chance of muscular strain. A proper cool down period helps remove the end products of exercise, including lactic acid, and will reduce muscle soreness.

CHART GUIDE FOR MAXIMUM HEART RATE

Exercising too hard or not hard enough can be ineffective. For best results, determine your maximum heart rate range by subtracting your age from 220:

   **220-(your age) = (maximum heart rate)

If your goal is FAT LOSS, use the following formula to determine your training zone:

   **(maximum heart rate) x 60% = Lower limit
   **(maximum heart rate) x 75% = Upper limit

If your goal is CARDIO-RESPIRATORY FITNESS, your effective training zone will be higher. Use the following formula to determine your training zone:

   **(maximum heart rate) x 75% = Lower limit
   **(maximum heart rate) x 85% = Upper limit

EXAMPLE: Age 35 (220-35 = 185)
   FAT LOSS TRAINING:
   185 x .60 = 111 beats/min. (lower limit)
   185 x .75 = 139 beats/min. (upper limit)

   CARDIO-RESPIRATORY TRAINING:
   185 x .75 = 139 beats/min. (lower limit)
   185 x .85 = 157 beats/min. (upper limit)

Strength Training: Strength training increases your muscle strength (your ability to lift heavy objects) and muscular endurance (your ability to repeat a movement requiring strength). Regular strength training can help build strength, power and endurance, control weight, lower body fat, improve appearance and build self-confidence. It helps lower the risk of injury to muscles, ligaments and tendons. Properly conditioned muscles are also essential to carry out the activities of your daily life and vital to a safer performance in sports and aerobic conditioning programs. A well-rounded fitness program will include both strength and endurance programs.

Tips before you lift weights include: start at a comfortable level, warm up properly, learn the proper lifting techniques, exercise major muscle groups, exercise large muscles first (chest, back and abdomen prior to biceps, triceps and smaller muscle groups), alternate muscle groups to reduce risk of injury, challenge yourself by increasing weight and resistance over time, and give yourself at least a day of rest between workouts.

PROPER EATING

Weight loss has been one of the major issues we have discussed within our group because it is a battle we all face. Though not a nutritionist, I have learned that excessive fat grams in a diet make weight loss nearly impossible. Unfortunately, everything I enjoy eating is loaded with fat grams. Janna has helped me be more conscious of the things I eat, and my accountability group has helped keep me focused on my goals. Eating habits need to be disciplined and monitored on a regular basis. In fact, a few years ago my group helped me lose 40 pounds in a 40-week period by bringing a weigh scale to our weekly meetings to help track my progress. It was a great encouragement!!

Instead of counting calories, pay attention to where they come from. Calories from carbohydrates are less likely to be stored as fat and more likely to energize muscles than calories from fat. Ideally your diet should be made up of 55-60% carbohydrates, 10-15% protein and less than 30% fat. High-carbohydrate foods include bread, cereal, pasta, crackers and rice. Fats, oils and sweets should be avoided while reasonable levels of vegetables, fruits, milk products, meat, poultry and fish should be included as part of your nutrition.

SLEEPING HABITS

Don't snicker...this one is also important. One of the keys to my entire day is how well and how much sleep I got the night before. I would love to get a solid eight hours a night. Unfortunately, my love for the late night makes this almost an impossibility. Janna has helped me to be aware of this area as well.

God has created each of us with a certain requirement for rest. Too little sleep or too much leaves us fatigued. Determine your optimum sleep pattern and then plan backwards. Fit your responsibilities into the remaining time. We shouldn't be embarrassed to face this need and to plan our schedule accordingly.

KEYS TO SUCCESS

The following guidelines are ideas to help better manage these three areas (exercise, eating and sleeping):

1. *Begin.* "I'll start tomorrow" does not work. It is important to identify your need, and begin today. Set aside time to properly stretch, and begin a regular walking, jogging or workout program as part of your daily schedule. Exercise experts say physical activity by itself makes us leaner and healthier, sleep more deeply and more resilient to stress.

2. *Look for daily activity.* Some type of activity seems to help suppress appetites. "The exercising body knows what it should eat, when to sleep, why it shouldn't smoke and how much alcohol to drink," says Dwight Gaal, an exercise physiologist who designs fitness programs for the UAW, Ford Motor Co. and other employers. "I firmly believe, once somebody finds exercise and adopts it, then everything else falls into place," Gaal says.

3. *Work briskly.* Try to complete your activity within 45 minutes. Include some resistance exercise like lifting weights as part of your workout.

4. *Diets don't always work, but low-fat nutrition can.* Once you start to exercise, you will increase weight loss by trimming fat from your diet.

5. *Participate in activities you enjoy, and ask friends to join you.*
Exercising with a friend will encourage you to work out.
6. *Record your progress.* Keep a log, and develop a reward system
for outstanding efforts and accomplishments. Tell others. Going
public with a goal helps you stay with it.
7. *Think long-term.* Exercise, eating right and getting the right
amount of sleep can't be just a one-month deal. Shoot for the long-
term. Be realistic in your goal-setting.

ALCOHOL, SMOKING AND ILLEGAL DRUGS

Fortunately, our group does not have people in it who are bat-
tling addictions to alcohol, smoking or illegal drugs, so little if any
time has been dedicated to these subjects. If anyone in your group
needs help in any of these areas, develop accountability questions
that would help those in need and encourage a professional support group if necessary.

There are guidelines that each of us should consider when
faced with these temptations.

1. *When prohibited by law, do not use.* If you are under age, in a
county where it is illegal, or if it is a crime, this is a no-brainer.
Don't do it!
2. *Consider others.* Doing something may not seem wrong to you,
but it may cause a serious "stumbling block" to someone else.
Consider the following Scriptures:

"And if anyone causes one of these little ones who believe in
me to sin, it would be better for him to be thrown into the sea
with a large millstone tied around his neck" (Mark 9:42).

"So I strive always to keep my conscience clear before God and
man" (Acts 24:16).

"So then, each of us will give an account of himself to God.
Therefore let us stop passing judgment on one another. Instead,
make up your mind not to put any stumbling block or obstacle in
your brother's way" (Romans 14:12-13).

"'Everything is permissible'—but not everything is beneficial.
'Everything is permissible'—but not everything is constructive.

Nobody should seek his own good, but the good of others"
(1 Corinthians 10:23-24).

3. *Be careful and honest with yourself.* I have known people who
have innocently begun using alcohol and/or drugs and either
became addicted and/or greatly influenced to the point where it
changed them (temporarily or permanently). This is particularly
true with alcohol use. Personally, I feel strongly that there is no
reason to use alcohol or drugs. Also, I believe a commitment to
abstinence opens up opportunities to tell others about Christ and
eliminates many of the negative consequences.

In Summary

The key word in taking care of your body is discipline. A disciplined person is able to stand up on his or her own two feet and
make wise choices. Men and women who are disciplined are easily
distinguished from those who are not. A high level of character and
leadership qualities emerge.

It takes much dedication and discipline to change the habits of
a lifetime. Someone once observed that it takes seven times longer
to unlearn a bad habit and learn a new good one than it would
have taken to learn the good new one in the beginning. We have to
start where we are—today and right now!

Habits are built a day, and even a moment, at a time. A dozen
times a day, we choose to do things the old way or a new way. We
may be motivated by any number of things: we want to live alcohol and drug-free; we are tired of constantly being on a diet; we
want to not be so tired during the day; or we want to be in shape.
When we are motivated, we set goals. These goals need to be realistic and attainable. If they are too high and grandiose, we'll probably fail and quit trying. If they are too easy, we will lose interest.

In establishing goals consider answering these two crucial questions: (1) What are you responsible for? (2) What are you not
responsible for? People are responsible for their own behavior, their
own choices, and their own responses to problems. We aren't
responsible for other people's behavior, choices and responses. I

urge people to consider three keys to successful goal setting: Pray, Post and Publicize. First of all, ask God for his help. Second, post your goals in a visible place where you see them frequently. Finally, tell other people about what you're planning to do. In doing these three things you involve God and others in the process. Goal-setting sounds easy, but in fact, it's one of the hardest things for people who lack discipline. Proper goal setting can help you stay on track and in making real progress.

The changes we desire will emerge when we put ourselves in positive environments rather than the old areas where we constantly are tempted or have experienced struggles. Some leaders demand compliance through a set of legalistic standards. Paul wrote, "All things are lawful for me, but all things are not helpful. All things are lawful for me, but I will not be brought under the power of any" (1 Corinthians 6:12). Hopefully we will be able to make wise decisions and understand the consequences whether they are good or bad.

When we attempt something new or challenging as we seek to be disciplined, we will either experience the thrill of victory or the agony of defeat. We might be vulnerable to tremendous highs and lows. These swings are accentuated by the volatility of life. Remember, we are not perfect!!

The Lord knows how difficult it is to do something new because the Scriptures are full of admonitions to be strong and courageous. The unknown is often frightening. Even a stouthearted, proven man like Joshua needed the Lord's encouragement: "Have I not commanded you? Be strong and of good courage; do not be afraid, nor be dismayed, for the Lord your God is with you wherever you go" (Joshua 1:9).

EIGHT POINTS TO LIVING A CONSISTENT CHRISTIAN WALK
by Harold Reynolds, former Major League Baseball player

Author's Note: I heard Harold give this talk at an FCA event and felt there were many practical applications to this chapter. "Vision" can be defined as something (or anything) that you want to accomplish.

1. *Have a vision.* Habakkuk 2:2 says to write your vision down, so you'll recognize it when it unfolds. We have to know our reason for living.
2. *Commit to the vision.* Just like focusing a camera, making a commitment focuses our vision, making it clearer and clearer to us. It helps to begin with the end in mind which will allow us to see the outcome before others see it.
3. *Don't get distracted or discouraged from the vision.* Jesus came so we could have life, but Satan wants to kill and to destroy.
4. *Stay on the right path because it builds confidence.* Proverbs 4:18 says, "The path of the righteous is like the first gleam of dawn, shining ever brighter till the full light of day." The further you go along, the clearer things will get.
5. *Allow the vision to mature.* Sometimes we give up too fast—like marriages where everything is great during the initial months, but the couple divorces within a year. It takes nine months for a baby to develop and mature within the womb before it is born. As Christians, we need to have patience in our spiritual growth. Growth takes time. We should remember this when we bring people to Christ. We must provide for follow-up, not just say, "I'm glad you've made a commitment. Now grow up."
6. *Develop good work habits.* Excellence in any area of life demands good work habits...whether it's prayer, Bible reading or baseball. I've worked on my swing and developed good habits in baseball, and even though I'll still have rough times, those good baseball habits will get me through.
7. *Run through the tape.* You've all seen sprinters lean into the tape at the end of the race. In the spiritual race of life it's not how well you start but who endures to the end and leans to the tape (1 Corinthians 9:24-25).
8. *Remember the vision because the vision keeps you alive.* Proverbs 29:18 reminds us that when there is no vision, we perish.

God has uniquely gifted you with the personality, talent and experience to accomplish more than you can even dream or imagine (Ephesians 3:20). Today, let us understand that we must act on our God-given vision. Author and pastor Andy Stanley reminds us, "If God has birthed a vision in your heart, the day will come when

186 CHARACTER THAT COUNTS—WHO'S COUNTING YOURS?

you will be called upon to make a sacrifice to achieve it. And you will have to make the sacrifice with no guarantee of success." We know that the sowing of great sacrifices is required for the reaping of great rewards.

Stanley puts it this way: "Vision requires the commitment of a parachutist. You don't 'sort of' parachute. You are either in the plane or in the air." I challenge you to take the risks and make the sacrifices needed in order to move toward the vision God has put in your heart.

Notes

Author's Note: Much of the information pertaining to exercise was supplied by Kathy Van Horn, who is an exercise physiologist/personal trainer in the Kansas City area. In 2002, Kathy was appointed to the President's Council on Physical Fitness and Sports.

Chapter Sixteen

JOY AND HAPPINESS

Have you allowed any person or circumstance to rob you of your joy?

"Therefore, since we are surrounded by such a great cloud of witnesses, let us throw off everything that hinders and the sin that so easily entangles, and let us run with perseverance the race marked out for us. Let us fix our eyes on Jesus, the author and perfecter of our faith, who for the joy set before him endured the cross, scorning its shame, and sat down at the right hand of the throne of God. Consider him who endured such opposition from sinful men, so that you will not grow weary and lose heart" (Hebrews 12:1-3).

This question was recommended to me by former FCA staff member Van Normand and helped complete our ten questions. There is a distinct difference between joy and happiness. It has been said that happiness is when you are happy because of your circumstances while joy is when you are happy in spite of your circumstances. Joy can also be described as "feeling contentment and peace inside because God's in charge outside." Joy isn't based on emotional feelings or events. It is a deep, ongoing certainty and feeling of peace that no matter how rotten life is, God's still in control through every situation. Though your self-image may take a beating, real joy is knowing God loves you deeply and unconditionally.

Happiness is often based on external circumstances or temporary situations. For instance, if the weather is lousy or a friend is rude, it can ruin our day. In our daily routine are there incidents when we allow people or circumstances to rob us of our joy? This can range from frustrations in driving in slow traffic, having a flooded basement, working with a difficult employee or a variety of other reasons.

How you react to these difficult situations can have a tremendous impact not only on your own spirit but also on the spirit and attitude of those around you.

Author Paul Sailhammer says, "Joy is that deep settled confidence that God is in control of every area of my life." Tim Hansel believes, "Joy is not a feeling; it is a choice. It is not based upon circumstances; it is based upon attitude. It is free, but it is not cheap. It is the by-product of a growing relationship with Jesus Christ. It is a promise, not a deal. It is available to us when we make ourselves available to Him. It is something that we can receive by invitation and by choice. It requires commitment, courage and endurance." He also states, "Pain is inevitable, but misery is optional. We cannot avoid pain, but we can avoid joy. God has given us such immense freedom that He will allow us to be as miserable as we want to be." John MacArthur points out, "There is no event or circumstance that can occur in the life of any Christian that should diminish that Christian's joy."

There is no question that the day-to-day grind of life is difficult. In John 16:33 Jesus reminds us that in the world we will experience trouble. There will be tribulation, but we are not merely to endure it but to "be of good cheer" for He has overcome the world. You cannot avoid the stresses and pressures this world brings. The pulls of the world are strong. Therefore, we need to be disciplined and prepared to fight the spiritual battles and defeat our enemy.

Being "successful" in the eyes of the world doesn't necessarily mean you will experience joy. Many in the world have achieved riches, power, fame and popularity, yet they are miserable. The attainment of success resulted in the high price of losing their families, friends and even their own souls. Steve Largent, NFL Hall of Famer, warns about climbing the ladder of success and discovering at the top rung that the ladder had been leaning against the wrong structure. How tragic when people make this discovery.

Many of us go through life searching for things that are meaningless—especially in the spiritual realm. We seek meaning in life without ever including God in our search. It is only through Him that we can have abundant life (John 10:10). We seek security in material possessions which will soon decay and forget to "store up for yourselves treasures in heaven, where moth and rust do not destroy" (Matthew 6:20). We seek happiness in the pleasures of this world and forget the source of true happiness. The Psalmist said, "You have made known to me the path of life; you will fill me with joy in your presence, with eternal pleasures at your right hand" (Psalm 16:11).

We all go through life seeking something. Some will come to the end of their lives and admit their search turned up nothing of lasting, eternal value.

True success is walking in obedience with God, meditating on His Word day and night (Joshua 1:7-8). And as Dal Shealy, admonishes, "It's your attitude, not your aptitude, that allows you to get to a higher altitude, if you have enough intestinal fortitude."

Joy Robbing?

When it comes to joy robbers, I've got a memorable weekend in October 1997 that ranks up there with the all-time greats. My adventure began in Lubbock, Texas on a Friday afternoon as I sat in the terminal awaiting a United Airlines flight back to Kansas City through Denver. I should've seen the ominous signs emerging when the plane I was about to board was pouring out black smoky clouds as it pulled up to the gate. After several hours of maintenance, we loaded up and headed for Denver.

The short flight to Denver was an adventure. The winds were whipping us causing our plane to bounce and shake, but we finally landed just about the time a heavy blizzard was striking the new Denver airport. Within minutes of arriving in the terminal it was announced that all departing flights had been cancelled for the remainder of the evening. As I stood in lengthy lines, I discovered that the only road from the airport to the rest of civilization was closed due to a number of accidents. No one could get in to the airport from the outside world, nor could we get out.

After grabbing a sheet and a pillow about the size of my hand from airport personnel, myself and thousands of other passengers settled in for a night of sleep on the hard, cold concourse. When Saturday morning arrived it was still snowing. In total, over 30 inches of snow fell from start to finish. A sense of panic descended when people began to realize that we were in for the long haul, and available food was scarce to none. Women with small children needed diapers and formula. All the airport restaurants and gift shops were closed because employees couldn't get to the airport. Within a short period of time all the vending machines in the airport were completely empty. I watched a group of men and women discuss whether to break through the glass of one snack shop in order to get food. Around noon, one shop opened up and I stood in a line for over an hour to pay for a couple of candy bars and a bag of chips. When I finally got to the cash register, I found out that they were only taking cash because the credit card machines weren't working. Much to my dismay, I discovered that I had less than $5.00 in my pocket so I ended up borrowing a couple of bucks from another passenger in the line.

A huge bummer was that we were told that absolutely no flights were leaving on Saturday, but mysteriously, as we looked out, we saw snowmobiles transporting the Denver Broncos team to an awaiting plane where airport personnel scrambled for hours trying to help the team make their game the next day on the East Coast. Thousands of people ferociously booed as the plane finally departed with all of us left behind in snowy Denver.

Saturday night, I huddled along with my new friends and watched Game #6 of the World Series on a television set that barely worked. It was about this time that I noticed how terrible I looked and smelled. I desperately needed a toothbrush. My checked luggage was somewhere in the bowels of the Denver airport, and all I had with me was a small shoulder bag with some paperwork enclosed. Hungry, smelly and sore was how I went to bed still clutching my sheet and pillow from the night before.

I awoke at 3:00 a.m. on Sunday morning with a brand new strategy. I wasn't concerned about getting to Kansas City....I just wanted out of Denver. I figured that if I could catch a flight to Chicago, then I could easily get a connecting flight to Kansas City. The reader boards in the terminal indicated that there was a flight at 8:00 a.m. that was scheduled to depart on time. Yippee!! But it was about this time that I realized that my watch had a different time than the reader board. Oh no; it was "turn your clock back weekend" and instead of being 3:00 a.m., it was really only 2:00

a.m. Undeterred, I got in line with about 50 other passengers in front of me to wait six hours for the Chicago flight.

As the sun came up in Denver, I realized that my plan wasn't going to work as well as I had thought. There were people arriving at the airport who had been in their cozy homes all weekend with confirmed flights that took priority over thousands of us who had been stranded all weekend. Helplessly I watched people board the flight while I stood by. After everyone boarded it was announced that they would begin a stand-by list for the handful who remained in line. I got a number and waited and waited. I knew if I moved to another line in the airport, I would probably be in the same dilemma. I also watched the reader board as flight after flight was cancelled throughout the day.

Finally at noon, my name was called from the list and I boarded the 8:00 a.m. flight to Chicago (yes, some of the people had boarded this flight over four hours earlier). One single seat—a middle one—on the back row awaited me. I was thrilled. Around 3:00 p.m. that flight finally became airborne and I touched down in Chicago just before dinner time.

Once in Chicago, I realized how bad I looked. My clothes and hair were in terrible shape. My breath was bad, and I was unshaven. Compared to people in Denver, I looked normal but here in Chicago, I looked like a man just arriving from the jungle. All flights were packed to Kansas City, and I was put on a stand-by list. For the next few hours, I watched Game #7 of the World Series as three different flights departed for Kansas City. Finally, at 11:00 p.m. my name was called, and I was headed home! I arrived back at my home 57 hours after I boarded the flight in Lubbock, Texas. PTL!

How did I do? Remarkably well!! This potential joy robbing experience became a time to share my faith with others, to listen to people, and to pray. Though I was a mess physically, I learned a lot about myself and life that weekend. In spite of the difficulties, I never lost my joy that weekend. Years later, I can laugh about the experience and realize that my current dilemmas are nothing compared to all I went through in the Denver airport. By the way, my luggage arrived on Monday afternoon when the first flight from Denver following the storm touched down in Kansas City.

CHOOSING CHEERFULNESS

Being cheerful can brighten anyone's day. There are physical, psychological and spiritual rewards of cheerfulness because it is contagious. It is one of those rare treasures which is multiplied when given away.

Barnabas was known for his cheerfulness. In fact his name is translated as "son of encourager." He had a way of blessing everyone he interacted with and drawing out the best in them. In the book of Acts, Paul and Barnabas worked together well but one day they had a conflict about taking John Mark with them on a mission trip. Barnabas was willing to reach out to people who were less than perfect. The young John Mark had abandoned his ministry duties on an earlier trip to Cyprus, but Barnabas never gave up on him. Through Barnabas's encouragement, John Mark was given a second chance.

Barnabas had the unique ability to change the atmosphere around him, because he encouraged people. Whenever people were around Barnabas, their spirits were lifted, and their faith was strengthened. Guidance, help and direction is never a solo search. Growth in our lives occurs when we are surrounded and immersed in cheerful relationships. We get better and find our way in groups, not by ourselves. Positive connection with others provides guidance, encouragement and prayer support. There is lots of laughter when we are in the midst of cheerful people. Living life with others is just plain fun.

What produces cheerfulness? Cheerfulness is not the absence of trouble, but the presence of Christ. Our greatest source of cheer is eternal salvation. Because cheerfulness comes from having a genuine relationship with Christ, anything hindering that fellowship will diminish it. Jesus reminds us that cheerfulness comes by keeping commands of the Lord (read John 15:10-13).

OVERCOMING OBSTACLES

Jesus exhorted His disciples when persecuted and in encountering all sorts of evil to "rejoice and be exceedingly glad." The original Greek says it this way, "Rejoice and leap for joy." In other words, when everything is at its worst, you should have a happiness which leaps. Jesus was glad even to the end. Even in the upper room, when death was only a few hours away, He went right on speaking of the joy that was bubbling up in His heart, and He prayed the same joy would abound in the hearts of those who love Him. He wanted them to have joy and that their joy might be full. It's a daily decision to choose joy.

In the midst of disappointments, frustrations and crushed hopes and dreams, joy comes down to having a deep, personal relationship with God. Ephesians 4:23 tells us, "Be renewed in the spirit of your mind." I urge you to adopt an attitude of enthusiasm and gladness. Emory Ward once remarked, "Enthusiasm, like measles, mumps and the common cold, is highly contagious." Today, commit to pursue gladness no matter what the obstacles.

The following poem depicts the attitude we should display as we meet various obstacles in life.

THE RACE

"Quit! Give up, you're beaten," they shout and plead,
"There's just too much against you now. This time you can't succeed."
And as I start to hang my head in front of failure's face,
My downward fall is broken by the memory of a race.
And hope refills my weakened will as I recall that scene,
For just the thought of that short race rejuvenates my being.
A children's race, young boys, young men; how I remember well,
Excitement sure, but also fear, it wasn't hard to tell.
They all lined up so full of hope. Each thought to win that race,
Or tie for first, or if not that, at least take second place.
And fathers watched from off the side, each cheering for his son,
And each boy hoped to show his dad that he would be the one.
    The whistle blew, and off they went, young hearts and hopes of fire.
To win, to be the hero there, was each young boy's desire.
And one boy in particular, his dad was in the crowd,
Was running near the lead and thought, "My dad will be so proud."
But as he speeded down the field across a shallow dip,
The little boy who thought to win, lost his step and slipped.
Trying hard to catch himself, his hands flew out to brace,
And mid the laughter of the crowd, he fell flat on his face.
So down he fell and with him hope. He couldn't win it now.
Embarrassed, sad, he only wished to disappear somehow.
But, as he fell, his dad stood up and showed his anxious face,

Which to the boy so clearly said, "Get up and win that race!"
    He quickly rose, no damage done, behind a bit that's all,
And ran with all his mind and might to make up for his fall.
So anxious to restore himself, to catch up and to win,
His mind went faster than his legs. He slipped and fell again.
He wished that he had quit before with only one disgrace.
"I'm hopeless as a runner now. I shouldn't try to race."
But in the laughing crowd he searched and found his father's face,
That steady look that said again, "Get up and win that race!"
    So he jumped up to try again, ten yards behind the last.
"If I'm to gain those yards," he thought, "I've got to run real fast."
Exceeding everything he had, he regained eight or ten,
But trying so hard to catch the lead, he slipped and fell again.
Defeat!! He lay there silently, a tear dropped from his eye.
"There's no sense running anymore—three strikes, I'm out—why try?"
The will to rise had disappeared, all hope had fled away,
So far behind, so error prone, closer all the way.
"I've lost, so what's the use," he thought, "I'll live with my disgrace."
But then he thought about his dad who soon he'd have to face.
"Get up," an echo sounded low, "Get up and take your place.
You were not meant for failure here. Get up and win that race."
    With borrowed will, "Get up," it said, "You haven't lost at all,
For winning's not more than this—to rise each time you fall."
So up he rose to win once more, and with a new commit,
He resolved that win or lose, at least he wouldn't quit.
So far behind the others now, the most he'd ever been,
Still he gave it all he had and ran as though to win.
Three times he'd fallen stumbling, three times he rose again,
Too far behind to hope to win, he still ran to the end.
    They cheered the winning runner as he crossed, first place,
Head high and proud and happy; no falling, no disgrace.
But when the fallen youngster crossed the line, last place,
The crowd gave him the greater cheer for finishing the race.
And even though he came in last, with head bowed low, unproud;
You would have thought he won the race, to listen to the crowd.
And to his dad he sadly said, "I didn't do so well."
"To me, you won," his father said, "You rose each time you fell."
    And now when things seem dark and hard and difficult to face,
The memory of that little boy helps me in my own race.
For all of life is like that race, with ups and downs and all,
And all you have to do to win is rise each time you fall.
"Quit! Give up, you're beaten," they still shout in my face.
But another voice within me says, "Get up and win that race."[1]

Notes

[1] D.H. Groberg.

Chapter Seventeen

WRAPPING IT UP

Have you lied to us on any of your answers today?

Each week, we close our time together by asking this deliberate question. I can only recall once when we got down to this question and one of our members had to confess that he needed to come clean on a previous answer.

As mentioned earlier, accountability helps play a very important role in our Christian growth. I have grown so much over the past several years by being answerable to people in areas of my public, personal and private life. I encourage you to seek out others who share your desire to also be accountable. I pray you will be as blessed as I have been.

No two groups will be identical because every person brings a unique personality and set of talents, along with a different background and maturity level. Utilize the concepts and questions in this book to develop a model which will ultimately bring you closer to Jesus Christ.

One of the practical steps you can take within your group is to have each member write out a personal mission statement. This one-page document should include spiritual, relational, financial, physical and social goals. This activity can help establish a game plan to give direction and purpose and also help you to focus on what is really important. The most effective statements are one sentence long, can be understood by a 12-year-old and would be able to be recited at gunpoint.

I've heard that 90 percent of all millionaires have a personal mission statement, yet fewer than three percent of all other individuals have one. A mission statement helps people discover what drives them, where their passions are and what brings energy and focus. It is a compass or a road map with a concept of life long learning and personal development. It constantly needs to be reevaluated. I encourage you to share your mission statement with your group and family. They can then periodically refer back to your statement in holding you accountable. My personal mission statement is noted in Appendix G.

One of my favorite FCA Summer Camp Themes was "Go The Distance." God desires each of us to be strong to the finish so we can stand as Paul did at the end of his life and proclaim, "I have fought the good fight. I have finished the race. I have kept the faith" (2 Timothy 4:7). Caleb was an example of a man who finished strong. In Joshua 14:6-12, at 85 years old he still had a clear vision, an incredible passion and was ready to take action. He exclaimed, "I want this hill!" The fire was still burning in him as he continued to trust and believe in God.

In 1968, the country of Tanzania selected John Stephen Akhwari to represent it in the Mexico City Olympics. Along the racecourse for the marathon, Akhwari stumbled and fell, severely injuring his knee and ankle. By 7 p.m., a runner from Ethiopia had won the race, and all other competitors had finished and been cared for. Just a few thousand spectators were left in the huge stadium when a police siren at the gate caught their attention. Limping through the gate came number 36, Akhwari, his leg wrapped in a bloody bandage. Those present began to cheer as the courageous man completed the final lap of the race. Later, a reporter asked Akhwari the question on everyone's mind: "Why did you continue the race after you were so badly injured?" He replied: "My country did not send me 7,000 miles to begin a race; they sent me to finish the race."

May that be our motto as believers in Christ. Not to just start the Christian race but to finish. Andy Stanley once said, "Giftedness ensures a good start; accountability ensures a good finish."[1] I would welcome the words of Jesus at the end of my life: "Well done, good and faithful servant."

SURRENDER ALL

For most people, the word surrender represents defeat. Many times, the initial image is a scared, timid individual who has no backbone to withstand a difficult situation. This picture is not accurate from God's perspective.

The need to surrender to God's will is a central theme in the Bible. Abraham obeyed God's call to migrate to a foreign land. Moses yielded himself to God and led the Israelites to freedom, out of their Egyptian bondage. Joshua convinced his army to lay down their weapons when they approached the fortified city of Jericho. Jesus, when agonizing in the Garden of Gethsemane, prayed, "Not my will, but yours be done." (Luke 22:42). By surrendering to God's will, each of these men experienced the fullness of God's plan for their life.

Jonathan Edwards wrote a prayer that says, in part: "I claim no right to myself—no right to understanding, this will, and these affections that are in me; neither do I have any right to this body or its members—any right to this tongue, to these hands, feet, ears, or eyes. I have given myself clear away and not retained anything of my own. To God this morning I have given myself wholly—I purpose to be absolutely His."

Total dedication and surrender best happens one day at a time. In fact, obedient surrendering must happen one choice at a time. I vividly remember learning this lesson when I was the chaplain of the Seattle SuperSonics back in the mid-1980's. On this particular night, only one player, John Lucas, showed up for chapel. John was a talented ballplayer, but he had struggled initially in his career with a drug addiction. When he met Jesus Christ, he began a new journey of sobriety. I was talking that night about daily dying to self. As I shared this truth, John's eyes lit up. I asked John, "Do you ever think about going back to your old lifestyle—the drugs and all those other addictive habits?" John's honest response has stayed with me to this day. He replied, "Yes, I think about returning every single day but I remind myself that with God's strength I can say no to these temptations." He then quoted Galatians 2:20 and Luke 9:23-24.

John Lucas recognized his need to surrender to God's will. He knew the reality of his sin and his desire to be obedient to God's truth. Like John, when we surrender, God will bless us. Giving ourselves to Him, on a daily basis, allows us experience the abundant life which Jesus promises us (see John 10:10). No longer do we need to be controlled by our sinful urges.

As an example of this, read Romans 7:14-25. How many times did you read the words, "I, me or myself" in this text? In my Bible, 36 times these words are mentioned. The Apostle Paul is honestly pouring out the reality of his sin and the battle he faces every second to choose God's will. He recognizes he is incapable apart from Christ and the work of the Holy Spirit. Now, read Romans 8:1-17. How many times is "I, me or myself" uttered here? In my Bible, the answer is zero. Instead, the word "Spirit" is used 27 times. The message here is that God's spirit will aid you as you daily surrender to Him. Today, surrender yourself to God. It is the key to experiencing true success.

FINISHING WELL
by Bobby Clinton, Fuller Seminary

Biblical studies show only one in three finishing well. Finishing well means different things to different people. The classic Old Testament character who finished well and demonstrated all of the characteristics was Daniel. The classic New Testament character who finished well is Paul. Here are six major characteristics that help assess a good finish:

1. They maintain a *personal vibrant relationship* with God right up to the end.
2. They maintain a *learning posture* and can learn from various kinds of sources—life especially.
3. They evidence *Christlikeness in character* (godliness—you like to be around them).
4. Truth is lived out in their lives so that *convictions* and promises of God are seen to be real.
5. They leave behind one or more *ultimate contributions* (saints, stylistic practitioners, mentors, public rhetoricians, pioneers, crusaders, artists, founders, stabilizers, researchers, writers, promoters).
6. They walk with a growing awareness of a *sense of destiny* and see some or all of it fulfilled.

Notes
1   Andy Stanley, audio cassette "Accountability" from the Reach Out Ministries Conference in April 1993.

BIBLE STUDY GUIDE

I n t r o d u c t i o n   t o   B i b l e   S t u d y   G u i d e

Have you ever wondered why, fifty days after Jesus elevated back to His Father, He sent us "a Comforter" instead of a Discipliner, Accuser, or an Intimidator?

Do you crave to be accountable? Hardly. It's not in our DNA. We didn't inherit it from our first parents in Eden nor have we evolved into people who run toward God. From the Father's call "Adam, where are you?" to Paul's thunderous conclusion that "no man seeks after God," we're seen as creatures who run from, not toward responsibility.

Yet, knowing that, Jesus didn't send us a heavenly Bronc Rider to "break" us and make us ready to be ridden. He sent us a Comforter, the Holy Spirit, God Himself who takes up residence in the life of every follower of Christ. We don't have to run "from" God. We can't…because wherever we go, there He is! To make it easy for us to be accountable to God, He lives within us. This is what you call your "ultimate accountability partner."

But God created us to be in relationship to our fellow humans as well. Since 1984 He has graciously given me four other brothers-in-Christ to walk through this life with, men to whom I've voluntarily become accountable. God knew I didn't need friends like Job's–Eliphaz, Bildad and Zophar had the right idea, but they blew it big time.

You know the story. When they learn that their buddy Job has lost everything, they race to his side. Shocked at the degree to which his sufferings have wasted Job, they sit with him in stunned silence for seven days. Instead of easing their forlorn friend's pain, they lay more on him, burying him in guilt. Even a younger-but-not-wiser Elihu has nothing to offer to relieve Job of his misery.

Ultimately, God leads Job through a list of questions, perhaps the prototype of those which my friend Rod Handley poses for us in these pages. Through his personal encounter with the Creator, Job (on whom God had lavished the highest praise, saying there was none other like him in the world) finally understands God. And in so doing, he recognizes he's a sinner desperately in need of the Heavenly Father.

Isn't this the whole point of being answerable? That is, seeing God for who He is, and seeing ourselves for who we are. My friend Tom Shrader, who came to Christ as an adult and hit the ground running, says, "I've spent a lot of years studying about this, and I've come to this conclusion— there is a God and I'm not Him!"

These men whom God gave me in 1984 have been His visible angels assigned to my case, helping me through life, death, ominous family illnesses, family transitions, career highs and lows, spiritual victories and wastelands. Through it all, instead of acting like Job's friends, they've held up my arms in battle. If I only could, I'd find three or four such men for you, sir, or women for you, ma'am. Then I'd give you a copy of *"Character That Counts: Who's Counting Yours?"* with the corresponding study guide and watch you survive and thrive!

Then I could say of you, as James said of our ancient friend, "You have heard of Job's perseverance and have seen what the Lord finally brought about. The Lord is full of compassion and mercy." (James 5:11)

George Toles
Owner
The Toles Company
Edmonds, Washington

The Quiz

I've figured out why powerful people often wear sunglasses. The spotlight blinds them to reality, and they suffer from a delusion that power means something. They believe that titles make a difference and are under the impression that their earthly authority will make a heavenly difference.

Take this quiz:
* Name the five wealthiest people in the world.
* Name the last ten Heisman trophy winners.
* Name the last four winners of the Miss America contest.
* Name eight people who have won the Nobel or Pulitzer prize.
* How about the last ten Academy Award winners for best picture, or
* The last decade's worth of World Series winners?

How did you do? I didn't do well either. With the exception of you trivia hounds, none of us remember the headliners of yesterday too well. Surprising how quickly we forget, isn't it? And what I've mentioned above are not second-rate achievements. These are the best in their fields. But the applause dies. Awards tarnish. Achievements are forgotten. Accolades and certificates are buried with their owners.

Here's another quiz. See how you do on this one:
* Think of three people you enjoy spending time with.
* Name ten people who have taught you something worthwhile.
* Name five friends who have helped you in a difficult time.
* List a few teachers who have aided your journey through school.
* Name half-a-dozen heroes whose stories have inspired you.

Easier? It was for me, too. The lesson? The people who make a difference are not the ones with the credentials, but the ones with the concern.[1]

Why Was This Study Guide Written?

The *"Character That Counts: Who's Counting Yours?"* study guide is about connecting with God and others. Getting beyond credentials, titles and accolades and getting to the hearts and souls of people. If you want to get real with yourself, people and God, this study guide will take you there. This material will be challenging, yet I believe God is calling us to raise the standard of our lives to excellence, not mediocrity. Obviously none of us will ever attain perfection, yet we should strive and pray to be all that God desires.

Just this week, I read the story of an internationally famous athlete who had fallen publicly through a moral failure. Although he has been a vocal witness for Jesus Christ, several hundred million people who follow this international sport are reading about him, his sin and the contradiction of his professed faith in Christ. His story isn't the first, nor will it be the last. These brutally painful, embarrassing failures bring a black eye to Christianity. In fact, the Old and New Testaments are full of men and women who believed but also failed. The fact of the matter is that every one of us is also capable of falling.

Therefore, we need to create an environment in which every person can find help. The continual development of character and seeking accountability are two disciplines we all should vigorously pursue. Don't be the next casualty. The principles laid out for you in this study guide will go a long way toward protecting you and helping you "finish the race" of life. It all begins with a willingness to be honest with yourself and God. If you are willing to start with this mindset, you're ready to get into the race.

In addition, this study was developed to take people from a group discussion back to the privacy of their homes, and particularly to their marriages. From years of study and research, I know how character development and accountability take place individually, but I never grasped or fully understood how to connect my wife and children to these principles. With the help of couples' from my church and the input of others across the country, I've created a model where valuable communication can take place within a marriage. This study led my wife and me to discuss areas that we had never considered or talked about. As we've wrestled through the lessons ourselves, our conversations have been more meaningful and intimate. The same positive reaction has come from others as well.

Since 1990, I've been blessed to be in a group of guys who've helped me navigate through many life experiences. They've been instrumental in my growth, and they continue to pray diligently for me. Now as a husband and father, they are my advisors, and they keep me on the "straight and narrow" path. Believe me, my family benefits from their input. I eagerly look forward to our weekly time together because I know I'll be sharper and better equipped to fulfill the calling God has on my life.

I challenge you to consider taking at least two action steps: (1) Identify at least one intimate friend to whom you can be accountable; and (2) Increase the level of intimacy in your marriage. Norm and Bobbe Evans always conclude Pro Athletes Conferences with these words, "We know you've been bombarded with a zillion great ideas this week, enough to make your head spin for months. We suggest that you select just one or two for now, the ones most relevant to where you are at this moment, and concentrate on them. Once you've assimilated them into your lifestyle, go back to your notes and choose one or two more to munch on." Perhaps these wise words will apply to you as you embark on this study guide.

How To Use This Study Guide

Each study guide chapter has an opening summary before introducing three sets of questions and the "extra points."

1) GROUP QUESTIONS: These questions would be appropriate for a men's or women's group, a couples' study or even a mixed (male/female) setting for all ages. The first question is an ice-breaker to help get discussion started. Feel free to add or delete questions as necessary based on how your group responds to one another and the material.

2) BETWEEN YOU AND YOUR SPOUSE: If you're married, answer these questions privately between husband and wife but only after group discussion questions have been answered. If you're in a couples' study, you'll be familiar with what was discussed in the group setting. If you're not in a couples' study or only one of you is in a group study, please have your spouse read the chapter so you can discuss this set of questions. There are some very invigorating exercises to spur on conversation with your life partner.

3) BETWEEN YOU AND GOD: These questions are meant to be answered alone before God. Prayerfully and honestly come into His presence.

4) EXTRA POINTS: Practical "take home" applications for the entire group, couple or individual.

If you're married, I encourage you to work through all three sets of questions. For those who are single using this study, don't be alarmed by the section specifically for married couples'. If you're single, the "Group Questions" and "Between You and God" should be answered. Engaged couples' or those who are seriously dating would be encouraged to think through and discuss the principles outlined in "Between You and Your Spouse."

In advance of the study, read the chapter and be prepared to answer the "Group Questions." Bring back to the group any insights gained from what you did at home with your spouse or with God from the prior lesson. This is a great way to get immediate feedback from your group.

During the first meeting, allow group members to get to know one another. You will want to spend time going over the purpose of the group and some of the ground rules for group discussion. Some ground rule recommendations should include:

*Talk only about yourself, your feelings and your thoughts, not those of your spouse or others.

*No one will be forced to participate in a discussion or answer a question aloud.

*Always maintain confidentiality. Names, words, actions, observations and impressions are not to be repeated outside the group.

*Avoid giving advice. Instead, look for opportunities to provide mutual support and care.

*Read the materials, including the Scripture passages, before you come so you'll be prepared.

Epilogue

This study guide was initiated by twelve couples' from Lee's Summit Community Church. The goal was to use *"Character That Counts: Who's Counting Yours?"* and work together to develop materials that would benefit couples'. What ultimately resulted was a three-in-one study guide, a series of questions designed for groups, couples and individuals. My wife Janna and I knew a few of the couples' who participated in our study, but most of the people we didn't know well. We met every other week for an hour and a half over a nine month period, and during that time we developed some significant life long friendships.

In our case, there was more information and questions to get through than available time. In fact, rarely did we get through every question. It was purposefully designed this way to push beyond the status quo. We challenged the couples' to continue the discussion at home while completing the other sections of the study. Every group is unique, and the time available varies, so we urge you to personalize the process.

Many times I felt the freedom to deviate from the questions and supply additional materials or thoughts which would bring interest and excitement to the group. Gary Smalley, David Ferguson, Chuck and Barb Snyder, Clarence Shuler and others have outstanding materials designed just for couples, and we benefited from their writings. In addition, in Chapter 9 dealing with sex languages, we had each couple provide feedback anonymously. The results were compiled into a bar graph chart and we discussed the findings. It was a wonderful way to talk through a very seldom discussed topic. Using Chapter 14, we had a very honest dialogue about how fearful many were to engage in personal evangelism. In fact, one person couldn't remember telling anyone about Christ for years, using the reasoning that personal faith could be a silent witness. Yet the reality was that they had been far too quiet. We encouraged people to actively pursue the "Extra Point" from this chapter and during our next session we had stories to tell. We also had every couple give us their personal set of accountability questions from Chapter 6. These are just a few examples of how we used this guide.

Perhaps the greatest encouragement has come from watching couples grow closer throughout the year. As a result of developing their questions, one couple has begun meeting together at 6:00 a.m. every Wednesday to pray and read Scripture together. Another couple who's been married for close to twenty years has had some of the most significant conversations of their entire marriage. One family has experienced tremendous grief through the loss of several children at birth and this study has helped bring healing and encouragement to their marriage. One man identified an accountability partner after watching our group interact throughout the year.

We have received numerous positive reports around the country from groups testing the material. How exciting to see God work and to see marriages and relationships being restored and renewed by God's grace and power. Do you desire to take yourself and your relationships to a whole new level? If yes, then take this tremendous opportunity and eagerly await God's leading and blessing as you work through this study guide, as you search the Scriptures and dedicate your life to prayer. Are you ready? On your mark, get set, go!!

Chapter 1 • Character Counts

H istorically Quakers have resisted being sworn in before testifying in court. Their rationale is simple. If they have to promise to be honest for the next few minutes, the obvious implication is that they are dishonest the rest of the time. And if such is the case, why should anyone trust the oath they make? A person's integrity should be such that no one would ever ask whether she or he will speak "the truth, the whole truth, and nothing but the truth." Jesus made the same point in Matthew 5:37 when He told His listeners, "But let your statement be, 'Yes, yes' or 'No, no.'" In other words, be a person of such integrity that when you speak, the community will never have reason to doubt what you say.[2]

This chapter seeks to answer the age old question…does character count? In today's society we see and hear examples that would lead us to believe that character and integrity simply don't matter anymore. Yet many people are seeing gaping "character" holes in others as well as their own personal lives. No matter which of following categories may apply (men/women, young/old, married/single, believer/non-believer), we should be concerned and eager to take steps to better understand and apply character. We will attempt to not only understand what character is but also the ample benefits which emerge when true character is developed.

GROUP QUESTIONS:

1) What adjectives would you use to describe yourself?

2) How would you define "character," "integrity" and "reputation"? How are they different? Are they the same? Develop a definition that all members can agree upon.

3) Think of someone who gives a genuine picture of Christian integrity/character. Why did you choose him/her?

4) The New Testament gives us several examples of couples who displayed tremendous character and at least one who did not. Look up the following passages and discuss the benefits and consequences of these couples' decisions to "do the right thing." Why is it important to "do the right thing?"
    *Mary & Joseph: Matthew 1:18-25
    *Ananias & Sapphira: Acts 5:1-11
    *Aquila & Priscilla: Acts 18:1-3, 18, 24-28; Romans 16:3-4;
        1 Corinthians 16:19; 2 Timothy 4:19

5) Disappointments, difficulties, conflict, adversity, pain, failure, humbling moments, obscurity and successes are some of the ways that God chooses to mold and develop our character. Whether they are big or small, it is often a major time of growth. Name a specific example in your life where God worked through one of these ways and how you can now see the positive results of this character-building time.

6) We live our lives in three different arenas…public, personal and private. Some say we have no right to meddle in other people's lives; that what Sal, Joe, Preston, media stars, politicians and the Christians next to you do is their own business. Do you agree or disagree and why? How does what you do in private impact what you do in public?

7) What are steps you can take to make sure that your public, personal and private lives are congruent? What steps of integrity could you take to protect yourself from temptation and to make certain your input to others is positive?

8) Describe the importance of integrity/character in a marriage? With your children?

9) How can you show integrity:
    * In your marriage
    * With relatives

* With friends and neighbors
* With your children
* On your job
* At church

BETWEEN YOU AND YOUR SPOUSE:

1) "What" and/or "whom" has God used in your life to give you perspective about marriage, family and home life?
2) How do you resolve conflicts? Look at both how you handle those between one another and those you handle as a team. If you are newly married and haven't experienced conflict yet, talk about the boundaries that you would like to set up now.
3) Do you have the right and responsibility to approach one another with a character flaw? How do you currently do this, and is this done in a proper, biblical way?
4) What expectations of integrity do you have for your marriage?
5) What legacy are you passing on to your spouse and children? What character qualities are you now emphasizing as you "train up your children?" (See Appendix A on pages 249-252 for examples).
6) What positive character traits does your family exhibit? In what area would you like to see your family become a better example?
7) One way I can demonstrate how important my spouse is to me is by

   _____

   _____.

BETWEEN YOU AND GOD:

1) What do those closest to you say about your character? How well does what they say match how you are on the inside?
2) Does your life honor God, or are you focusing on putting forth an image?
3) How have you helped someone by demonstrating integrity? How have you honored God by demonstrating integrity? How have you blessed your spouse by demonstrating integrity?
4) How have you hurt someone by your lack of integrity? How have you hurt God by your lack of integrity? How have you hurt your spouse by your lack of integrity?
5) What inspires you about letting God deepen your personal integrity?
6) What circumstances does God seem to be using in your life to strengthen your character? What changes do you sense God desires to make in you?
7) When I consider my integrity, I know I need to _____

   _____

   _____.

EXTRA POINTS: Review Appendix A noting three character qualities in your life where you are doing well and three where you need to improve.

Chapter 2 • A Call to Accountability

My personal experience with accountability is that the word is used frequently by many people in a variety of different situations, yet very few truly understand true accountability. Virtually every day I encounter the word used in the newspaper or in daily conversation. Bosses urge employees to be accountable in meeting a deadline; teachers give tests to students and expect accountability in not looking at their neighbor's answers; police officers hold drivers accountable for speed limits; mortgage companies hold homeowners accountable to make timely payments; high profile personalities/athletes/politicians are expected to be accountable for their conduct. However, within the local church rarely is accountability addressed directly. It is often referred to but not easily encouraged or enforced. James McDonald once said, "It's so shocking to look back and see how frequently people are excited about accountability until they are the one who needs it."

Choosing to become accountable may sound like walking into a prison and giving someone else the key. But accountability is actually freeing. It gives you benefits you find no other way. This chapter will address the necessity of accountability and describe its rewards. You are in for a tremendous blessing when you embrace accountability.

GROUP QUESTIONS:

1) To whom do you listen to most closely for advice? Why?
2) Without identifying names or revealing details, think of someone who professed to be a Christian but fell into inappropriate behavior. Why did their actions bother you?
3) Explain the reasons for accountability using absolutely no religious or churchy words. (If you can explain it without theological words, you truly understand it). Then tell your group which one most compels you to be accountable.

   ❏ Satan's schemes   ❏ Holiness
   ❏ Remain right with God   ❏ Mutual encouragement
   ❏ God's judgment   ❏ Stumbling block

4) Page 37 says, "Remember, accountability will not remove sin or keep you from sin, but it helps you to become aware of your sin and helps point and focus you back on Jesus Christ. Being accountable takes honesty, and if honesty doesn't exist, accountability will be a meaningless experience." How would you respond to this statement?

5) Six benefits to accountability are noted on pages 43-45. Comment on these six reasons—can you identify more benefits? How would you convince an extremely resistant person that these benefits make it worthwhile to choose accountability?
6) How can Christians encourage each other to do right without sounding judgmental, condescending or parental?
7) How could you incorporate accountability into the life of your family?
8) Why is isolation so easy and accountability so hard? Why is there power in confessing sin to another person?

BETWEEN YOU AND YOUR SPOUSE:

1) Debrief with your spouse on the subject of accountability and ask for their input on what specifically are areas where accountability could pay great dividends. Also, discuss possible candidates to whom you could be accountable who are not in your immediate family.
2) Talk with your spouse about a time you were overwhelmed by a sin, and you didn't feel you could talk to anyone about it. If appropriate, invite your spouse to give you an action plan to stay out of a similar trap now and in the future.
3) To what extent should you be accountable to your spouse and children?
4) It really means a lot to me when my spouse_____
_____.

BETWEEN YOU AND GOD:

1) Are you ready to face a holy God? Why or why not?
2) The key to accountability is to determine areas of your life where you need immediate and specific help. What are these areas for you?
3) Are you currently part of an accountability group? Why or why not?
4) Someone who could hold me accountable is_____.
5) When I consider areas of my life known only by God and me, I know I need to_____.

EXTRA POINTS: In the next session we are going to give everyone in the group an opportunity to talk about their current relationship with Jesus Christ. Prior to attending, be thinking about what you might want to relate to the group within a five minute period.

Chapter 3 • A Look At Our Group

Everyone has a different reason for wanting accountability. Some include a desire for purity, handling temptation, social reasons, emotional help, spiritual guidance and deeper friendships. The bottom line is that they've received help in their time of need. But beginning the process of being personally accountable starts with a willingness to receive Jesus Christ as Savior and Lord. He is the reason for our pursuit of accountability.

Before you go further in this study, ask yourself: Am I certain that I know Christ as my personal Savior? The following statements can help you answer this question. Place a check beside those you can answer yes.

❏   I believe the Bible, God's Word, is our guide to salvation and eternal life.
❏   I believe the Bible when it tells me I am a sinner and that the penalty for sin is eternal separation from God.
❏   I believe that Jesus is the Son of God, that He died on the cross to pay the penalty for my sin, and that He rose from the grave to give new life for all who place their faith in Him.

Did you answer yes to each question? Do you want to have eternal life? The Bible tells how to have eternal life, as noted on page 54. If you take these steps, you will have personal salvation in Jesus Christ. Call on Him in prayer right now. Then reveal your decision to a pastor, a Christian friend or spouse. Seek to grow in your faith through regular Bible study, prayer, worship, service and Christian fellowship.

GROUP QUESTIONS:

1) What's one of the greatest things your friends have ever done for you?
2) As stated on pages 53-54, accountability is a by-product of a personal relationship with Jesus Christ and a desire to follow Him obediently. Break your group into four's (or two couples) and have each person describe his/her journey of faith up to this point. Have each person take no more than 5 minutes. After 20 minutes, reconvene the small groups into the larger group to answer the remaining questions. NOTE: Consider doing the line graph on Question #1 below, "Between You & God," if appropriate.
3) What personal attitudes, habits and priorities have been changed within you in the last few years? Did God use specific people to bring about these changes? Any particular events? Any specific Scripture passages?

4) Identify people in the group who've had an accountability partner and/or group. Have several members talk about their personal experience with accountability. What value did it bring to them?
5) Cam Meers and Darla DeBacker both told of the impact that an accountability group has had upon their marriages on pages 50 and 52. For those who have had a spouse involved in accountability, please relate the impact it has had upon your marriage.
6) Ecclesiastes 4:9-10 says, "Two are better than one because they have a good return for their labor. For if either falls, the one will lift up his companion. But woe to the one who falls when there is not another to lift him up. Furthermore, if two lie down together they keep warm, but how can one be warm alone? And if one can overpower him who is alone, two can resist him. A cord of three strands is not quickly torn apart." Why do you believe this verse? Describe situations when you've seen this verse in action.
7) Ideally, accountability engages three relationships (if married): To God, to a person or person(s) of the same sex and to your spouse. What are the benefits of engaging all three? What happens when you don't engage in all three?
8) Who is one of the greatest people of faith you've ever met? What touched you about that person's life?

BETWEEN YOU AND YOUR SPOUSE:

1) Take as much time as needed to review exactly where you are in your relationship with Jesus Christ. If necessary, retrace the five steps on page 54 for receiving Jesus into your life. If you've never prayed this prayer and you desire to, you and your spouse can make this commitment right now before God and each another.
2) Review Ecclesiastes 4:9-12 and tell each other why you know, from your marriage, the value of this passage. Re-affirm that God has called you to be a helpmate to your spouse, and thank him/her for being a perfect compliment for you.
3) How could you be more accountable to one another?
4) Respond to this statement: "To live an unaccountable life is to flirt with danger." Why is this true or false?
5) I really feel loved by my spouse when_____
_____.

BETWEEN YOU AND GOD:

1) Draw a line graph from your birth up to the present time. Chart your spiritual growth, showing your salvation experience, times of rapid growth, "backsliding," plateaus, etc. Now show where you'd like to be "spiritually" at the end of the next year.

212 CHARACTER THAT COUNTS—WHO'S COUNTING YOURS?

2) Come clean with God and tell Him exactly where you are currently in your journey of faith. What are areas that you need to confess to God? How can God become the center of your life?
3) Read Ecclesiastes 4:9-12. Biblical examples abound of people getting into trouble because they tried to go it on their own. What trouble did these Bible characters create for themselves by trying to be Lone Rangers? (In addition to the verses you remember, use a Bible concordance to look up others).
4) What are your reasons for embracing or resisting accountability? If you're not accountable, what would motivate you to become so?
5) What people will I call upon to help me grow in Christian maturity?
6) When I consider accountability, I know I need to_____
_____.

EXTRA POINTS: Show your line graph to a trusted friend—and ask him/her to do the same. It will be difficult to proceed with this study without having a personal relationship with Jesus Christ. Have you made that decision?

Chapter 4 • Teamwork That Works

When children are born, parents quickly learn about the dependence of a child. Apart from crying, sucking and dirtying their diapers, newborns are helpless and extremely dependent upon mom and dad for everything. Too soon, these little ones begin to seek independence. They want to prove that they can do things on their own. But God didn't design us to be dependent or independent—His desire is that we would be interdependent. This chapter will help you learn the value of interdependence.

So many believers have no idea how crucial this is to their Christian growth as well as being a tremendous protector of their faith. The exciting part is that God has been promoting it from the beginning of time. Though we are each individually responsible, we can call upon people of faith to help us navigate through the perils of life. The Bible is filled with numerous examples of people who connected themselves to others. They made better decisions and were more obedient to God when they submitted their lives to others.

Each of us needs to be connected to a team of people. When this takes place, then synergy occurs. When synergy occurs, the sky is the limit.

GROUP QUESTIONS:

1) Tell the group the most successful team you've ever been part of (sports, business, church, etc.). What made this team such a winner?

2) What are your impressions of the accountability model of John Wesley in the 1700's? What would happen if people were subject to these types of questions on a weekly basis?
3) We'd all like to think that our faith is enough to help us live the Christian life. Why are you more prone to sin if you think no one will find out?
4) What initially comes to mind when you hear the word "submission"? Did your views of "submission" change when you read pages 57–59? Why or why not?
5) Discuss the differences between dependence, independence and inter-dependence. Identify examples (and the results) in your life when you have allowed one of these three to have an upper hand.
6) Have you ever been part of a synergistic effort? What specifically happened?
7) What are the keys of working well with others?

BETWEEN YOU AND YOUR SPOUSE:

1) If you were to describe your marriage in terms of a winning percentage, where would you stand (between 0-100%)? Are you satisfied with that number? What could you do to improve it?
2) What is a recent example of when you really worked together well as a team? What is a recent example of when you didn't work well together as a team?
3) Before you were married, what were your views of submission? Have those views changed since then? How are you doing in submitting one to another?
4) Have each spouse list 5-6 strengths for each of you. Compare lists and discuss. What areas are you relying heavily upon your spouse to handle in your marriage? Identify areas where your spouse is relying heavily upon you. (NOTE: This question is designed to not only look at strengths you bring to a marriage but also evaluate dependency/inter-dependency issues).
5) In the context of your marriage, what are your three greatest needs? What are your spouses' three greatest needs? What opportunities have you had recently to meet these needs? Answer these separately before discussing.
6) Do you know what your mate's "life vision" is? How can you complement that vision?
7) One way I can give more of myself to my spouse is by_____
_____
_____.

8) What did you learn about your marriage by answering questions #1-#7?_____

_____

_____.

BETWEEN YOU AND GOD:

1) Who was one of the best partners or teammates you ever had? What made that person so effective?
2) Read Jeremiah 17:9. Because "the heart is deceitful above all things" we can be easily deceived. When we give a report or must explain our actions to someone, we are more likely to do the right thing. Recall a time when you were deceived in:
    ❑ a relationship or friendship ❑ a choice ❑ by leadership ❑ by ego
    Did another Christian help you see things clearly?
    How were you prompted to make the needed changes?
3) Do you find yourself primarily in a dependent, independent or interdependent environment? Why? Would you like to be more interdependent? Why or why not?
4) What are your reasons for embracing or resisting interdependence? If you're not interdependent, what would motivate you to become so?
5) When I consider becoming a better teammate, I know I need to_____

_____.

EXTRA POINTS: Make a list of successful qualities of teams, businesses, churches, marriages, etc. There are many common parallels among them. Share this list with someone who really could benefit from your observations.

Chapter 5 • How To Get Started

We've discussed many character issues in these past chapters. You've looked at your commitment to God and how accountability can help you live that out. You've discovered ways to let Jesus become the center of your life. You've discussed what integrity means in your private and public worlds.

At some point, it is important to get beyond the theory to the practical. This chapter will help you map a strategy for getting started. It will also discuss several foundational keys of successful groups. Remember, no two accountability groups will be identical because every person brings unique skills and talents, a different background and a different maturity level.

Accountability has played a very important role in my Christian growth. I've been strengthened and challenged over the past decade by being answerable to people. I encourage you to seek out others who share your desire to be accountable. I pray you will be blessed as I have been.

GROUP QUESTIONS:

1) What is one of the biggest challenges you've ever faced? How successfully did you face it? What resources helped you?

2) Would you describe yourself as a "good starter" when faced with new relationships, projects, challenges or changes to your normal routine? Why or why not?

3) Comment on the truths noted by Chuck Swindoll (The Truth About Friends) on pages 68-69. Explain how you have seen the difference between acquaintances, casual friends, close friends and intimate friends in your own relationship world. What kind of spirit and attitudes are crucial in making intimate friends?

4) How can you overcome the natural tendencies of making your relationships look like the iceberg on page 70?

5) How can an accountability group maintain balance in the following areas, as guided by Galatians 6:1-10, Philippians 2:4 and Luke 6:41?
    ❑ Growing in Christ
    ❑ Awareness of your own needs while helping others with theirs
    ❑ Addressing successes as well as failures
    ❑ Looking at the present as well as the past

6) A written covenant can be a powerful tool for a successful accountability group. Have you ever formally adopted a written covenant? If so, what was the result? If not, would you consider doing one? What would be the most important components of a successful covenant?

7) There are several important issues discussed in this chapter such as: the need for transparency, confidentiality and dealing with conflict. Discuss these three issues and other key components that emerged from reading this chapter.

BETWEEN YOU AND YOUR SPOUSE:

1) Have each spouse do a quick inventory of the people he/she spends the most time with. Place each person in one of the four friendship categories: acquaintances, casual friends, close friends and intimate friends. Review and compare the list with one another and discuss the breakdown.

2) Do you have a copy of your marriage vows? If not, find them!! By having them in your possession, you can review these with your spouse and discuss how each of you is doing in fulfilling these vows. We suggest you do this exercise at least annually.

3) Have each partner take the fifteen covenants listed on pages 78-80 and put them in the order of personal importance (1 to 15) in your marriage. Compare your list with your spouse and be attentive to your spouse's top three areas of need (covenants) during the next 30 days. Plan to keep these covenants fresh.

4) How do you handle transparency, confidentiality and conflict resolution in your marriage? Are you effectively working through these delicate issues?

5) The communication with my spouse is greatly increased when we do a simple, nightly exercise called "Couch Time." It is time for us to sit eyeball to eyeball for at least five minutes with no interruptions or distractions and talk through our day, as well as plan for tomorrow. Consider doing this in your own home and see what might happens.

6) Together with my spouse, I would enjoy_____.

BETWEEN YOU AND GOD:

1) What dreams do you have for your personal, spiritual and professional life?

2) Review the list on page 66 (Reasons People Refuse Accountability). Have you used any of these excuses in the past? Are there other reasons you could add to this list?

3) What temptations, time pressures and demands do you face? How might accountability to other Christians help you manage these?

4) Relationship building is at the core of accountability. However, maintaining healthy relationships isn't easy. Our spouses, children, parents, friends or roommates give us plenty of opportunity for conflict, resentment, deception and outright dishonesty. What qualities, besides Christian commitment, does God want you to seek in friends? Are these qualities visible in your life? Describe the kind of friend you are to others.

5) Name someone who helps you be a better friend. How does he or she do this?

6) Jot down the name of one or more like-minded believers with whom you might form an accountability group. Prayerfully consider what God may be leading you to do.

7) When I consider establishing or living up to covenants, I need to _____
_____.

EXTRA POINTS: Covenant living examples (personally and for a group) are also found in Appendix B & C. Develop covenants which would work personally within your marriage and/or within an accountability group.

Chapter 6 • Developing Your Questions

What a thrill it is to hear how people around the country have taken personal ownership of the accountability process and have spent prayerful time working on developing questions which apply specifically to them. The ten questions our group designed work for us, but they represent just one model. The steps taken to identify specific issues and questions can be one of the richest experiences ever encountered. For many, it brings deliverance and joy.

Betsy King's story is worth repeating. As one of the most recognizable people in America, Betsy knows that her celebrity status has great benefits and potential pitfalls. Shortly after reading *"Character That Counts,"* Betsy felt the need to find an accountability partner, and Kathy Malone emerged as someone with whom mutual accountability could occur.

Betsy and Kathy designed questions which would apply to them and identified Scripture which corresponded to the questions. Today, Betsy and Kathy continue to have a rich friendship which has strengthened them personally and spiritually because of the questions they regularly ask each other.

GROUP QUESTIONS:

1) What's been one of the most miraculous deliverances you've ever experienced (i.e. from death, an illness, a bad habit, a tough situation, etc.)? How did it happen?
2) What is your first impression of reading the ten questions that are noted on the back of this book and repeated on page 83? What would happen in your life if you were regularly asked these types of questions?
3) As you ponder submitting to a Christian who can help you grow in integrity, think about the questions you could ask each other. How could you voluntarily yield to another person in ways that would help you live for Christ more authentically?
4) 2 Peter 1:10 says, "for as long as you practice these things, you will never stumble." What is this verse referring to, and how could you be protected from stumbling?
5) What is the difference between restoring someone gently and confronting them in a sanctimonious or harsh way?
6) On pages 84-85 you'll find some daily goals that help keep me on track. What daily routines (disciplines) have you incorporated into your life to help keep you personally accountable?
7) How do you handle the "gray" areas of life? Refer to the examples on page 90 to spur on conversation.

BETWEEN YOU AND YOUR SPOUSE:

1) How would each of you answer these four questions:
    a) Can I expect God to meet my needs and still vulnerably share them with my spouse?
    b) Can I openly and lovingly communicate my needs to my spouse as well as to others?
    c) It really means a lot to me when my spouse _____
        _____.
    d) One way I can demonstrate how important my spouse is to me is by_____.
2) What dreams do you have for your marriage and family life?
3) What do you view as the two biggest turning points or breakthroughs in your life? Why these?
4) Create a set of accountability questions that would work for you and your spouse to answer together on a weekly basis. Look at pages 246-247 for examples.

Feel free to use all the sample questions in this chapter to develop ones which would work for you. Having done that, determine the best time and setting to do this on a regular basis. Make sure both husband and wife are in complete agreement with this to insure the highest level of follow-through.

BETWEEN YOU AND GOD:

1) What steps of integrity could you take, beginning today, to protect yourself from temptation and to make certain your impact on others is positive? Note one step in each of these areas:
    ❑ Honesty ❑ Sexual conduct ❑ Work ❑ Money
    ❑ Friendships/Dating ❑ Family
2) Imagine that you are standing in front of Jesus Christ. What picture does your life present to Jesus? Is it an accurate picture? Is it shallow or deep?
3) Answer the ten accountability questions noted earlier, either alone or with a trusted Christian friend. What did you learn about yourself and your friend from doing this?
4) Create accountability questions that fit you. Feel free to use my group's questions as a model.
5) What specific changes do you hope for in yourself as you pursue personal accountability? In your spouse? In your children?
6) I really feel cared for when _____
    _____.
    Describe your answer to a good friend.

EXTRA POINTS: (1) Think through the types of questions you would like to begin asking within an accountability group or your marriage. Don't leave this session without putting some questions on paper. Make a commitment to yourself to regularly re-visit these questions with a friend. (2) Several groups I know have come up with creative names for their accountability group such as PIGS (Pretty Important Guy Stuff); FIT 5 (five men meeting at 5:00 a.m. for the purpose of being physically and spiritually fit); THE LOSERS (they are losing their lives for Christ's sake); BAND OF BROTHERS; MEN OF VALOR; DREAM TEAM; etc. If you have an accountability group, come up with a creative name for your group.

Chapter 7 • Satan and His Strategy

We have an enemy, and his name is Satan. Even before Genesis 1:1, a war was waged in heaven between God and His most beautiful angel (Satan). God won the victory, and Satan's ultimate destruction is promised. Until that day of final judgment, the evil one considers all believers in Jesus Christ a threat. Thus he'll try anything to bring them down. He has many strategies, and he is powerful, but his power is limited, and believers in Christ are equipped to win.

You don't need to fear Satan. Instead place your hope and trust in Jesus Christ and stay focused on Him. Satan will do anything to block you from living a Christ-centered life. He makes "wrong" look "right" and "sin" look "fun." He waters down what really matters, so we'll settle for cheap imitations of God's best.

Isolation is one of Satan's most powerful tools. Accountability can help us stay on course. The banana pulled from the bunch is the one that gets peeled. Don't isolate yourself from the Body of Christ. Stay connected!!

GROUP QUESTIONS:

1) Who were your enemies when you were in school? What did they do to you? Did you ever retaliate?
2) Satan's strategy is well planned, but the Christian's weapons are more powerful. What weapons do we have against Satan? (See Ephesians 6:10-18 for ideas). Give examples of how these pieces of armor can defeat Satan.
3) How can you make certain you don't isolate yourself, leaving you open to Satan's attacks?
4) Perhaps you feel safe because you don't dabble in satanic "stuff". But one of Satan's lies is that God isn't concerned with your daily life–only with church attendance. Satan tries to segment your life so you

separate worship from other activities. As a result, subtle compromises can creep in. What are some disciplines you could make to connect what you do at church to the rest of your week?

5) How does the study of God's Word and prayer defeat Satan's schemes? How does working for the glory of God defeat Satan?

6) On page 95, are two reminders of "Remember, We Win!" What are some additional promises that we know will ultimately play out for us and our defeated enemy?

BETWEEN YOU AND YOUR SPOUSE:

1) Discuss with your spouse which area you are most likely to get caught in by Satan:
   ❏ you don't pay enough attention to his schemes
   ❏ you deliberately toy with sin/wrong
   ❏ you don't equip yourself with the armor of God
   ❏ you have a hard time trusting God
   ❏ you get isolated and independent
   What could you do to get help in this area of potential danger?

2) Satan would love to pull you and your spouse apart and ultimately destroy your marriage. Identify precautions you could establish to not allow Satan's schemes to endanger your marriage? Take time to pray together asking God to help you follow through with this commitment.

BETWEEN YOU AND GOD:

1) Read John 8:44. Which lies of Satan's have you believed in the past? What did you learn from this?

2) Read 1 Peter 5:8-9; Ephesians 6:10-18; Colossians 3:2-10. List out the specific strategies for defeating Satan.

3) An area where I've allowed Satan to have victory in my life in the past is_____.
   What can you do to address this issue today in making the needed changes?_____.

4) When I consider closets of my life known only by God and me, I know I need to_____.

EXTRA POINTS: We've addressed a number of danger spots where Satan could gain a foothold. What can you do today to stop that from happening?

Chapter 8 · Daily Time With Christ

Prayer and the Word of God are inseparable and should always go together. In His Word God speaks to me, and in prayer I speak to God. If there is to be true communication, God and I must both take part. If I simply pray without using God's Word, I am apt to use my own words and thoughts. Taking God's thoughts from His Word and presenting them before Him really gives prayer its power. God's Word is indispensable for all true prayer!

Through the Word the Holy Spirit shows me who God is. The Word also teaches me how sinful I am. It reveals to me all the wonders that God will do for me and the strength He will give me to do His will. The Word teaches me how to pray—with a strong desire, a firm faith, and constant perseverance. The Word teaches me not only who I am but who I may become. Above all it reminds me that Christ is the great intercessor and allows me to pray in His name.

Learn to renew your strength each day in God's Word and to pray according to His will. *Dear Father, I pray that when I read Your Word I may understand it. May the Holy Spirit teach me to know and use the Bible correctly, and may I see in it that Christ is all in all and will be all in me. May my prayers be consistent with what You have said in Your Word. In Jesus' name, amen.*[3]

GROUP QUESTIONS:

1) Just as a car needs fuel to run, a believer needs a "quiet time" to keep running effectively. Obviously, there is a correlation between the amount of fuel and the likelihood of getting to your destination. Does anyone have a "running out of gas" story to tell?
2) Who gave you your first Bible, and how old were you when you received it? How did it influence your life?
3) Jeremiah 29:12-13 promises, "Then you will call upon me and come and pray to me, and I will listen to you. You will seek me and find me when you seek me with all your heart." What does seeking God "with all your heart" mean and what are the implications of the word "all"?
4) A quiet time can be defined as spending time alone with God and allowing Him to speak to you through His Word. Why is time alone with God a crucial foundation to integrity and personal spiritual growth?
5) Who are some of your role models when it comes to a quiet time (parents, relatives, friends, roommates, etc)? What, if any, was their impact on your life?
6) Share tips you've discovered on how to have an effective quiet time, such as the devotional guide(s) you use, the places you go, the way you stay focused, etc. What are keys to being consistent in prayer and Bible study in our busy lives?

7) Several prayer models are mentioned in this chapter. Here's another one to consider, using the fingers on your hand. The **thumb** because it is nearest to the body is a reminder to pray for those near and dear, such as family and close friends. The **second, or pointer finger**, is for those who direct and manage and reminds us to pray for supervisors. The **third finger**, tallest of all, stands for those in high positions of leadership in government and church. The **fourth finger**, the weakest, is a reminder to pray for those who are suffering and weak. Finally, the **little finger**, last and smallest of all, is for ourselves. Thus with meekness, our needs are considered last. What are some other prayer models that you utilize?

8) What are ways you could grow in your prayer life, devotional time, Bible study, memorization of Scripture and worship? Which one of these could you begin today?

BETWEEN YOU AND YOUR SPOUSE:

1) How could you encourage one another to develop a consistent quiet time?

2) Write a letter to God expressing your needs, feelings and desires for your marriage. Let Him know what you want. Sit quietly and give Him the opportunity to show you how He can make an immeasurable difference in your life and in your home. Be transparently honest. Start your letter like this, "Dear God: When it comes to my marriage, my deepest desire is that_____."

    After developing this letter on your own, look for the right opportunity to share the contents with your spouse.

3) Spiritual intimacy may include (but not be limited to): praying together, working on a mission trip or service project, discussing the devotional readings you've shared throughout the week, memorizing Scripture together, etc. Identify areas where you could connect more frequently developing spiritual intimacy.

4) What ministry goals and plans do you have as a couple?

5) Specific goals we would like to undertake in our spiritual life during the next year are_____.

BETWEEN YOU AND GOD:

1) Do you currently have a quiet time? Why or why not? If you do, how much time are you spending reading and praying?

2) Is there anyone who could help motivate you to have a consistent quiet time? How will you invite him or her to do this?

3) How can you find the time necessary to grow in Christ?
4) In what ways and areas are you now growing spiritually?
5) Psalm 119 is God's commercial for the Bible. What do the following verses say about Scripture from Psalm 119? 5-6; 9-11; 23-24; 27-28; 36-37; 45-46; 61-63; 67-68; 92-93; 98-99.
6) Name the place and time you'll have your quiet time for the next four weeks.

EXTRA POINTS: Scripture memory is one of the best offensive weapons we have at our disposal. This next week, memorize at least one verse that will help you in your daily routine.

Chapter 9 • Sexual Temptations and Lust

We live in a society inundated with sex. Regularly we are told that sex outside of marriage is acceptable, expected and the primary sign of "true love." Our longings for love and our God-given passions push us toward physical expression of our feelings. For me, it is exciting to know that God created sex for us, but it was intended to be reserved solely for our mate within the context of marriage. We must guard ourselves and be answerable regarding our behaviors and attitudes in this area, which have separated so many from their relationship to God.

In God's Word, sexual contact prior to marriage is called "fornication" and sex beyond the bonds of marriage is called "adultery." Many feel that if you avoid these two areas, all is okay, but Scripture indicates that our sexual desires are not only with bodily actions, but with our minds and hearts.

If you are single, commit to dating relationships that will honor God and maintain purity. If you are married, pursue your spouse with the same desire and fervency you had during your courting days.

GROUP QUESTIONS:

1) What are your memories from your first date? If married, describe your first date with your spouse.
2) How does sexual purity honor God? How does sexual purity honor ourselves and our marriage, on our fiancee or dating partner?
3) Review the Scripture found on pages 108-109. Create a list of ways group members can encourage one another to sexual purity. Consider the following questions to spur on your list:
   a) What seems to be the key to sexual purity?
   b) How does the temptation process work?
   c) What are some of the principles God gives us regarding temptations and proper sexual conduct?

    d)   How does God view inappropriate sexual activities?

    e)   What are flirtatious or lustful attitudes? How are they expressed by people?

4)   This chapter points out many of the potential pitfalls related to sexual temptation, and on pages 117-118 we get some practical advice from someone who stumbled. What lessons can we learn from this chapter? Identify ways you can demonstrate integrity through your sexual conduct at home, in your workplace, social settings, etc.

5)   For those who are married, why are many couples ashamed or reluctant to discuss sex? How would your spouse respond if you were completely transparent regarding your sexual issues and desires?

6)   One night your 19-year old nephew calls you to get help in his personal life. He shares that he's being sexually tempted and wants some advice on how to "control his sex drive" so that he won't sin. After clearing your throat and wiping your brow, what would you say to him?

7)   What is the greatest example of love you've ever experienced? How did it make you feel?

BETWEEN YOU AND YOUR SPOUSE:

1)   How often do you verbalize your sexual desires and needs to your spouse? Do you know what sexually satisfies your spouse? Are you meeting his/her sexual needs?

2)   Many times the courting ends when the wedding begins. Do you and your spouse regularly go out on dates, including overnights away from home? Develop a plan for making dating your spouse a priority.

3)   As sex becomes more intimate, you begin to emphasize sharing and affirming each other's feelings. Each feels cherished and valued as important and meaningful. Disagreements about sex is mentioned as one of the top four problems couples bring to marriage counselors and "quantity of sex" is the most frequent complaint. Dr. David Ferguson encourages couples to: *Improve lovemaking quality and quantity resolves itself.* He advocates beginning acts of tenderness when you part in the morning, expressing your desire to be together that night, so that throughout the day you can both anticipate the pleasurable evening ahead. He talks about adding variety, varying your sexual routine, openly communicating, increasing your nonsexual touches and seeking to stimulate one another. How are you doing sexually with your spouse?

4)   Many spouses are not aware of the best way to demonstrate love to their mate (sex languages). It is important to understand what makes your partner feel loved and cared for. To help identify what you and your spouse enjoy, review the list below and note those that appeal to your mate and those that appeal to you. Rank the top five, pay careful attention to and respectfully consider each other's answers.

*Holding hands   *Going for a walk   *An unexpected hug   *Finding a love note
*A surprise date   *Being told "I love you"   *Helping with the kids   *Saying "thank you"
*Being approached sexually   *Taking a shower together   *Getting a back rub
*Being praised for achievements   *Receiving a surprise gift,   *Having dinner out
*Having a quiet conversation   *Being served a favorite meal
*Helping out around the house   *Receiving compliments on your looks

BETWEEN YOU AND GOD:

1) Read 1 Corinthians 6:12-20. This passage was written to the Corinthians, many of whom felt that what they did in the "flesh" wouldn't affect their spirit.
   a) What is meant by the phrase, "Everything is permissible...but not everything is beneficial"?
   b) Verse 18 instructs us to "flee from sexual immorality." Why did God choose the word "flee" as opposed to "walk away from" or "leave?"
   c) What excuses do you make for not following this guideline?
2) Too often, we view sexual temptation as a game. How far can I go with flirting and/or inappropriate sexual behavior and still be pure? Can I walk "on the line" and still not go "all the way?" How does honoring God and your future mate (if single) or your spouse (if married) give you a better game plan?
3) Which of the following pulls you down in maintaining sexual purity: movies, music, the internet, books or magazines and/or specific people? What changes do you need to make?
4) I could become sexually pure if I would _____.
5) The next special date I have planned is on _____ and it will include_____.

EXTRA POINTS: I urge you to develop some written standards to keep you on the straight and narrow pertaining to sexual conduct. Take time to document your standards and then share your commitments with a trusted friend to help hold you accountable.

Chapter 10 • Financial Dealings

It may surprise you to learn that the issue of money is the most discussed topic in Scripture. The way we handle money affects us spiritually, emotionally and physically. Contrary to popular belief, the Bible is relevant for today's economy and complex financial system. In His Word, God promises to provide all we need, and He does! The problems begin when we fail to manage the provision of resources carefully and we become lethargic to the principles God has designed for its use.

You can sum up God's principles into three truths: (1) God Owns All You Have - Psalm 24:1; Haggai 2:8; Deuteronomy 8:18. We are merely stewards. (2) God Controls All You Have - 1 Chronicles 29:11-12; Daniel 4:34-35. He is sovereign over all. (3) God Provides All You Need - Luke 12:30-31. He'll meet all your needs, not necessarily your wants.

Matthew 6:19-21 tells us, "Do not store up for yourselves treasures on earth, where moth and rust destroy, and where thieves break in and steal. But store up for yourselves treasures in heaven, where moth and rust do not destroy, and where thieves do not break in and steal. For where your treasure is, there your heart will be also." Finding balance in your pursuit of money and living a life of integrity with the money you possess as a steward can be challenging. Ask the Lord to give you wisdom and insight into this critical area.

GROUP QUESTIONS:

1) How would you describe your philosophy on money: a spender, a saver, a tightwad, frugal, generous, "just charge it," coupons only or _____(select one of your own)? Tell the group why you made this choice.

2) The way money is handled is such a personal matter, yet there are truths you can learn from others. Discuss the following issues and look for suggestions to improve your own understanding.
   a) How helpful is following a budget? What are ways to establish and follow a budget?
   b) How do you determine how much to give to your church, other ministries and those in need? How could you increase your giving?
   c) How could you save or invest money on a more consistent basis?
   d) Should you buy things now and make monthly payments or save the money first and pay cash? How do you handle credit card purchases and other debt?
   e) What are some of the plans you have made to establish a will or a trust? What is your philosophy and plan for retirement?
   f) How can you better establish a record keeping system?
   g) How do you steer clear of scams and "get rich" schemes?

3) Disagreements over financial decisions can be a major cause of marital discord. If married, have you ever made a significant financial decision without your spouse's approval? If so, what was the result?

4) Page 121 says, "If we are faithful in our stewardship, God makes certain promises to us including peace, provision and prosperity." Describe how you've seen this happen in your own life.

5) Pages 129-131 identifies "28 Money Saving Tips." Add at least ten additional ones with the help of the entire group.

BETWEEN YOU AND YOUR SPOUSE:

1) Here's a series of tough questions to consider for every marriage:
   a) How responsible is your partner about spending money?
   b) How much money can you spend without getting permission from your spouse?
   c) Do you have a specific plan for spending each month?
   d) Do one or both of you know how to budget? If so, are you following it?
   e) Are you satisfied with how much you are saving?
   f) Are there any unpaid debts that concern you?
   g) Are you worried that your income is insufficient?
   h) Do you have trouble deciding what is most important to spend money on?
   i) Do you usually agree on how to spend money?
   j) Who has the main responsibility for handling the money?
   k) Do you give or lend money or resources to others in need?
   l) Do you require your children to regularly give (money, toys, clothes, etc.)? Why or why not?
   m) If you questioned your extended family or neighbors would they describe you and your family as a "giver" or a "taker"?

2) What are your family's financial plans for eliminating credit card or personal debt? What about your plans for saving toward your children's college education? What's the next major household expenditure you've agreed on making?

3) What percentage of your income do you give to your church, other ministries and worthwhile causes? Are you in agreement with your spouse on these amounts and the organizations you are supporting?

4) What financial goals and dreams do you have? Are you on track with these goals?

5) If something suddenly happened to your spouse, how would you answer the following:
   a) Do you have life insurance? How much? With whom?
   b) What would you do about funeral arrangements? Have you established a will and trust?

c) Do you know if and where you (and your spouse) have savings accounts, bonds, stocks, property or other sources of income?
d) Do you know if and to whom you and your spouse owe money? This list could include: auto and house payments, personal loans, bank loans, credit cards, college loans, etc.

BETWEEN YOU AND GOD:

1) Does your income exceed your expenses? Do you feel you and/or your family are spending money appropriately? If not, how should you adjust your priorities?
2) Christians have as many problems with money issues as non-Christians. The following are five Scriptural truths concerning money (Proverbs 22:7; Proverbs 23:5; James 3:16; 1 Timothy 6:10; Malachi 3:10). What does each tell us? How can these verses help you get money problems under control?
3) What are your strong and weak points related to money use?
4) If you aren't above reproach in your financial dealings, why? What are some things you can do to correct the situation?
5) The percentage of my income that I currently give away is ____. I would like to give away ____. In order to do this, I'm going to _____.
6) The greatest financial challenge I'm currently facing is_____.

EXTRA POINTS: (1) Read a book on Christian financial principles; (2) Develop a financial statement, budget and a system to keep track of your plan; (3) Determine how you could become a generous ("hilarious") giver as described in 2 Corinthians 9:7.

Chapter 11 • Quality Relationships

Good communication is the most important part of every relationship. Studies have shown that 55% of communication is through body language, 35% through tone of voice, 2% is intuitive and only 8% through words. If body language, vocal tone and words don't match, proper communication cannot occur. Healthy relationships don't develop quickly, they take work and communication is at the core.

We must deliberately seek out relationships and nurture them. Cultivate the kind of togetherness the Bible calls fellowship (Acts 2:42 and 2 Corinthians 6:14). Friends and family are vitally important to our well-being because they are the ones with whom we travel through life. They are the ones who live, cry and rejoice with us, as well as encourage and teach us. Hebrews 10:25 says, "Let us not give up meeting together, as some are in the habit of doing, but let us encourage one another—and all the more as you see the day approaching."

Finally, are your relationships draining or replenishing? Draining friendships take more than they give. You may enjoy these people, but when they're gone, you're spent. On the flip side, replenishing friendships leave you feeling cheerful, energized and motivated. They strengthen and help equip you to face life. You do the same for them. You must balance relationships with at least as many "replenishers" as "drainers."

GROUP QUESTIONS:

1) What are your memories of your first "best" friend? What attracted you to him/her?
2) How would you define "quality" relationship time?
3) Relationships have to be intentional...rarely do they happen without spending time together. Develop a creative list of ways by which you could initiate and improve friendships. If you're married, what are ways you could enhance your time with your spouse and children? Exchange "quality" time ideas.
4) Who helps you to be a better friend? How does he or she do this? What qualities does God want you to seek in friends?
5) What does it mean to have "replenishing" or "draining" friendships? Without naming specific people, discuss this concept with your group.
6) John 15:12-13 reminds us to lay down our lives for our friends. Give examples of ways you have laid down your life for a friend, then examples of ways friends have done the same for you.
7) Describe how your relationship with your family has changed since you moved away from home (assuming that you have done so). How are you doing in your relationships with your parents, siblings and other relatives?
8) We've discussed a number of important relationships during this chapter. Which ones do you feel you need to strengthen? Why did you choose these and what are ways you can deepen it?

BETWEEN YOU AND YOUR SPOUSE:

1) Emotional intimacy with your spouse develops as you share lifelong dreams, express your deepest emotions, enjoy common interests, pursue one another, pray together, etc. What dreams do you have for your marriage and family life? How are you doing in developing emotional intimacy with one another?
2) Have you ever told your mate that you're committed to him/her no matter what the differences are or what happens? Have you assured your spouse that you'll never forsake him or her? If not, why not do that now?

3)   Should you go out on more "dates" and/or "get-away weekends" together? How often? Where? When? List some of the topics you'd like to discuss on your next outing.

4)   Name ten couples whom you regularly spend time with and determine whether each relationship is draining or replenishing. With which married couple friends are you purposefully developing close relationships with? What are you doing to enhance each relationship?

5)   What character qualities are you now emphasizing as you "train up your children?" Refer to Appendix A if you need help.

6)   We've discussed a number of different relationships in this chapter. To which relationships do you and your family need to be most attentive? What could you do to strengthen them?

7)   As I think about the many relationships our family will have in the future, I hope we will be attentive to_____.

BETWEEN YOU AND GOD:

1)   Name a way you can keep the following relationships strong:
❏ Parents and siblings ❏ Spouse and children
❏ Pastor and other spiritual mentors ❏ Close friends
❏ Co-workers ❏ High school or college friends
❏ Relatives outside of immediate family ❏ Neighbors

2)   The book of Ruth tells about a family relationship that endured through hardships. The love and loyalty that led Ruth to stay with her mother-in-law can be a model for how we relate with our family. Read all four chapters of Ruth and answer the following questions:
a)   How did Ruth and Naomi become close?
b)   These two women were from different lands and families. When Naomi's son died, Naomi urged Ruth to return to her people and find another husband. Why did Ruth refuse?
c)   How did they survive in this new place? What is intriguing about their story? How did they demonstrate integrity and accountability to one another?
d)   Their story has a happy ending, but loyalty to friends and family is valuable even without a happy ending. When could this be true? Describe a relationship you are in that needs more loyalty. Name specific actions God wants you to take in order to demonstrate loyalty: _____.

3)   Name ten people with whom you spend time, and determine whether each relationship is draining or replenishing. How can you build replenishing relationships rather than draining ones? What is God telling you to do about it?

4)   In terms of people skills, what are your strong and weak areas?

5) Who are two of your most faithful friends? How have they supported you in the last year? How have you shown your appreciation to them?
6) When I consider my relationships, I know I need to_____.

EXTRA POINTS: From the following relationship actions, choose three that God is prompting you to develop over the next six months. What will you do to fulfill this commitment?

*Including new people in my friendship circle   *Considering others' feelings
*Balancing time with family, friends and myself   *Keeping in touch with family
*Strengthening my personal integrity   *Giving people more time
*Finding a way to serve other people   *Listening skills
*Showing friendship to those who need Christ   *Speaking encouraging words
*Communicating more through email, letters or phone calls

Chapter 12 • Our 100% Best

Minor league—it's a phrase that is synonymous with second-rate, unimportant, inconsequential. Yet in professional baseball, progressing through the minor league ranks is a necessary training process for the aspiring major-leaguer. It's where the young player demonstrates his abilities and hones his skills. To the public at large, the minors are only a warm-up to the "main event," but in reality they are the proving grounds of the sport. Mike Sweeney spent five years in the Kansas City Royals minor league system building his skills and abilities before becoming a major league star.

Almost every profession or trade has its "minor leagues". Many times the respected CEO starts out, not in the boardroom, but in the mailroom. Every famous architect began somewhere as a draftsman, and every renowned surgeon pulled down the grueling hours of a medical residency. Every master plumber or carpenter began as a lowly apprentice, and every plant foreman began by pushing a broom or working on the assembly line. Each step of achievement was executed with a 100% effort.

For the Christian, our training ground is learning to fully utilize our time, talent and treasure to glorify God. Christ's ultimate game plan is for us to receive responsibilities and rewards far greater than any earthly achievements. Eternal rewards are earned by faithfulness in the "small" areas of life. Do we make ethical deals? Do we borrow company equipment or supplies? Do we cut corners to get ahead? Are we always on the lookout for a loophole, for the opportunity to help ourselves, even if it costs our employer? No matter how successful we may appear, we'll never make it out of the spiritual minor leagues without integrity.[4]

GROUP QUESTIONS:

1) What's been the hardest job you've ever had? What made it so difficult?

2) Is it possible to always give 100%? Why or why not? Tell the group about a time when you gave your 100% best (a project, a game, a relationship, a conversation, etc.).

3) Playing to an audience of One is a powerful concept as noted in Colossians 3:17, 23-24. Practically, how can you strive to do this day in and day out?

4) Read 1 Thessalonians 4:11-12. Many people equate ambition with self-seeking and wealth-gaining. But true ambition goes much deeper. Define true ambition. How does that differ from the world's definition? Describe a time you "won the respect of outsiders" through something you did?

5) How can Christians demonstrate their commitment to live a life of excellence that is above the ordinary? How would commitment to excellence impact a non-believer? Give examples.

6) How do you distinguish between the important and urgent needs that come up daily? What are some of the keys to getting a handle on your day and balancing your responsibilities and needs?

7) Can you say "no" when you begin to feel over-extended? How can you help others who struggle with saying "no"? How does God help you manage your time rather than add more pressure to it?

8) If you are in a classroom environment, share ideas for finding prime time to study, complete group or individual projects, and write papers.

BETWEEN YOU AND YOUR SPOUSE:

1) Are you giving a 100% effort in your marriage? Are you meeting his/her needs?

2) How does it feel when you meet your mate's needs? How does it feel to "receive" from your spouse? Give a specific example of when you met each other's needs.

3) Amos 3:3 poses the question, "Can two walk together, unless they are agreed?" Agreeing on where you're headed is essential to oneness in relationships. You can start with a simple agreement that neither one makes a time commitment involving the other without first discussing and agreeing on the matter. Setting goals are also crucial for unity and it can involve family nights, household planning sessions, vacation ideas, etc. Without established goals, confusion, contradiction and conflict will result. Take time to reflect on the benefits of goal setting in your home and answer the following questions:

a)   I remember how important it was to me when my spouse and I came to a mutual understanding and agreement concerning _____

b)   One area I hope we can come to a supportive agreement on is ___

c)   One way we can eliminate confusion and misunderstanding is by _____

d)   I often go overboard in giving too much attention or concern to (for example: job, kids, finances, hobbies, shopping, etc.) _____ .

e)   I would like to consistently place a higher priority on _____ .

f)   When I/we finish an important project or goal, I feel _____ .

4)   In what ways do you encourage and support your mate in his or her career/domestic responsibilities? How could you improve? What are ways you could become a cheerleader for your spouse?

5)   What can you and your spouse do to continue developing your vocational growth and goals, such as reading, seminars, projects and so forth?

6)   What are some specific things you would like to accomplish this year in your vocation/domestic responsibilities?

7)   Do you make good use of time around the house? For example, do you watch too much television? Should you read more or spend more time on hobbies or just relaxing?

BETWEEN YOU AND GOD:

1)   Review Colossians 3:17, 23-24 and the comments on page 147. Think about the different actions and routines that fill your day. How could you perform each of these tasks in the name of the Lord? How could you show God's goodness and demonstrate integrity in each action?

2)   Related to your work habits, what % effort (0-100) would your employer and co-workers grade you? Do you work too much? What work changes does God want you to make in your life?

3)   Name obstacles that keep you from doing your best? How will you overcome these obstacles?

4)   List your current commitments and the time each takes. Do changes need to be made? Map out the changes you will make.

5)   What plans do you have for personal development through education, self study or career enhancement?

6)   When I consider my work and/or school, I know I need to _____ .

EXTRA POINTS: For the next week on your job, imagine that your boss is Jesus Christ. At the end of the week, answer this question: How did your attitude regarding work change?

Chapter 13 • Half-Truths and Outright Lies

Every relationship has its share of hurtful words, lies, misunderstandings, dashed expectations and unmet needs. If these problems aren't properly resolved, they will develop into bitterness and resentment. The only way to keep your emotional cup from emptying is to regularly seek forgiveness, confessing your inappropriate words and actions.

Speaking the truth "in love" can be challenging. You may have a tendency to hide your feelings, to pretend that nothing is wrong, while you silently brood over perceived or actual offenses. Then when you've hit the last straw, you explode like a grenade. The other extreme is to tell the truth but not do so in love. There may be nuggets of accuracy in the attacks you dish out, but if the truth is hurled like a weapon, it deeply wounds. Neither of these extremes breeds closeness.

If you tend to speak without love, to gossip, to exaggerate, to lie or to move your lips without first choosing your words carefully, consider the following suggestions:
  * Think before you speak–just because you think something, you
  don't have to say it! (Psalm 141:3; James 1:19, 26)
  * Take wrong and inaccurate thoughts "captive" before God.
  Instead of blurting them out to others, confessing them to God
  helps get them out of your system and gives time to remind you
  of the truth. (Colossians 3:8-17; Proverbs 21:23)
  * Replace these thoughts with new ones which more accurately
  represent the situation. (Proverbs 12:17-19; Philippians 4:8)
  * Choose to speak edifying, accurate words that are soaked in love.
  (Ephesians 4:29; Colossians 4:6)

GROUP QUESTIONS:

1) Have you ever been caught in a lie which spiraled out of control and eventually crashed? What ultimately occurred, and what did you learn from this incident?
2) How do you handle "gossip" that comes your way? What are keys to killing gossip?
3) What does it mean to speak the truth in love?
4) Occasional misunderstandings, irritations and impatient words are inevitable in relationships. The critical issue is healing the hurts through genuine apologies and forgiveness.

a) What are some keys to bringing timely reconciliation when hurts have occurred? What happens when this doesn't occur? Give examples of when you have seen forgiveness work.

b) Pride and self-righteousness often get in the way of our asking for forgiveness. Yet forgiveness brings such healing to relationships. What are Jesus' instructions in Matthew 5:23-24 about healing relationships? What is our responsibility in forgiving others? According to Ephesians 4:32 and Colossians 3:12-13, what is our basis for forgiveness? What kind of heart attitude are we to have?

c) If someone has wounded you and doesn't ask for forgiveness, what should be your response? What does Luke 6:35-37 say you are to do? What does God promise to those who obey this verse? To whom does God show kindness?

d) The word for pardon or forgive can also be translated "release" or "set at liberty." Someone has said, "Forgiveness is setting a prisoner free and finding out that prisoner was me." Give an example of an instance when that was true in your life.

5) Define humility. Is it possible to be humble in today's society? Why or why not? How can we live out "real" humility?

6) Why is being a person of integrity one of the first of many qualities you need in yourself and in friendships? Why should you care about integrity and character?

BETWEEN YOU AND YOUR SPOUSE:

1) Look at the above Group Question #4 pertaining to forgiveness. Is there anything you need to ask your mate to forgive? Make a list of the ways you know you've offended or hurt your spouse through words or actions. Then get alone and ask for forgiveness.

2) Privately discuss areas within your marriage where you are demonstrating integrity. How often do you affirm your marriage partner with positive comments, pertaining to integrity issues? After you've identified several, brag on each other in front of your children, other relatives and friends.

3) How do you communicate respect and admiration to your spouse, specifically related to leadership and decision making?

4) If you have noticed evidence of unhealthy thinking patterns or negative feelings or behaviors in your spouse lately, what personal need(s) may have gone unmet? Verbalize these needs to one another.

5) One of the greatest ways we can meet our partner's needs is to fully appreciate him/her. Appreciation is best understood as a process of discovering and expressing your gratefulness for another person in

terms of what they do and for who they are. Appreciation can be expressed privately as well as publicly. It can be expressed verbally, in writing, or in other creative ways. Tell your spouse some of the reasons you were originally attracted to them. What are some of the areas you've learned to appreciate since you got married?

BETWEEN YOU AND GOD:

1) Secrecy is an enemy of integrity. We may assume if no one knows our sin, there's no problem. After all, a little wrongdoing won't matter and if it does, we can always get forgiveness, right? King David found himself allowing one compromise after another to entrap him in a terrible predicament in 2 Samuel 11, which ultimately led to a major confrontation with Nathan in the next chapter. Read these two chapters and answer these questions:
    a) What level of integrity did David display and why?
    b) What was David's first sin? How could he have stopped there? What were his other sins? How could he have drawn the line after each one before going further?
    c) How did David respond to Uriah's integrity?
    d) How did David pull Joab into the deceptive pattern?
    e) How did David try to cover up his sin? What made David think he could get away with these sins?
    f) What can you learn from Nathan's confrontation with David?
2) How do you convince yourself that you cannot be caught in sin? How do you rationalize it in your mind?
3) Do you lie and exaggerate to others and self? Do you participate in or stop gossip? Do you try to be humble? How will you become clean in each of these areas?
4) Often it is the small actions that catch people's attention rather than the large events. What can you do to build a reputation marked by integrity?
5) I have not taken responsibility for asking forgiveness for hurting _____ because _____. I'm going to confess this now and make it right by doing the following:_____
    _____.
6) In considering the biblical admonition concerning an "unbridled tongue" (James 1:26), I realize I need to_____
    _____.
7) I hurt_____recently with my words when I said, "_____." Now I realize what I should have said was,"_____
    _____."

EXTRA POINTS: Identify at least one person whom you have hurt and where reconciliation is sorely needed. Seek to do whatever is necessary to correct this situation.

Chapter 14 · Sharing The Gospel

H ere's the story of Eric and Jean Homer. Like others who had moved into our neighborhood, we greeted them with friendly waves and a "welcome" cookie plate. We initiated contact and prayed about an opportunity to share our Christian faith with them. One day, Janna engaged in a spiritual conversation with Jean, and it appeared they might have interest in going to church with us.

A number of times we asked them to church or to some church function, yet months went by without them coming. But progress seemed to be taking place through numerous conversations. Eventually they accepted an invitation by a friend to attend another church in our community. Within a few weeks the Homers decided to follow Jesus Christ. We were thrilled with their decision and much to our surprise, we learned later that our efforts to reach them had not been in vain. They described their spiritual journey at a church service and mentioned that our family had played an important part in their faith commitment. God has done a wonderful work in their life and we have a dear friendship with them.

You never know what seeds you are planting in the lives of people. Just pray faithfully and ask God to give you natural opportunities to tell people about Jesus Christ.

GROUP QUESTIONS:

1) Rebecca Manley Pippert in *"Out of the Salt Shaker"* said: "Christians and non-Christians have something in common: we're both uptight about evangelism." Why is this true for non-Christians? Why is this true for Christians?

2) You've heard the phrase: "You're the only Jesus some people may ever see." We certainly aren't perfect, but when we obey Christ, people notice. Many will be attracted to Him by observing our actions and words. But many more are repelled when they see us living hypocritical lives. What are some of the keys to leading a life which will be attractive to non-believers?

3) Jesus Christ made it a point of initiating contact with non-believers, such as Zacchaeus, the woman at the well, prostitutes, tax collectors, etc. We should not spend our life exclusively with Christians, as we need to also have pre-Christian friends. Why is this important? How can you strike a balance between the two, yet maintain Christlike character?

4) Transmitting God's love means being willing to tell our story. Consider the blind man in John 9. When questioned by the authorities as to what had happened to him, he did not know all the answers, but the one thing he did know was revealed in verse 25: "I was blind but now I see." Like the blind man, we don't have to know all the answers, but we do need to prepare. Working on verbalizing our testimony is important. We should always be ready to tell what God has done for us!

    a) How do you respond when you don't know answers to specific questions?

    b) How often do you get the opportunity to talk about your faith with others?

    c) What are ways to initiate conversations with non-believers about your relationship with Christ?

    d) If someone approached you and asked how they could become a Christian, are you prepared? What would you say?

5) What are the basic points of the Gospel? What does it mean to "witness"? To "evangelize"? To "make disciples?"

6) What is your role in bringing someone to Christ? Does the admonition: "We are not responsible for what results when we tell others about our faith," take some of the pressure off?

7) Tell about a time when you gave someone your testimony. How did the opportunity develop? How did you feel at the time? What did you learn from the experience?

8) What are some of the Christian terms that you should avoid when talking to a non-believer? Why would this be important?

9) Describe the background and events surrounding how you came to a personal relationship with Christ. If this is something you're still pondering, tell where you are in this journey.

BETWEEN YOU AND YOUR SPOUSE:

1) What ideas do you have for serving Christ together as a couple?

2) What special talents, gifts, training or life experiences do you see in your spouse that could be a blessing to others?

3) As a couple, who are some of the non-Christians with whom you have an opportunity to influence spiritually and discuss Jesus Christ? What are you currently doing to make a difference in their lives?

4) How might your home become a place of ministry to other couples, families, children or teenagers?

5) How knowledgeable are you in discussing other religions and/or cults? If someone knocked on your door to tell you about their faith, would you be prepared to respond? What would you say?

6) Practice relating your testimony with one another using the guidelines established on pages 172-173.

BETWEEN YOU AND GOD:

1) What dreams do you have for serving God?
2) Review the following verses–Matthew 28:18-20; 1 Timothy 2:1-7; 1 Timothy 4:1-16; Romans 15:1-6. What guidelines and principles for Christian service do you find in these verses?
3) Do you know the specific steps involved in leading someone to Christ? It should include: recognition of the need for Christ, turning away from sin, accepting Christ's forgiveness for your sin, and embracing Jesus Christ as Savior and Lord. Look up verses to support each of these points (For example, "The Four Spiritual Laws" or the "More Than Winning" tract).
4) There are many times when believers attend a Bible study or Sunday school class and give all the right answers, and then go out into the real world and struggle with living out their faith. How could you benefit from "real" discussion with other Christians in Bible study, home groups, worship, etc. and really live it out when you leave a Christian setting?
5) Identify several non-Christian friends that you spend time with on a regular basis. I'm going to begin to pray about sharing my faith with

_____.

6) Write out your personal testimony. Practice by telling it to a friend.

EXTRA POINTS: Between now and the next session, commit to praying the following prayer each morning: "Lord, lead me to someone who needs to hear about Jesus, and please give me the courage and sensitivity to tell them about You through Your power." Start off the next session by telling what God did in answering this prayer.

Chapter 15 • Exercising, Eating and Sleeping

s a young boy, I had aspirations of becoming a professional athlete but I didn't make it because I wasn't gifted with breakaway speed and jumping ability. However, I gained an edge over my competition by maintaining certain disciplines, such as not drinking, smoking and doing drugs. On the field, I pushed my body to the limits during grueling workouts. Off the field, I ate the right foods and got plenty of rest.

Though my dreams of becoming a pro athlete never came to fruition, I was able to play college football. I believe God honored my efforts and

I'm thankful He gave me the abilities and strength to compete. Not only did these disciplines help me on the field, but it's also a mindset I've carried on beyond athletics. In fact, 1 Timothy 4:7-8 says, "...train yourself to be godly. For physical training is of some value, but godliness has value for all things, holding promise for both the present life and the life to come."

Today, my body doesn't respond as quickly as it did when I was a teenager and a young adult, but I'm still striving to make sure that my body gets the proper attention it needs. After all, it's the only body I'll have on this earth until I get a new one in heaven.

GROUP QUESTIONS:

1) When have you been in the best physical shape? How did you reach this point?

2) What physical discipline is the toughest for you: exercising, getting adequate rest, eating properly or _____ (fill in your own answer)? Why?

3) What does it mean to "honor the Lord with your body" (1 Corinthians 6:19-20)?

4) Describe your current exercise/workout routine compared to your workout goals. How can you incorporate more exercise into your daily life?

5) Do you get enough sleep? Why or why not? If so, what are some of the obstacles you face in getting enough rest?

6) What are some challenges you face in managing what you eat? How could you improve your eating habits?

7) On pages 181-182, there are seven practical suggestions to help you in improving your "battle of the body." With the help of your group, what are additional tips you could add to this list. What are the benefits of regular exercise, proper eating and sleeping habits (physical, spiritual, mental, etc.)?

8) Discuss the principles noted on pages 182-183 related to alcohol, smoking and illegal drugs. Do you agree or disagree with the points made? Why?

9) One of the keys to living a consistent Christian walk is to have "vision" as described by Harold Reynolds. What are your keys for living out your "vision"?

BETWEEN YOU AND YOUR SPOUSE:

1) Should you improve your eating habits, with more nutritional foods, fewer sweets and healthier meals together at home? If so, what can you do to make this happen?

2) What are your goals related to physical health? How could we spur on one another to establish a more consistent exercise time?

3) What is a fitness level and/or ideal weight that you would like to maintain? How can you accomplish this?

4) Are you more of a late night or an early morning person? What could be done to help each other get more rest individually?

5) From Page 179, calculate your maximum heart rate for one another.

6) How often do you compliment your mate related to physical appearance? Is this frequent enough?

BETWEEN YOU AND GOD:

1) What improvements in your physical fitness or appearance would you like to make?

2) How are you doing with sleeping, exercising and eating? If you are not pleased with your current situation, what do you plan to do about it? Fill in the blanks below if you are struggling in meeting your personal goals and objectives in each of these areas:

   a) I don't get enough sleep because _____. What I need to do to get more sleep is_____
   _____.

   b) I don't exercise enough because _____. What I need to do to exercise more is to _____
   _____.

   c) Related to eating, I destroy my body by regularly_____.
   What I need to do is_____.

3) If you drink alcoholic beverages, smoke or take illegal drugs list your reasons for doing so. Then list what you gain from these practices. If you don't do any of these things, ask these questions to someone who does.

4) When it comes to caring for my body, I do these things well: _____. I do not do these things well:
   _____.

5) If the Lord spoke to you in a vision tonight about your circumstances and what He has in mind for you, what would He probably say? Why?

EXTRA POINTS: Establish an action plan for getting on top of your exercise, eating and sleeping patterns. Write down your goals and tell them to someone who would be willing to help you.

Chapter 16 • Joy and Happiness

ho's the most joyful person you know? One of the people who immediately comes to my mind is Tanya Crevier. Tanya is known as the World's Greatest Female Basketball Handler.

Her ability to spin up to eleven balls simultaneously and do all kinds of tricks with basketballs is remarkable. Her performances around the country have caught the attention of fans and players, including Michael Jordan.

When you first meet Tanya you are struck with the joy that pours from every fiber of her body. And it isn't fake, it's genuine and contagious. Tanya has the "joy of the Lord" in her life. Certainly she faces moments of unhappiness, but because of her faith in Jesus Christ, she "counts it all joy" in all she does.

Shouldn't every believer in Christ have the same joy that Tanya exhibits? Why are so many Christians sulking through life, allowing their circumstances to rob them of their joy? Today, renew your commitment to pursue joy no matter what obstacles or opportunities come your way.

GROUP QUESTIONS:

1) Identify several people whom you would describe as "joyful." What causes them to be that way?

2) Discuss the differences between joy and happiness. Is it possible to have joy and not be happy?

3) How do you react to this statement: "Joy and bitterness are choices, not simply emotions." Why do you react this way?

4) Satan will try to capitalize on every negative circumstance in your life to bring you down–to steal your joy. We must be forewarned and forearmed. What are some of the keys to keeping a positive attitude in the midst of difficult situations?

5) Being a person who pursues truth is one of the greatest antidotes for joy because you don't live a double life, full of secrets. Abiding in truth reveals God's power. Describe a time you were truthful or you acted on truth, and joy followed. Why does this show God's power? What else does it show about God?

6) When have you allowed your joy to be robbed by choosing to believe a lie or not fully trusting God? What will you do in the future when you encounter these types of situations?

7) Living for Christ is the most dynamic, exciting and fulfilling journey you'll ever experience. How could you explain Christian joy to a non-believer?

BETWEEN YOU AND YOUR SPOUSE:

1) Have you experienced any of the following emotions recently? Doubt (John 10:26-29); Worry (Philippians 4:6-9); Anger (Ephesians 4:26-27); Fear (Matthew 10:24-31); Frustration (John 14:26-27); Foolishness (Ephesians 5:15-17); Guilt (Psalm 103:8-13); Heartache (Psalm 13). If so, discuss them and look at the corresponding Scriptures.

2)   What person in your family seems best able to cope with trouble and hardship? What is his/her secret?

3)   How often do you argue or fight with your spouse? Are your arguments or fights controlled or out of control? Do you have pre-established rules for managing your disagreements? Consider how a set of rules would help reduce tension in your relationship.

4)   Have you witnessed the effects of divorce on yourself, family or with friends? How would you feel if you were suddenly divorced? Who would be affected and how? Pray today for God's strength and wisdom to deal with any issues that threaten your marriage.

5)   How often do you tell your spouse, "I love you"? What could you do make this a habit?

BETWEEN YOU AND GOD:

1)   What does Psalm 119:1-8 tell us about experiencing joy?

2)   Would you describe yourself as "joyful?" Why or why not?

3)   What are a few of the joy robbers that you currently face? What could you ask Jesus to help you do to overcome it? Where do you go when life gets too heavy for you? Why?

4)   Do you struggle with a spirit of anger or bitterness? If so, why?

5)   If you were going to choose four other people to help you in a tough situation, whom would you choose? Why?

6)   What is the worst suffering you've ever experienced? What has God taught you through suffering?

7)   When I consider my joy, I need to_____.

EXTRA POINTS: Spend time with a joyful person (phone or face to face). Candidly ask them to tell you the secret to their attitude.

Chapter 17 • Wrapping It Up

While there is so much to celebrate in society, there also are many disturbing trends to worry us. You know the list: crime, breakdown of the family, leaders we can't trust, a general loss of faith in "the system," poverty, racism, drugs, and so forth. As a society we have lost our way. People are confused and frustrated. Actually, these trends are simply the consequences of sin that lies deep within each of us. It is the cumulative effect of the gradual erosion of values that has left us without a moral rudder. In general, people have been losing their moral and spiritual roots for a long time, and the result is that our souls are in pain. It's time not only to take stock, but to recommit ourselves to what is right and helpful, and then finish strong.

Are you prepared to do what it takes to be a strong finisher? Is your legacy in shape? What are you leaving behind for those who follow you?

Like it or not, you will leave something behind. Unfortunately, sometimes what we leave is an inheritance that contributes to the evaporation of goodness. Character building isn't something that can be inherited or ignored. It's not done whenever it's convenient or by pretending. Character is the reflection of the whole person and is lived out consistently. Like a cyclist who automatically leans in the right direction to maintain balance, the person of good character knows intuitively how to speak the truth, care for others and live a life that exemplifies the love of Christ.

The message is simple. Be candid in who you are when opening your life to others. If you do, future generations will know who you really were, and what virtues were central to your life.[5]

GROUP QUESTIONS:

1) What's the closest you've ever come to death? What happened? How did you survive?
2) If you died today, what would people say that you had contributed to society? What would you like carved on your tombstone?
3) Would you describe yourself as a "good finisher?" Why or why not?
4) From all you've discussed in the previous sixteen chapters, discuss the pros and cons of accountability.
5) Has anyone gone through the process of developing a personal or family mission statement? If so, describe how you did it, the amount of time you invested in the process and the results. If not, what would motivate you to develop a mission statement?
6) What are the most important lessons you've learned from this study? What do you plan on doing from this point on?

BETWEEN YOU AND YOUR SPOUSE:

1) Interview some long-lasting married people from your family or church. What are some of the secrets that have made their marriages prosperous? What can you learn from their advice? What do you believe are the keys to a happy marriage?
2) List the projects you would like you and/or your mate to start or finish in the next few months. After you've discussed them, hang them on your refrigerator as a reminder to each of you.
3) What special insights or new sensitivities have you developed toward God and your spouse during this study?
4) If you've never do so, take the time to develop a family mission statement.

BETWEEN YOU AND GOD:

1) As a result of this study, what changes have you noticed in your perception and understanding of yourself? If you are married and have children, what changes have you seen in your spouse and children? Be specific.
2) How do you do at establishing goals? Do you put them in writing? How often do you compare your results to your goals?
3) What legacy do you want others to remember about you?
4) What types of customs, traditions and attitudes do you want to pass on to your children and grandchildren?
5) If you've never done so, take the time to develop a personal mission statement. If you have one, review it and make sure it is up-to-date.
6) When I consider finishing well, I need to_____
_____.

EXTRA POINTS: Develop your plan for starting or continuing an accountability group, putting together all you've discussed in this book.

Bible Study Guide Footnotes:
   [1] Adapted from unknown source on the internet.
   [2] Adapted from Don M. Aycock, *God's Man* (Grand Rapids, MI: Kregel Publications, 1998), p. 17-18.
   [3] Edward A. Elliott, *The Best of Andrew Murray on Prayer* (Uhrichsville, OH: Barbour Publishing, Inc., 1996), p. 8.
   [4] Adapted from Don M. Aycock, *God's Man*, p. 152.
   [5] Adapted from Richard G. Capen, Jr., *Finish Strong*, (Grand Rapids, MI: Zondervan Publishing, 1998), p. xxv and 49-52.

Other resources utilized not specifically footnoted:
Incompatibility: Grounds for a Great Marriage, Chuck and Barb Snyder (Sisters, OR: Questar Publishers, Inc., 1988).

Intimate Encounters, Dr. David and Teresa Ferguson and Dr. Chris and Holly Thurman (Nashville, TN: Thomas Nelson, Inc., 1994).

Transparent Living: Living a Life of Integrity, Rod Handley (Nashville, TN: Lifeway Christian Resources, 1998).

With Thanks and Appreciation:
*Gordon Thiessen: As my publisher and friend, Gordon continues to have tremendous vision for the "character and accountability" materials.
*George Toles, Don Hilkemeier, Mike DeBacker, Laura Maxwell and my wife Janna: A marvelous group of editors, with keen insights and wisdom.

*Rick and Karen Bass, Mark and Angie Byler, Mike and Darla DeBacker, Mark and Heidi Fantauzzi, Roger and Sheryl Fender, Wade and Karen Jacobsma, Joe and Carla Krebs, Kent and Sue Kuss, Dale and Laura Maxwell, Mark and Patty McWilliams, Bruce and Sheri Rehmer and Tom and Mary Tischer: The twelve couples from our church who served a testing group for the study. The questions that they developed for their own marriages are noted below.

Sample Couple Questions:

1) Have we prayed together this week? as a couple? as a family?
2) Has there been romance in our relationship this week?
3) Has our snacking and soda intake been reasonable this week?
4) Have we spent daily individual time with the Lord? in the Word? in prayer?
5) Have we encouraged our children and each other this week? compliments?
6) Did we leave work on time today?
7) Did we spend time at home wisely?
8) Did we brighten someone's day?
9) Did we exercise three times this week?
10) Did we spend time with God this week, not counting Sunday?
11) What are you reading? What is your Secondary readings? (Read to kids; Psalms/Proverbs over breakfast; Book at night; When is our family reading night?)
12) Have you made a positive emotional deposit with our kids and to each other?
    *Did you get your 5 second kiss/hug today?
    *Did you give the kids a 5 second hug?
13) Have you eaten properly today and drank enough water?
14) Have we had ample "couch time" this week? (See Chapter 5 for explanation of "couch time.")
15) Have we made our schedule for this month's social events?
16) Have we made an effort to schedule an evening or time with friends (at least twice a month), especially with friends we've lost touch with or don't frequently see?
17) Have you scheduled one social event with a friend away from family this month?
18) Have you spent quality alone time socially with our children?
19) Have you "lost it" with your family this week?
20) Have you spent beyond your budget?
21) Have you attempted to feed your family in a nutritious manner on a daily basis (sit down meal with whole family)?

22) Has anything upset you in the last week that I should know about?
23) What are your expectations for this week?
24) Have we chosen to speak "wholesome words" and be a role model for our family, church and community?
25) What kind of "quality and quantity" time have we had together as a couple and with our children?
26) What is our top "issue or problem" for this month?
27) Are we purposefully filling our mind with the knowledge of God's word—knowledge we can give away to others?
28) What has God been saying to you this week?
29) Does your body belong to God, to be groomed, cared for disciplined for maximum usefulness and His glory (including water intake, sleep, exercise, nutrition, sex, manicure, facial, pedicure, floss, potassium)?
30) Are we nurturing love to others—thinking, speaking and acting toward them as Christ would? (spouse, children, friends, family).
31) Who are we going to have over this week? Write a note to? Make a phone call to?
32) Are we spending and accounting for the money God has given us as good stewards? Are we giving cheerfully to God's work?
33) Are we anxious about anything? How can I help you? Share a success or something that added to your joy this week.
34) Have you removed something from your procrastination list? What?
35) Did you do something this week that you wanted which was fun and made you laugh?
36) What do you have planned for the coming week?
37) When is our next date night?
38) What did you wish for that came true this week?
39) What surprised you this week?
40) Although it requires energy and creativity, have we taken advantage of every 'teachable moment' with our children?
41) Have we responded appropriately to people who have approached us with a need? (really listening for understanding, not just the 'sympathetic nod,' and not overlooking the opportunities to witness?"

APPENDIX A

ENCYCLOPEDIA OF CHARACTER QUALITIES

ACCOUNTABILITY: Being answerable to God and at least one other person for my behavior.

ALERTNESS: Being keenly aware of the events taking place around me so that I can have the right responses to them.

AMENDS (Repentance): Humbly acknowledging how you have fallen short of God's standard and seeking His forgiveness to make things right.

ATTENTIVENESS: Showing the worth of a person or task by giving my undivided concentration and effort.

AUTHENTICITY: Being exactly who you claim to be with honesty and transparency.

AVAILABILITY: Making my own schedule and priorities secondary to the wishes of those I serve.

BENEVOLENCE: Giving to others, basic needs without expectations of personal reward.

BOLDNESS: Demonstrating the confidence and courage that doing what is right will bring ultimate victory regardless of present opposition.

BONDING: Connecting with one another in an authentic way, avoiding unhealthy isolation.

BOUNDARIES: Creating a "safe place" or limitations that protect me from potentially unmanageable temptation.

BREADTH: Having depth and broadness, in words and deeds, within the heart and mind.

BROTHERLINESS: Exhibiting a kinship and disposition to render help because of a relationship.

CANDOR: Speaking the truth at the time when the truth should be spoken.

CAUTION: Knowing to be alert in a hazardous or dangerous situation.

CHEERFUL: Expressing encouragement, approval or congratulations at the proper time.

CHIVALRY: Protecting the weak, the suffering and the neglected by maintaining justice and rightness.

COMMITMENT: Devoting myself to following up on my words (promises, pledges or vows) with action.

COMPASSION: Investing whatever is necessary to heal the hurts of others by the willingness to bear their pain.

CONFIDENCE: Placing full trust and belief in the reliability of a person or thing.

CONSISTENCY: Following constantly the same principles, course or form in all circumstances; holding together.

CONTENTMENT: Accepting myself as God created me with my gifts, talents, abilities and opportunities.

COURAGE: Fulfilling my responsibilities and standing up for convictions in spite of being afraid.

CREATIVITY: Approaching a need, a task or an idea from a new perspective.

DECISIVENESS: Learning to finalize difficult decisions on the basis of what is right, not on what's popular or tempting.

DEFERENCE: Limiting my freedom to speak and act in order to not offend the tastes of others.

DEPENDABILITY: Fulfilling what I consented to do even if it means unexpected sacrifice.

DETERMINATION: Working intently to accomplish goals regardless of the opposition.

DILIGENCE: Visualizing each task as a special assignment and using all my energies to accomplish it.

DISCERNMENT: Seeking to use intuitive ability to judge situations and people; understanding why things happen to me and others.

DISCIPLINE: Receiving instruction and correction in a positive way; maintaining and enforcing proper conduct in accordance with the guidelines and rules.

DISCRETION: Recognizing and avoiding words, actions and attitudes which could result in undesirable consequences.

ENDURANCE: Exercising inward strength to withstand stress and do my best in managing what occurs in my life.

ENTHUSIASM: Expressing lively, absorbing interest in each task as I give it my best effort.

FAIRNESS (EQUITY): Looking at a decision from the viewpoint of each person involved.

FAITH: Developing an unshakable confidence in God and acting upon it.

FAITHFULNESS: Being thorough in the performance of my duties; being true to my words, promises and vows.

FEAR OF THE LORD: Having a sense of awe and respect for Almighty God which goes above and beyond anyone or anything else.

FIRMNESS: Exerting a tenacity of will with strength and resoluteness. A willingness to run counter to the traditions and fashions of the world.

FLEXIBILITY: Learning how to cheerfully change plans when unexpected conditions require it.

FORGIVENESS: Clearing the record of those who have wronged me and not holding their past offenses against them.

FRIENDSHIP: Coming alongside another person for mutual support and encouragement.

GENEROSITY: Realizing that all I have (time, talents and treasures) belongs to God and freely giving to benefit others.

GENTLENESS: Learning to respond to needs with kindness, personal care and love.

GLADNESS: Abounding in joy, jubilation and cheerfulness.

GOAL-ORIENTED: Achieving maximum results toward the area where my effort is directed.

GOODNESS: Having moral excellence and a virtuous lifestyle; a general quality of proper conduct.

GRATEFULNESS: Making known to others by my words and actions how they have benefited my life.

GREATNESS: Demonstrating an extraordinary capacity for achievement.

HOLINESS: Being whole with no blemish or stain.

HONESTY: Proclaiming the truth with sincerity and frankness in all situations.

HONOR: Respecting those in leadership because of the higher authorities they represent.

HOPE: Feeling that my deepest desire will be realized and that events will turn out for the best.

HOSPITALITY: Sharing cheerfully food, shelter and life with those with whom I come in contact.

HUMILITY: Seeing the contrast between what is perfect and my inability to achieve that perfection.

INDIGNATION: Channeling the driving passion of righteous anger without sinning.

INITIATIVE: Recognizing and doing what needs to be done before I am asked to do it.

INTEGRITY: Being whole and complete in moral and ethical principles.

JOYFULNESS: Choosing to be pleasant regardless of outside circumstances, which ultimately lifts the spirits of others.

JUSTICE: Taking personal responsibility to uphold what is pure, right and true.

KINDNESS: Demonstrating a gentle, sympathetic attitude towards others.

KNOWLEDGE: Becoming acquainted with facts, truths or principles through study and investigation.

LEADERSHIP: Guiding others toward a positive conclusion.

LOVE: Having a deep personal attachment and affection for another person.

LOYALTY: Using difficult times to demonstrate my commitment to others or to what is right.

MEEKNESS: Yielding my power, personal rights and expectations humbly with a desire to serve.

NARROWNESS: Staying within established boundaries and limits.

NURTURE: Caring for the physical, mental and spiritual needs of others.

OBEDIENCE: Fulfilling instructions so that the one I am serving will be fully satisfied and pleased.

OPTIMISM: Confident, hopeful and never doubtful.

ORDERLINESS: Learning to organize and care for personal possessions to achieve greater efficiency.

ORIGINALITY: Creating "new" thinking, ideas and expanding truths from an independent viewpoint.

PASSIONATE: Having an intense, powerful or compelling emotion and feelings towards others or something.

PATIENCE: Accepting difficult situations and without demanding a deadline to remove it.

PEACEFUL: Being at rest with myself and others.

PERSEVERANCE: A continuing effort to do or achieve something despite difficulties, failure and opposition.

PERSUASIVENESS: Guiding another's mental roadblocks by using words which cause the listener's spirit to confirm the spoken truth.

POISE: Being totally balanced in mind, body and spirit.

PRAYERFUL: Communing with God spiritually through adoration, confession, thanksgiving and supplication.

PROSPERITY: Flourishing or being successful, especially pertaining to financial issues.

PRUDENCE: Exhibiting caution, humbleness and wisdom in regards to practical matters.

PUNCTUALITY: Showing respect for other people by respectfully using the limited time they have.

PURE SPEECH: Speaking words that are clean, spotless and without blemish.

PURITY: Freeing yourself from anything that contaminates or adulterates.

PURPOSEFUL: Exercising determination to stay on track until the goal is achieved.

REASONABLENESS: Having a sound mind by being level headed, sane and demonstrating common sense.

RENEWAL: Restoration of strength through recovery and replenishment.

RESOURCEFULNESS: Using wisely that which others would normally overlook or discard.

RESTORATION: Getting a fresh start, or new beginning.

RESPECT: Honoring and esteeming another person due to deep admiration.

RESPONSIBILITY: Knowing and doing what is expected from me.

REVERENCE: Giving honor where it is due and respecting the possessions and property of others.

RIGHTEOUSNESS: Acting in a moral and upright way that honors God, regardless of who is watching.

SECURITY: Structuring my life around what is eternal and cannot be destroyed or taken away.

SELF-CONTROL: Bringing my thoughts, words, actions and attitudes into constant obedience in order to benefit others.

SENSITIVITY: Being aware and attentive to the true attitudes and emotional needs of those around me.

SERVANTHOOD: Caring for and meeting the needs of others before caring for self.

SINCERITY: Endeavoring to do what is right, without ulterior motives.

SURRENDER: Yielding to the authority, guidance and direction of God in my life.

STEWARDSHIP: Administering and managing personal and financial affairs effectively.

STRENGTH: Having power, force and vigor for the task assigned.

TEACHABILITY: Demonstrating a willingness to learn or be trained without any reservations or hindrances.

THANKFULNESS: Expressing deep gratitude and appreciation to people and to God.

THOROUGHNESS: Executing something perfectly with the realization that each of my tasks will be reviewed.

THOUGHTFULNESS: Showing consideration for others through acts of kindness and/or words.

THRIFTINESS: Preventing myself or others from spending money unnecessarily.

TOLERANCE: Learning to accept others as valuable individuals regardless of their maturity.

TRANSPARENCY: Allowing others to shine a light on my life for the purpose of being accountable.

TRUTHFULNESS: Earning future trust by accurately reporting past facts.

TRUST or TRUSTWORTHY: Believing completely and totally in someone or something.

UNDERSTANDING: Exhibiting strong intelligence and a sound mind in comprehending and discerning matters.
UNSTOPPABLE: The freedom to perform at your highest level without any restraints.
VIRTUE: Building personal moral standards which will cause others to desire a greater moral life.
VISIONARY: Dreaming not inhibited by the unknown. Looking beyond problems by creating successful solutions.
VULNERABILITY: Being open to receive constructive criticism and guidance.
WISDOM: Learning to see and respond correctly to life situations with keen judgment; the application of knowledge.
WORSHIP: Honoring God reverently.

Adapted from several sources including, *Institute in Basic Conflicts,* by Bruce Bickel; *Character First!* program and, *The Character of Jesus,* by Charles Edward Jefferson.

AUTHOR'S NOTE: The character definitions noted above have been illustrated in two different series of books, "Character Counts For Quiet Time & Small Groups, Volumes 1-3" and "Team Studies on Character, Volumes 1-7." Each volume features 16 different character quality teachings. For more information on how to order these books, contact Rod Handley or Cross Training Publishing.

Team Studies on Character Volume 1, 2, 3, 4, 5, 6 & 7

The purpose of this book is to identify character qualities that will make a winning difference in your life. Make it your plan to examine at least one character quality each week. The book is designed to interact with your teammates. If you are leading a group, create an environment where you can freely exchange thoughts and ideas. $6.99 retail (per book) with quantity discounts, 72 pages, 1-929478-65-8.

Character Counts for Quiet Time and Small Groups Volume 1,2,3

Each of these lessons includes biblical illustrations along with interactive questions and application exercises. An excellent book for either personal or group study. $6.99 retail (per book) with quantity discounts, 1-929478-27-5.

APPENDIX B

ACCOUNTABILITY COVENANTS

1. My commitment of **AFFIRMATION**
   - I will affirm and love you regardless of your past.
   - I will encourage you in your commitment to Christ.
2. My commitment to **AVAILABILITY**
   - My time and the resources God has given me are at your disposal.
3. My commitment to **REGULARITY**
   - I promise to attend our meetings whenever possible.
   - I consider our meeting one of the highest priorities on my schedule.
   - I promise to be prepared by reflecting on the week prior to meeting.
4. My commitment to **PRAYER**
   - I promise to pray for and uphold the group.
   - I promise to have a weekly prayer partner.
5. My commitment of **TRANSPARENCY**
   - I will be open with you to let you know who I am and what I believe and stand for.
6. My commitment to **HONESTY**
   - I will be honest on all my answers and comments.
7. My commitment of **CONFIDENTIALITY**
   - I will be trustworthy with the answers and comments shared in the group.
   - I will say nothing that may be traced back or that could bring injury or embarrassment to my accountability partners.
8. My commitment of **ACCOUNTABILITY**
   - You have a right to expect growth from me so that I may show you the fullness of the gifts which God has given me and fulfill my God created designs. You have my permission to ask me about the goals I set with God, family, work and community. I expect you to lovingly not "let me off the hook."
   - You have the right to share with me areas in my life that do not reflect Jesus Christ because I want to grow in personal holiness.

AUTHOR'S NOTE: This is a sample of the written covenant which our group established in August 1997. I would urge your group to develop a written covenant which is agreed upon by the members, spelling out the group's purpose and operating procedures. This will help clarify expectations, reinforce direction, monitor progress and evaluate the group experience. I was greatly encouraged by a group I met in St. Louis who felt so strongly about their written covenant that they also had the document notarized.

AN ANTI-GOSSIP PLEDGE

"A talebearer reveals secrets, but he who is faithful conceals a matter." Proverbs 11:13

In 1752, a group of Methodist men, including John Wesley, signed a pact that each man agreed to hang on his wall. The six articles of their pact were as follows:

- "Be it agreed that we will not listen or willingly inquire after ill concerning one another;
- That if we do hear any ill of each other, we will not believe it.
- That as soon as possible we will communicate what we hear of the other by speaking or writing to the person concerned;
- We further agree that, until we have done so, we will not write or speak a word of it to any other person;
- Neither will we, after having done our duty, make mention of the matter to any other person;
- And finally, that we make not exception to this pact unless we believe ourselves absolutely obliged for the common good, and then only after having conferred with those good men who place their names below."

Signed:

_____   _____

_____   _____

The CrossSeekers™ Covenant

"You will seek me and find me when you seek me with all your heart."
Jeremiah 29:13

As a seeker of the cross of Christ, I am called to break away from trite, nonchalant, laissez-faire Christian living. I accept the challenge to divine daring, to consecrated recklessness for Christ, to devout adventure in the face of ridiculing contemporaries. Created in the image of God and committed to excellence as a disciple of Jesus Christ,

I will be a person of integrity

"Do your best to present yourself to God as one approved, a workman who does not need to be ashamed and who correctly handles the word of truth." 2 Timothy 2:15

My attitudes and actions reveal my commitment to live the kind of life Christ modeled for me—to speak the truth in love, to stand firm in my convictions, to be honest and trustworthy.

I will pursue consistent spiritual growth

"So then, just as you received Christ Jesus as Lord, continue to live in him, rooted and built up in him, strengthened in the faith as you were taught, and overflowing with thankfulness." Colossians 2:6-7

The Christian life is a continuing journey, and I am committed to a consistent, personal relationship with Jesus Christ, to faithful study of His Word, and to regular corporate spiritual growth through the ministry of the New Testament church.

I will speak and live a relevant, authentic, and consistent witness

"Always be prepared to give an answer to everyone who asks you to give the reason for the hope that you have." 1 Peter 3:15

I will tell others the story of how Jesus changed my life, and I will seek to live a radically changed life each day. I will share the good news of Jesus Christ with courage and boldness.

I will seek opportunities to serve in Christ's name

"The Spirit of the Lord is on me, because he has anointed me to preach good news to the poor. He has sent me to proclaim freedom for the prisoners and recovery of sight for the blind, to release the oppressed, to proclaim the year of the Lord's favor." Luke 4:18-19

I believe that God desires to draw all people into a loving, redeeming relationship with Him. As His disciple, I will give myself to be His hands to reach others in ministry and missions.

I will honor my body as the temple of God, dedicated to a lifestyle of purity

"Do you not know that your body is a temple of the Holy Spirit, who is in you, whom you have received from God? You are not your own; you were bought at a price. Therefore honor God with your body." 1 Corinthians 6:19-20

Following the example of Christ, I will keep my body healthy and strong, avoiding temptations and destructive personal vices. I will honor the gift of life by keeping myself sexually pure and free from addictive drugs.

I will be godly in all things, Christlike in all relationships

"Therefore, as God's chosen people, holy and dearly loved, clothe yourselves with compassion, kindness, humility, gentleness and patience. Bear with each other and forgive whatever grievances you may have against one another. Forgive as the Lord forgave you. And over all these virtues put on love, which binds them all together in perfect unity." Colossians 3:12-14

In every relationship and in every situation, I will seek to live as Christ would. I will work to heal brokenness, to value each person as a child of God, to avoid petty quarrels and harsh words, to let go of bitterness and resentment that hinder genuine Christian love.

AUTHOR'S NOTE: National Student Ministries (NSM) adopted the above covenant to correspond with the national "CrossSeekers" event which was initially held in New Orleans during Labor Day 1998. To learn more about future events sponsored by NSM, please call 1-615-251-2783. This covenant is a marvelous example of how to develop a personal mission statement.

APPENDIX D

LORD'S PRAYER GUIDE

"Our Father who art in heaven, Hallowed be Thy name. Thy kingdom come. Thy will be done on earth as it is in heaven. Give us this day our daily bread. And forgive us our debts, as we also have forgiven our debtors. And do not lead us into temptation, but deliver us from evil. For thine is the kingdom, and the power, and the glory forever. Amen" (Matthew 6:9-13).

1. Preliminaries..."Holy Spirit, help me pray!" (Romans 8:26).
2. Enter His Presence..."Father" (Romans 8:15-16).
3. Seek His Face..."Hallowed be Thy (Your) Name" (Psalm 100).
   a. YHWH-tsidkenu: The Lord our righteousness (Jeremiah 23:6).
   b. YHWH-m'kaddesh: the Lord our sanctification(Exodus 31:13).
   c. YHWH-shammah: the Lord is present (Ezekiel 48:35).
   d. YHWH-rohi: the Lord my shepherd (Psalm 23).
   e. YHWH-jireh: the Lord provides (Genesis 22:14).
   f. YHWH-rophe: the Lord who heals (Exodus 15:26).
   g. YHWH-nissi: the Lord my banner (Exodus 17:15).
   h. YHWH-shalom: the Lord is peace (Judges 6:24).
4. Appropriate Intervention..."Thy Kingdom come...Thy Will be done" (Acts 12).
   a. In my life
   b. In my family
   c. In my church
   d. In my city/state/nation
   e. In my world
5. Appropriate Provision..."Give us this day our daily bread" (Psalm 144:1-15).
   a. Specific needs
   b. Sources of anxiety
   c. Kingdom prosperity
6. Appropriate Forgiveness..."forgive us our debts (sin)..." (Psalm 51).
   a. Confession
   b. Forgive offenses
7. Appropriate Protection..."Do not lead us...Deliver us..." (2 Kings 6:8-18).
   a. Armor of God (Ephesians 6).
   b. Presence of God (Psalm 91).
   c. Host of Heaven (Hebrews 1:14).

8. Reaffirm Truth
   a. "The Kingdom, the Power, the Glory!"
   b. Charge!!

AUTHOR'S NOTE: This prayer guide is modeled after the Lord's Prayer and breaks it down in a way where you can enter the presence of the Lord in a biblical progression. I became familiar with this model through the teachings of Bob Beltz and have found it to be a dynamite and practical way to pray. Reprinted (or adapted) from *Becoming a Man of Prayer*, @1996 by Bob Beltz. Used by permission of NavPress, Colorado Springs, Colorado. All rights reserved. For copies call (800) 366-7788.

APPENDIX E

BUSINESS BIBLICAL PRINCIPLES

1. God owns it all. God has a plan for your business. Leviticus 25:23; 1 Samuel 25:1-39; Psalm 24:1-2; Proverbs 8:10-11; Ecclesiastes 5:10-20.
2. God wants you accountable to others: spouse, church, government, peers. Proverbs 27:1-21; Ecclesiastes 4:7-12; Matthew 22:15-21; Romans 13:1-7; Ephesians 3:10-11; Ephesians 5:22-33.
3. God makes servants out of leaders and leaders out of servants. Exodus 3:11; Exodus 18:13-26; 1 Kings 3:5-14; Matthew 18:1-4; Matthew 20:20-28; John 13:1-13.
4. God wants you to be a good steward. Giving to others is part of His plan. Leviticus 19:9-10; Leviticus 25:35-37; Malachi 3:8-12; Luke 19:11-27; Luke 16:9-13; Luke 12:32-34.
5. God wants you out of debt. You can only have one master. Deuteronomy 15:1-6; Proverbs 22:7; Matthew 18:23-35.
6. God wants you to plan. God reveals your heart and His will when you do. Genesis 41:14-40; Proverbs 6:6-8; Luke 14:28-32.
7. God has a mission higher than profits for your business. Ecclesiastes 5:10-20; Luke 12:16-21; Luke 12:22-31.
8. God has a standard for excellence. What is his standard for you? Leviticus 23:3; Ecclesiastes 2:17-26; Ecclesiastes 3:9-12; Luke 10:38-42.
9. God wants you to make restitution. Exodus 22:1-15; Matthew 5:23-24; Luke 8:17; Luke 19:1-10.
10. God has called your business to an ethical standard higher than the market. Leviticus 35-36; Matthew 5:14-16; Matthew 5:25-26.

Integrity Resource Center has designed a 10-week Bible study which corresponds to each of these principles.

AUTHOR'S NOTE: This information was made available by Rick Boxx with Integrity Resource Center: PO Box 25301; Overland Park, KS 66225-5301. Phone: 913-782-9333 or 1-800-355-6071. Integrity Resource Center serves businesses, churches and nonprofits. They promote, practice and teach God's commands and Biblical principles to business leaders. They are a central connection for ministries and businesses throughout the world who are seeking Biblical counsel and resources. For more information contact: www.integrityMoments.com

APPENDIX F

WEEKLY TUNE-UP REPORT

Name: For the Weeks:

Prayer Requests/Personal Needs are:

Rate the following areas on a scale of 1 to 10:
    Spiritually _____Physically _____Emotionally _____

Past week's accomplishments were:
    1.
    2.
    3.
I need help/assistance/direction with:
    1.
    2.
    3.
My priorities for the next two weeks are:
    1.
    2.
    3.
The top priorities I will accomplish this month are:
    1.
    2.
    3.

Do you anticipate having any spare time this week?

If yes, what guidance/direction would you want from me?

Other concerns and issues:

Author's Note: This form has been adapted and utilized by FCA staff to provide an open forum for accountability. It was initially developed by Jeff Kern, Great Commission Ministries, in its staff training manual.

APPENDIX G

ROD HANDLEY'S PERSONAL MISSION STATEMENT

LOVE GOD WITH ALL MY HEART, SOUL, MIND & STRENGTH (Mark 12:30).

1. By maintaining my walk with God through spending time in prayer and reading His Word on a regular, daily basis.
2. By keeping my body physically fit through diet, exercise and involvement in high activity sports and proper sleeping habits.
3. By living out purity, integrity and honesty in my thoughts, deeds and actions.
4. By being accountable to other Christian men in regards to the welfare and balance of my life spiritually, emotionally, physically and financially.
5. By continuing in the ministry on a full-time basis, keeping that as my primary occupation while keeping all other areas of my life in proper priority.
6. By giving the "first fruits" of everything which comes in to God and His work.
7. By taking time on a regular basis to relax, refresh and renew.

LOVE MY NEIGHBOR AS MYSELF (Mark 12:31).

1. By maintaining a growing, vibrant relationship with my wife through regular "dates" and high priority time through strong communication.
2. By being a godly father to my kids. Consistently facilitating, training, bonding and providing fun times as a planned priority.
3. By providing completely for my family financially, even post-death, through short and long-term investments and savings.
4. By maintaining a growing relationship with my extended family.
5. By being involved with and ministering to a growing, loving community of friends through work, church, neighborhood and other common interests.
6. By ministering to people, letting them be a part of the rewards and challenges of financially supporting the Character That Counts (CTC) ministry.
7. By encouraging people in person and through regular contacts by phone and mail.

GO INTO ALL THE WORLD AND MAKE DISCIPLES (Matthew 28:19-20).

1. By reaching teens and adults with the good news of salvation through my role with CTC. Specifically, I will choose to have an "open door" policy and seek to be timely in responding to the needs and desires of people (and when appropriate, in writing and by phone).

2. By facilitating people growing in Christ by providing quality resources and materials.

3. By consistently seeking to improve CTC by being the best possible executive in the country.

4. By networking with others who have the same burden to reach teens and adults for Christ and seek out Kingdom purposes above organizational causes.

5. By putting "people" before "programs" in the ministry, seeking to train and equip them for long-term success in ministry.

6. By consistently brainstorming and experimenting with new and different ways to do a more effective job of reaching the World for Christ.

7. By encouraging people through my speaking and writing opportunities, maintaining a humble attitude and having God be my only audience.

APPENDIX H

CHARACTER MAXIMIZERS

M = **Make Things Happen**: Be a Difference Maker.
Speak the truth boldly (Romans 1:16-17).
Ask God to direct and lead your steps (Proverbs 3:5-6).

A = **Achieve Personal Significance**: What You See Is What You'll Be.
Live life confidently (Philippians 1:6).
Play to an audience of One (Colossians 3:17, 23-24).

X = **X Out The Negatives**: Don't Say Why, Say What.
Rejoice in the freedom of the cross (Galatians 5:13-15).
Humble yourself and seek His face (2 Chronicles 7:14, 16:7).

I = **Internalize Right Principles**: Do The Right Thing.
Accept the Bible as the final authority (2 Timothy 3:16-17).
Make godly decisions (Psalm 1:1-3).

M = **March To A Mission**: Go Beyond Success To Significance.
God has a plan for your life (Jeremiah 29:11-13).
Attempt to make the invisible God visible (Matthew 5:13-16).

I = **Integrate All Of Life**: You Can Have It All.
Practice integration over segmentation (Romans 12:1-2).
Expect suffering and grow from it (James 1:2-4).

Z = **Zero In On Caring For People**: Change People's Lives.
It's people, not programs (John 13:34-35; 15:12-13).
Encourage one another (1 Thessalonians 5:11; Romans 14:19).

E = **Energize Internally**: Experience Ultimate Power.
Learn to be content (1 Timothy 6:6-8; Philippians 4:11).
Thirst for daily renewal (2 Corinthians 4:16-18).

R = **Realign Rigorously**: Get From Point A To Point B The Right Way.
Give God your schedule (Proverbs 16:3).
Flexibility is a virtue (James 4:13-15).

S = **Stay The Course**: The Most Consistent Leadership Principle In The World.
Commit to life-long learning (Philippians 4:9).
Press on towards the goal by finishing the race (Philippians 3:14; 2 Timothy 4:7).

AUTHOR'S NOTE: The "Maximizers" acrostic was developed by Ron Jensen, taken from the book *Make A Life, Not Just A Living* (Thomas Nelson, 1995). The sub-points were added from a number of different sources.

APPENDIX I

BUILDING A WINNING TEAM

Today, many ministries, non-profit organizations and businesses are need-ing to restructure into flexible teams that focus on specific tasks or projects that produce the "corporate energy" beyond the day to day routine. But simply putting people together in a group and giving them a goal does not automatically create a "team." Teams must be intentionally built. Listed here are eight essential elements for building strong teams within your orga-nization. To help you remember them they are grouped in an acrostic— **TEAMWORK.**

T - Trust: Proverbs 28:20, "A faithful person will be richly blessed." This is the essential glue that binds people together. It produces confidence in oth-ers and encourages them to take risks and try new ways. On the other hand, mistrust creates stagnation. Trust is built by acting consistently. People must learn to trust you. The ultimate proof is when you delegate decision-mak-ing power to people. Freedom and trust go together.

E - Economize Energy: Proverbs 14:30, "A relaxed attitude lengthens a man's life." The quickest way to destroy a team is to burn it out. Every minute you are using up energy, and you only have a limited amount. Every new problem you give to a team adds a new drain emotionally, physically, relationally and spiritually. If you keep attaching more light bulbs to a bat-tery, you eventually end up with a dead battery! Be sensitive to the follow-ing factors on your team:

...don't expect every person to work at the same energy level at all times
...be aware of external drains (family, personal) and compensate
...plan your ministry year in energy cycles, with time to regroup
...work smarter, not harder...and focus on the long haul

A - Affirm and Appreciate: 1 Thessalonians 5:18, "In everything give thanks...this is God's will for you." William James said, "The deepest prin-ciple in human nature is the desire to be appreciated." Appreciation means to "raise in human value." Every time you appreciate team members, you increase their value to the team. There are four important areas to affirm in others:

...affirm their effort
...affirm their loyalty...it may be a miracle they've stayed with you
...affirm their ideas...even when you can't or don't use them
...affirm their differences...when two people agree on everything, one of them is unnecessary; when a group of people agree on everything, it usually means someone isn't thinking!

M - Manage Your Mistakes: Proverbs 24:16, "When righteous people fall seven times, they keep getting up." Mistakes are useful...they teach us what doesn't work. Tell your team, "I want everyone to make at least one mistake this week. If you aren't making any mistakes, you aren't taking any risks." Remove the fear of failure. Someone once wisely said, "I would rather fail than be mediocre. For in failure there are lessons to be learned, but mediocrity breeds false satisfaction."

W - Weekly Team Meetings: Ecclesiastes 4:9-12, "Two are better than one because together they can work more effectively. If one of them falls down, the other can help him up...Two can resist an attack that would defeat one man alone. And a rope of three cords is hard to break." At least every seven days your team members need significant contact with each other in some meaningful fashion. More often is better. Tremendous energy and creativity emerge when people committed to the same goals are allowed to think and plan and pray and play together.

O - Open Communication: Genesis 11:6, "If as one people speaking the same language they have begun to do this, then nothing they plan will be impossible for them." Poor communication is the No. 1 problem in most ministries. Problems occur when someone is not adequately informed. On the other hand, there is great power when all members of a team fully understand each other. There are three major barriers to open communication on a team:
1) Presumption—Proverbs 18:13, "It is stupid to decide before knowing the facts." Don't assume others think like you do. They don't! There is always more than one way to see things.
2) Impatience—James 1:19, "Let everyone be quick to listen and slow to speak."
3) Pride—Proverbs 13:10, "Pride always causes conflict." Pride makes us defensive to new ideas. We don't really hear what people are saying if we're thinking of ourselves.

R - Recognition and Reward: Proverbs 3:27, "Don't withhold good from those who deserve it, when it is in your power to act." Romans 12:10, "Let us have real, warm affection for each other...and a willingness to let the other man have the credit." Recognizing the efforts of team members always motivates and inspires everyone to do their best. Praise people sincerely and publicly. Much can be done through the person who doesn't care who gets the credit.

K - Keep on Learning: Proverbs 18:15, "The intelligent man is always open to new ideas. In fact, he looks for them." Provide continuing training and self-improvement opportunities for those on your team. Growing ministries are led by growing people.

NOTE: Where this information first originated is unknown. But it has been well used by the members of the Consulting Team of Life Enrichment, 14581 East Tufts Avenue, Aurora, CO 80015 (303-693-3954). It is our prayer that whoever put it together will be deeply blessed by our Lord, Jesus Christ, for their insight and creativity. This is a good reminder of how we need to think about teamwork in any group in which we participate or lead.

APPENDIX J

ACCOUNTABILITY'S TOP TEN

People expect religious organizations to abide by higher standards, according to Robert Thompson and Gerald Thompson in *Organizing for Accountability*. Here are Ten Commandments to build accountability into leaders:

1. No church is an island. Unethical conduct in business is also unethical in ministry. The best defense is to document all decisions in writing. Train your leaders to pay attention to paperwork.
2. There are no exceptions to management accountability. Some leaders have managerial weaknesses that shouldn't be ignored or hidden to protect the person or the church. Train leaders to confront each other when needed.
3. Not all management decisions are divinely inspired. Leaders should know how to gather reliable facts, review all options, and seek reputable professional services when needed.
4. Ministers need to rest, too. Sabbath means "rest." All leaders need time to rejuvenate, talk to God, and re-think situations and decisions.
5. Family comes first. Nurturing and protecting the ability of leaders to care for their families is the priority of every church.
6. There's more to life than ministry. There's no reason to snub or demean anyone who leaves your church. If you're experiencing a high turnover in your staff or congregation, it could mean your leaders aren't facing up to an accountability issue.
7. Religion and business make awkward partners. If a church gets involved in activities with a business or the community, the church's time, money and people are used for those pursuits. Because gaps in accountability can occur, make sure leaders of those organizations follow the accountability guidelines of your church.
8. Don't give to God what belongs to someone else. This happens when churches distribute copyrighted material without permission and when they keep non-ministerial assets for leaders' personal use.
9. Don't promise what you can't deliver. Build an organization where people tell the truth, give full disclosure on ministry and financial matters, and pay debts on time.
10. Don't covet what other churches have. Teach leaders to gather proper information and to seek wise counsel before they create or give support to projects or programs.

Author's Note: This great list appeared in *Vital Ministry*, 10/11/97.

APPENDIX K

PUTTING ON THE ARMOR OF GOD

The Apostle Paul tells us to "be strong in the Lord, and in the power of His might" (Ephesians 6:10). He expounds on this command for the next seven verses before telling us how to carry it out in verse 18. The individual who prays is the person who will become strong in the Lord. We are to put on God's whole armor by prayer. This strategy is to be used against the wiles of the devil. Even the technique of wrestling against principalities, powers, rulers of the devil's kingdom and against spiritual wickedness in high places is done through prayer.

Application of God's Word: Visualize yourself putting on each piece of armor--
• As strange as this may sound, I am told to put on a military girdle or the BELT OF TRUTH. This belt holds everything together and serves as a place to hang the armor. Jesus (the Truth) gives me freedom to walk uprightly in integrity.
• I put on the BREASTPLATE OF RIGHTEOUSNESS which shelters my heart from the assaults of the demonic powers. The breastplate is often called the "heart protector" as it covers from the neck to the thighs. Read Proverbs 4:23.
• I put on the SHOES OF PEACE to help me stand securely and walk out my faith, thereby being a credible witness to the Gospel of Jesus Christ.
• I put on the SHIELD OF FAITH to stop and extinguish the fiery arrows (temptations) aimed at me by the evil one. The shield was 4' high and 2 ½' wide and was designed to link with other soldiers to protect an entire row of soldiers.
• I put on the HELMET OF SALVATION which the Scripture reveals as hope. This provides safety from doubt and unbelief when the enemy attacks my mind.
• I put on the SWORD OF THE SPIRIT, which is the Word of God. This offensive weapon fights against the enemy's attacks and allows me to live a victorious life. Once the armor is on it is time to PRAY. It's time to go to battle in the spirit—praying all the time, on all occasions and with all your requests for others and yourself.

APPENDIX L

THE FELLOWSHIP OF CHRISTIAN ATHLETES AND ACCOUNTABILITY

It has been a wonderful honor and privilege to serve the Lord for a number of years through the work of the FCA. I have seen firsthand how the program can impact both adults and youth. Hundreds of thousands have been eternally transformed through the influence of FCA since beginning in 1954.

FCA is a Christ-centered ministry that is biblically based, helping people know and grow in Christ through the local church. The target audience are the junior high, high school and college campuses across the United States. Every FCA meeting (for coaches, athletes or adults) should be a comfortable place for the honest inquirer as well as the mature Christian.

For adults, the FCA Adult Chapter is a wonderful way to incorporate the accountability model. In addition to answering the questions, it also gives them an outlet for service to the youth of the community.

For youth, the FCA Huddle and Camp programs are places where they can relate intimately with peers and challenge one another to grow stronger in the faith. Specifically, FCA developed a program called "One Way 2 Play." This program is designed to help students withstand peer pressure through choosing to lead a drug/alcohol-free lifestyle. It is built as follows:

F - *Faith in Jesus Christ.* We believe God forgives us, gives us the wisdom to make good decisions and the strength to carry them out. Without faith in Christ, the commitments and accountability following would be shouldered by your own ability and not on God's strength.

C - *Commitment to say NO! to alcohol and drugs.* A pledge to be strong in the commitment and to help others be strong, too.

A - *Accountability to one another.* Hard questions are regularly asked by members who make the pledge to be drug/alcohol-free through the use of positive peer pressure.
  * Are you living and playing alcohol and drug-free?
  * Are you encouraging others to live and play that way?
  * Are you being honest with at least one mature person about your feelings and temptations?
  * Are you trusting Christ to meet your needs?
  * Are you honoring Him in your thoughts, words and actions?

Call 1-800-289-0909 to become aware of existing Huddle and/or Adult Chapter activities in your community, as well as the names of FCA staff personnel across the country. You can also write the FCA Home Office at 8701 Leeds Road, Kansas City, MO 64129.

INFORMATION ON CHARACTER THAT COUNTS

Character That Counts (CTC) was formally established in July 2000, but actually the roots of the organization date back to 1995. Since writing the initial version of *Character Counts: Who's Counting Yours?* (Cross Training Publishing, 1995), Rod Handley has had the privilege of sharing the message of character, integrity and accountability over 3,000 times in numerous settings and with diverse audiences. The information shared is fresh and insightful and people's responses have been overwhelmingly positive. Many have revealed that the words and principles communicated were exactly what they needed to hear to incorporate into their lives. Since 1995, over 250,000 CTC books have been sold. In addition, hundreds of testimonials have been shared to demonstrate the changes that have taken place as a result of hearing and reading these materials.

From 1995-2000, Rod's writing and speaking occurred while fulfilling his full-time responsibilities as the COO/CFO for the Fellowship of Christian Athletes (FCA). In June 2000, he resigned from FCA to commit complete energies to Character That Counts. Rod has additional staff members who are also available to speak in a variety of venues.

The **mission** and **vision** of Character That Counts is to: Communicate Life Principles of Integrity and Accountability. The ministry models this both personally and professionally. Over 100 character qualities identified on the website and in Appendix A (Pages 249-252) are consistently followed by the ministry. By the grace of God, true character is lived out. There are four key values of our work:

- **Teamwork:** This ministry needs a team of people working together, in relationship. Mr. Handley is not the ministry, nor is the ministry his alone. The board, staff members and volunteers are all key players in the ministry.
- **Excellence:** Everything done must be handled with professionalism, care and high quality. The name demands excellence.

- **Service:** The ministry will be attentive to the needs of people and strive to meet those needs.
- **Humility:** God will increase and we will decrease. All the credit and glory will go to God.

We believe that having a personal relationship with Jesus Christ and living out Biblical principles is foundational and essential to living out true character. Therefore, CTC is unashamed in pointing people to Christ and His Word. This is done both in Christian and secular settings. Opportunities to introduce people to Christ are plentiful. Materials will continue to be developed which share the love of Jesus Christ and His desire to bring people to spiritual maturity. Through Christ, character and integrity can be fully developed.

CTC's target market is focused on three audiences:

1) Athletes and coaches: Due to existing relationships with a number of professional, collegiate and high school teams across America, we have the opportunity to speak to them on a regular basis. Sports have an incredible influence on our society and these materials are making a significant difference in helping athletes fulfill their responsibility as a role model.

2) Children and teens: The students of this generation are confused in the areas of personal character and integrity. Many do not have positive role models. What we deem as "common sense" isn't easily determined, and it is difficult for them to distinguish between "right and wrong." Churches, parachurch ministries and the education systems (public, private and home schools) need high quality materials which go beyond saying "no" to drugs, alcohol and premarital sex. CTC provides a practical character curriculum to help students make the right choices.

3) Single and married men (above 18 years old): Men tend to gravitate towards conversations that only go as deep as news, weather and sports. We understand the needs of men, and we assist them in

discussing issues which result in deeper friendships. CTC isn't exclusively for men as many women (singles and married) also have been ministered to through seminars and publications.

In September 2001, CTC launched a new initiative called "Teaching God's Infinite Wisdom (TGIW)." This weekly Bible study format features a character word teaching from God's Word. Today, TGIW groups (for men and women) meet all over the world. To start a TGIW group in your church or city, contact the CTC office.

Through the work of Character That Counts, we envision men and women of all ages living out character and integrity, welcoming accountability in their relationships and professions. Being accountable has a profound impact on all sectors of life as people pursue character. It has been said that character takes a lifetime to build but a split second to lose. We are working to build a long lasting impact in the lives of people so that they can recognize when they face a compromising or precarious situation.

Character That Counts is a 501(c)(3), non-profit organization established in the state of Missouri. It is governed by a board of directors and advisory board members. From July 2000-December 2009, CTC operated under the umbrella of Lee's Summit Community Church based in Lee's Summit, MO. In January 2010, CTC received its own 501(c)(3) tax exemption number from the IRS.

If you're interested in having Rod Handley or any of the CTC Staff or Staff Associates speak to your organization, church or ministry please contact Rod at: www.characterthatcounts.org

ALSO FROM ROD HANDLEY
www.crosstrainingpublishing.com
www.characterthatcounts.org

Called to Coach Book One
Coaches are the most influential adults in the lives of many athletes. Evangelist Billy Graham said, "One coach will impact more young people in a year than the average person does in a lifetime." Called to Coach is a bible study series that is designed to help coaches and leaders at every level integrate their faith with coaching. There are a total of 12 lessons per book. This is the first book in a 3-book bible study series.
$7.99 paperback, 84 pages
978-0-9821652-6-3

Team Studies: In the Zone
Team Studies: In the Zone is the second book in the Team Character Series written by Rod Handley and Gordon Thiessen. Strong teams all have one key ingredient in common: character. Team Studies features 16 key character studies to use throughout the season as a discussion guide on how to build a championship team. The purpose of this book is to identify character qualities that will make a winning difference in your life and on your team.
Retail Price: $6.99, 96 pages
978-1-938254-01-7

Life In View of Eternity
This 316-page workbook features 35 character qualities. The workbook includes Quizzes, Exams, Essay, Bible Study, Daily Proverbs, along with Activities and Team Building Exercises. The book is ideal for use with a parent and a teenager; in a Sunday School class; or in a Christian School (suggested for grades 7-12). It can also be utilized by a small groups.
Retail Price: $24.99, 316 pages
978-0-9821652-2-5